WISDOM,
UNDERSTANDING,
—— AND ——
KNOWLEDGE

WISDOM,
UNDERSTANDING,
—— AND ——
KNOWLEDGE

BASIC CONCEPTS OF HASIDIC THOUGHT

Shmuel Boteach

JASON ARONSON INC.
Northvale, New Jersey
London

6|12

This book was set in 11 pt. Garamond by Alpha Graphics of Pittsfield, New Hampshire.

10 9 8 7 6 5 4 3 2 1

Library of Congress Cataloging-in-Publication Data

Boteach, Shmuel.
    Wisdom, understanding, and knowledge : basic concepts of hasidic thought / by Shmuel Boteach.
        p. cm.
    Includes index.
    ISBN 0-87668-557-2
    1. Hasidism.   2. Habad.   3. Judaism—Doctrines.   4. Mysticism— Judaism.   5. Schneersohn, Menahem Mendel, 1902- —Teachings.
    I. Title.
    BM198.2.B68   1995
    296.8'3322—dc20   95-6052

Manufactured in the United States of America. Jason Aronson Inc. offers books and cassettes. For information and catalog write to Jason Aronson Inc., 230 Livingston Street, Northvale, New Jersey 07647.

To the Great Leader and Lover of Israel,
Teacher of Godliness and Goodness to all Humanity,
Prince and Pride of the Jewish People

The Lubavitcher Rebbe

Rabbi Menachem Mendel Schneerson, O.B.M.

Who passed away during the production of this book
and whose memory continues to inspire everything I do
on behalf of others and every effort I make on behalf of
Judaism and my people

CONTENTS

ACKNOWLEDGMENTS

This book is based on the public orations of the Lubavitcher Rebbe, O. B. M., Rabbi Menachem Mendel Schneerson, which were compiled and presented by the great hasidic scholar Rabbi Yoel Kahn in his telephone lecture series known as *Nosim Beyahadus.* Rabbi Kahn's presentation was remarkable for its orderly sophistication and lucidity and in my opinion served as a model for how hasidic thought should always be taught. The thoughts in this book are extracts of nearly forty years of talks and commentary by the Lubavitcher Rebbe on Jewish mysticism and esoteric thought, and it is through the erudition and fluency of Rabbi Yoel Kahn that they have been anthologized into a series of essays in which each idea naturally flows from the ideas preceding it. These concepts, due to their profundity, remained largely inaccessible to the uninitiated scholars of hasidic thought, and so I have adapted them to make them appreciable by a contemporary audience that may have little knowledge of Jewish mysticism. At the same time, even those with a great knowledge of *Hasidus* should find most of the ideas in this book novel and stimulating.

Rather than attempt to describe here the penetrating depth that is characteristic of the Rebbe's gaze into all subjects, I will allow the reader to discover it for himself through the course of the book.

I am extremely grateful to Rabbi Kahn, who performed the difficult task of anthologizing the talks into a proper series. I also thank my loving wife for always doing her best to take upon herself my most urgent duties so that I might have time to write. Her devotion and companionship give me new life, and she is the greatest blessing that the Almighty, in His kindness, has ever bestowed upon me.

I would also like to thank the extremely devoted staff of the Oxford University L'Chaim Society—my three assistants, Kathy Brewis, Julie Markoff, and Faith Hill-King—who do their utmost to assume my daily office chores so that I might devote my time to teaching and counseling the students of Oxford University, to whom I serve as a rabbi. It is veritably through these constant exchanges with the brightest and most challenging of minds that so many of my ideas and understanding of Jewish thoughts are crystallized and fleshed out.

I am eternally grateful to my teacher, guide, and mentor, prince of the Jewish people, the Lubavitcher Rebbe, Rabbi Menachem M. Schneerson, O.B.M., who, to the great misfortune of the Jewish people and all of humanity, tragically passed away while this book was in its final editorial stages. The Rebbe, as he was lovingly known throughout the world, gave me the unique privilege of serving as one of his emissaries abroad, thus enabling me to see how the concepts of *Hasidus* actually have the power to touch, and in many cases radically alter, people's lives for the better. While the Rebbe lay critically ill in the hospital for many months, I prayed that this great and devoted leader of our nation be granted a full and complete recovery, and continue to lead our people. I ached for his sweet countenance to once again push us toward making this earth an arena of goodness and loving-kindness. Now, in the wake of his passing, I pray that we never forget him and his unparalleled love and dedication to the Jewish people and allow his memory to inspire our every effort to make the world a more decent and Godly place.

I also thank the residents and students of the University of Oxford, England, for welcoming me and my family into their lives, and challenging me to rethink and provide the answers that restimulate Jewish life. Most of all, I thank God Almighty for having given me the privilege of being one of those people who work so that Judaism might live and flourish again as in years gone by. I possess no deeper wish than to serve as an exponent of Judaism and to thereby enhance and enrich human life. God, in His infinite kindness, has granted me that wish. May the Almighty walk with and bless His people always.

Introduction

THE SEARCH FOR
THE MISSING CREATOR

What are we all doing on this God forsaken planet? My use of the term "God forsaken" in this instance is not intended as a cliché but as a precise encapsulation of the world's greatest problem: the Creator seems to enjoy hiding. So often does He conceal His presence one cannot be blamed if at times one feels utterly abandoned by the Creator. Has God found better things to do with His time than to spend it with humans? Throughout the ages the very first questions that have confronted men and women as they reached a responsible age are these: Where is my Creator? What is my source? From whence do I spring? And does my life have any purpose? I see such questions as they form in the hearts and minds of our students here at the University of Oxford. They question why they should spend so many hours studying and suffering through their exams. They're not sure that all the hard work is worth it or has a purpose. Were they really created to be lawyers? Does their existence have any intrinsic meaning, and would their absence be noticed by anyone at all? As I write these lines I think through the thousands of times that I too have contemplated these basic questions and come to the only plausible solution that both satisfies my curiosity and fires my passion for life. It goes like this:

The story of Creation, as narrated in the Bible, is quite simple. An eternal all-powerful God dreams up a world and sets about making it a reality. As one would expect, since God is perfect, the world He creates is very impressive. Everything seems ordered and complex. The heavens water the lush green vegetation, which in turn provide man and animal with food and sustenance. An ingenious immune system is included within the human body, which wages war against germs and infection. Every earthly inhabitant is provided with others to love, honor, and cherish through the institutions of marriage and parenthood. This is what it means to be a Creator: to make a world that is efficient and complete—a world that works. From the infinite Creator we would expect nothing less.

But things don't always proceed according to plan. At times, in fact, they go tragically wrong. The heavens sometimes fail to provide enough rain to irrigate the earth. Famine ensues and people die of starvation. The human body occasionally grows cancerous cells that its immune system is powerless to combat. A man and woman marry. Barely four months later they so loathe each other that they must live apart: the human need to feel special and irreplaceable is lost. Parents decide to have a child and in the midst of their happiness they discover that their child has leukemia, as one of my closest friends found just two years after his son was born. The world is not perfect and things go wrong. Mankind then asks, Where is God in the midst of such sorrow? He created the world, and He runs it, right? So why do so many things fail? God loves playing hide-and-seek and asks us to search for Him. But where are we to find Him when we need Him most? Does He truly listen to our prayers?

In a way, the Almighty is playing an unfair game of contradictions. On the one hand He gives us evidence that forces us to accept that He exists. The world is too complex, human love too perfect, the human mind too precise for it all to have arisen spontaneously or without design. On the other hand, too many things go wrong for us to accept that God is always in control or that He is always good and acting to our benefit. We are therefore, to paraphrase Franz Kafka, miserable animals: too aware of God's presence to deny His existence, yet too bothered by the misery and challenge of human life to always accept that He listens, loves, and cares. I have always believed that God loves and cares for me—that He is looking out for me. So why then does He allow those events which pain me? Our relationship with God is thus under constant scrutiny: one day we believe fervently in His omnipresence and existence, and the very next day we question whether or not He exists at all. It should not be surprising that the faith of the believer fluctuates so regularly. Everyday empirical experience seems to support the contradictory conclusions that God both exists and does not exist.

MAN MUST JOIN GOD AS PARTNER IN CREATION

Our mission as human beings on this planet is, therefore, to play the role of the living yet all-too-hidden God. Whenever and wherever something goes wrong in Creation it is *we* who must put it right. We must seek to gloss over all the bumps and inconsistencies in our world. When we witness a cancerous cell, it is *we* who must obliterate it and bring about its destruction before it claims a human life. When a husband and wife are rude to each other in public, it is we who must take up the ancient occupation of Aaron the High Priest, loving peace and pursuing peace. We must remind the husband and wife of their love and commitment to each other and thus ensure that tomorrow they awake reconciled in the same home. When we hear of children suffering in the midst of famine, war, or political corruption, it is *we* who must ensure that they are fed. We must become God for the moment, joining our father-in-heaven as junior partners in Creation.

This is not dissimilar to a family in which the father is the breadwinner and provider. He loves his family and provides for all their needs. One day he goes off on a business trip but, for whatever reason, does not return. As we are now unsure of his whereabouts, the oldest son must step into his shoes and run the family business, marry off his sisters, comfort his mother, and ensure that the family's quality of life is always preserved. The objective is not to wonder where the father has disappeared to. Rather, it is to immediately assume His work so that He may live and exist through our deeds. Man is a creator and by embracing the work of his Master he reveals His omnipresence within Creation.

Once a *hasid* asked his rebbe why God had allowed atheism in the world. Worse, the man said, God even allows His Creation to be used as support for atheistic claims. The world's indigenous processes and its geographical strata can be used to support such atheistic claims as the Aristotelian theory of the eternity of matter and Darwin's theory of evolution. "Atheism is necessary," answered the rebbe, "it is most welcome. This is why God has not only allowed it, but caused it to *flourish*." Then before the *hasid* even had a chance to raise his voice in protest to the strange words being spoken by his master, the rebbe continued. "If there were no atheism, then every time you witnessed someone starving you wouldn't feed them. Your attitude would be that God will take care of them. And every time you saw someone crying you might not comfort them. God will address their needs. And every time you saw someone drowning, you wouldn't save them, thinking that God will not allow them to perish. Therefore, every time we witness an innocent victim who is hungry, bereaved, or dying, we must at that moment believe that there is no God. If we do not help them, no one will. God will not come to their rescue because He does not exist. At that moment the only thing that exists and can grant salvation is *you*. Do not rely on God."

IN ANCIENT TIMES GOD REGULARLY
CAME OUT OF HIS HIDING PLACE

Here we have the purpose for man's Creation and his highest calling: to join the Almighty as a junior partner in Creation and be there whenever God is in hiding. There was a time, however, when man could afford to play a far more passive role in the world. When the Jews were enslaved in Egypt, for example, they barely needed to fight for their own freedom. God did it for them, with frogs, boils, locusts, and finally an avalanche of water crushing the Egyptian bones. God provided the fireworks. Humans had no need to interfere or really concern themselves. Take a seat and watch the show. You'll see God emerging from His camouflage and punishing the wicked. And as the Jews traveled through the wilderness, there was no need for human charity. There were loaves of bread raining from the heavens (or at least something similar). Someone's hungry: no problem. Cry out to God and then walk outside. All will be taken care of.

But then the Germans poured into Poland and Russia. Jews were herded up in cattle cars, and synagogues were set alight. Jews starved to death. They cried out then, too, but this time there was no bread from heaven, and there were no angels of mercy to save them. There was only a palpable and deafening silence. Where *was* God at Auschwitz? "Lord God, why hast Thou forsaken me?" Whence have You retreated? Your obscurity and seclusion is causing millions of Your abandoned children to doubt and deny Your existence!

WHEN GOD IS IN HIDING, MAN MUST BE VERY VISIBLE

Where is God when we need Him? This question, which is the most asked in latter twentieth-century theology and which I discuss in my previous book, *Wrestling with the Divine*, is, in the final analysis, unanswerable and unimportant to man. We have no time to ponder consequences during our crises. We are also responsible for Creation. We are God's partners. And when God is in hiding, we must be very visible. And whenever our Partner decides to take an unexplained hiatus, it is we who must fill in the gap. We must translate the hidden into the living, breathing God. *God exists wherever man exists.*

Hence one begins to understand the absolute centrality of works of kindness and goodness to Judaism, what we call *Gemilut chassadim.* The purpose of man on earth is to *reveal* God on earth–to slowly show His undeniable presence, just as the fruit ripens on the tree until its color causes it to be picked. God wants to be wanted. We are His press and publicity agents. We are the Divine graffiti. Why He allows suffering is beyond us: but if we can make a better world and if we can prevent holocausts, it will hardly be worth complaining.

God is above all else a provider. He is our Creator, He is our parent, and therefore He must look after us. But if He is the parent, then we are the nanny. Sometimes parents are nowhere to be found. And that can be construed as a crime and cause the child to feel deserted or rejected. But at the very least, the parent always leaves behind a nanny to act in their stead. Nannies are not as grand, as impressive, or as loving, but they are always there for us. Likewise God, in His kindness, did not place us on this earth alone. He gave us other humans, fellow brothers and sisters, to comfort and look after us—to love us and make us feel special. But this whole plan can only work, of course, if we truly feel that our next door neighbor is not a stranger, and certainly not an enemy. Rather, we share with them common parentage and common humanity. There is no more tangible way to become aware of God's existence and caring than for man to undertake and experience human acts of kindness on behalf of our God in hiding. The Baal Shem Tov said that love of God is expressed principally through love of man. Man is charged with a mission. He must pursue it passionately, vigorously, and with single-minded devotion. And the assignment? To be an angel of mercy. To allow the hidden God to be revealed through our constant acts of kindness and magnificence, performed at the command of the Supreme Creator.

Every one of us should feel a sense of urgency. The world needs our contribution and it cannot afford to wait. This is the central message of Judaism. Man is created to be a contributor, not just at his leisure and not just in his spare time: Now!! Always!! *This is what he is born to do*. Judaism wishes to educate the world's inhabitants about the need to use all their energies, aptitude, and ambition to help their fellowman and improve the state of the world. Aid to humanity is man's first and greatest calling. Students must study medicine, but with the overall aim of healing the sick. They must study business and banking, but with the chief aim of helping those who are destitute and in need of financial advice and funds. They must marry and have children, building a home in the mold of that of our forefather Abraham, which had no walls and was open to all passersby. Man must always remember that he is a partner in Creation. The Big Partner usually carries His load and assumes His responsibilities, but sometimes seems to overlook some of our needs. Those who are forsaken wonder why they specifically have been forgotten, and they look for comfort and rescue. They feel neglected by God and it is our job to support and embrace them with infinite love, *ahavas Yisroel*. Dare we fail them?

TO FIND AND EXPERIENCE GOD WITH ONE'S MIND

But Judaism has also maintained that it is insufficient to find and establish the hidden God through action alone. To be sure, action is the essence of Judaism, as we shall explain at length in the latter chapters of this book. But man must find God in his thought and speech *as well as* his action. Judaism tries to raise man to a higher level at which he comes into contact with the Divine in all his endeavors. The overall purpose of this book is to teach man to find the latent God with his mind and soul as well. To train his higher faculties to detect the omnipotent Creator in every aspect of his life and in every corner of the earth. This is the very purpose of Jewish mystical thought as embodied in *Hasidus*. To bring that which is hidden to the fore. *Hasidus* veritably lifts the curtain that separates human knowledge from Divine knowledge and the revealed from the concealed. It brings to life and makes intelligible that which we heretofore did not believe even existed. It is my hope, then, that this book, as it incorporates lofty hasidic ideas and ideals, will serve as the treasure map that leads to the grandest prize of all: the seemingly missing Creator. It will be observed that He will not be found merely at the conclusion of our journey, but, as in life itself, at every step along the way.

For centuries, it was concealed, accessible only to savants and spiritual giants of the generation. The esoteric and mystical Torah was never written and was passed down from mystical master to pupil all by word of mouth. The pupils were hand chosen and had to undergo extreme spiritual conditioning before being allowed to pursue the study of the secrets of the Torah. Few, if any, were permitted to enter this elite corps of mystics and scholars, and the daily regimen was as intense as it was enlightening. No one dared record these unfathomable mysteries of creation on paper, thus making them accessible to the ordinary laymen whose shallow perception threatened to grossly misrepresent them. Later, however, as the spiritual, scholarly, and moral fiber of the generations in general and the Jewish people in particular began to deteriorate, the mystical teachings of Judaism were finally written down in the form of what we today call the *Kabbalah*, the Jewish esoteric sciences and disciplines. There was one shortcoming, however. *Kabbalah*, for the most part, is too difficult to be truly intelligible to the masses. The achievement of the hasidic masters for the most part, especially the *Rabbeim* (Spiritual Masters) of the Chabad-Lubavitch movement, was to make it all intelligible. To do the seemingly impossible in taking that which is designed to transcend human comprehension and have it fit snugly within the constraints of human intelligence. *Hasidus,* then, brings the hidden God to life in the eye of the mind and in the heart of the soul.

THE TORAH AND THE JEWISH PEOPLE
ALSO POSSESS ASPECTS HIDDEN AND REVEALED

But in the process it also serves to clarify and add a deeper, more mystical dimension to our understanding of the Torah and the Jewish people as well. "Three are interconnected," says the *Zohar*, "the Jewish people, the Torah, and the Holy One, blessed be He, all have aspects hidden and revealed." How is God both hidden and revealed? As explained above, on the one hand, God is apparent and revealed to all. The magnificence of nature, the precision with which its various processes harmonize, reveals the presence of a purposeful Creator. On the other hand, this very instrument of nature with which God regulates His world makes it possible for some not to realize His presence behind nature. Nature serves more to mask than celebrate the Creator and most today pay homage to natural law for the wonders of nature rather than to the invisible benevolent Creator who lies behind its veil. Likewise the paradox that evil exists in a world created by a good God could lead some to similar conclusions. Nature thus not only reveals God's presence, it also conceals it. He is simultaneously both hidden and revealed.

The Torah and the Jewish people similarly have aspects that are revealed and external and others hidden and internal. The

Torah's revealed aspect, what we call *Nigleh*, is its halakhic, legal portion. These are the commandments and laws regulating the Jew's life, with the internal reasoning of these laws that determines how to carry them out in practice. This external portion is recorded in the *Mishnah*, and the Babylonian and Jerusalem Talmuds, halakhic midrashim, responsa literature, halakhic codes of law based upon all of these, and many authoritative commentaries on these works. The Torah's hidden, mystical portion, what we call *Nistar* or *Pnimius Ha Torah*, is those inner ideas of the Torah behind and beyond actual practice of its commandments. These ideas are the essence or "soul of the Torah," as the *Zohar* calls them. Most of these are alluded to in the so-called *Aggada* portions of the Talmud, collected in the masterful work *Ein Yaakov*, and in the nonhalakhic midrashim. Primarily, though, they are discussed in the Kabbalah. *Hasidus* is the ultimate expression of *Pnimius Ha Torah*, Torah's inner aspect. It draws on all authoritative Torah works of both *Nigleh* and *Nistar* to explain the depth of the internal, mystical portion of the Torah. Since the Torah is interconnected with the Almighty and with the souls of the Jewish people, as indicated in the above passage from the *Zohar*, *Hasidus*—revealing the inner aspect of the Torah—also reveals the inner aspect of the Almighty (as far as we can understand) and of the Jewish soul. *Hasidus* thus reveals the essence of the Jew and how it relates with what primarily governs his life: God and His Laws. The penetrating and sophisticated analysis that *Hasidus* provides of this relationship among God, His Torah, and His people affords a profound perspective of Judaism, exposing it in all its glory and depth. These powerful insights of hasidic thought are recorded in thousands of *Ma'amorim* (discourses) and hundreds of book-length works of the seven great Rebbes of Chabad *Hasidus* (also known as Lubavitch). This work draws on ideas of *Hasidus* in a form easy to grasp, though the ideas are essentially of great depth. We start with an analysis of the essence of the "Jew," moving on to a discussion of God, His Torah, and its commandments.

1

FROM HUMANITARIAN TO JEW: THE TRANSFORMATION OF ABRAHAM

THE FIRST MENTION OF ABRAHAM

The formation of the Jew as a distinct entity involved a number of fundamental stages. Most important was the Jewish people's acceptance of the Torah at Mount Sinai, which introduced an utterly new element into the essence of the Jew. However, long before the Divine revelation at Mount Sinai, our forefathers laid the foundation of the Jewish nation.

Abraham was the first Jew. To understand the essence of the Jew and how the Jewish people differ from the non-Jewish nations, we must examine the main events of Abraham's life.

The Torah's first detailed account of Abraham's life is the commandment he received from God: "Go for your sake from your land, from your birthplace, from your father's house, to the land that I shall show you" (Genesis 12:1).

In the Talmud and the *Midrash*, our sages extol Abraham's great self-sacrifice in disseminating the knowledge of God's existence even as a child. At the tender age of three, they tell us, he logically deduced the existence of the Mighty Creator. He rejected the prevailing idolatrous mores of his time; he postulated a God who lay behind nature, but regulated all created things and brought into existence all forms of life. Later, he systematically campaigned, wherever he could, to spread belief in one God and to urge mankind to abandon paganism and idolatry. Thus, Abraham singlehandedly gave the world monotheism and served as its most important exponent.

Abraham thereby placed his own life in danger. The *Midrash* relates, for example, how Nimrod, ruler of the known world at that time, had proclaimed himself a god. When Abraham's own father, Terach, denounced his child to Nimrod as a nonbeliever, the self-proclaimed deity Nimrod ordered Abraham thrown into a fiery furnace for seeking to undermine popular worship of him. Still the child did not give up his faith. He was ready to forfeit his life as a martyr for his cause. It was only a Divine miracle that saved him from death. This is just one of the many stories in the *Midrash* that display Abraham's complete and utter self-sacrifice on behalf of his beliefs.

In the light of Abraham's faithfulness, the commentators on the Torah ask a perplexing question: Why does the Bible ignore Abraham's long career of unprecedented self-sacrifice, only starting its account of Abraham's life when he received his first Divine revelation at the advanced age of seventy-five? Were his previous accomplishments somehow insignificant? Since the Bible seems not to consider his previous self-sacrifice even worthy of mention, it must have been in some way deficient. What then constitute the shortcomings in Abraham's self-sacrifice and self-negation before the age of seventy-five?

The answer given in Jewish mystical thought is that it is not the Torah's purpose to provide us with historical narratives, however stimulating they may be, even about the self-sacrifice of our great and wise patriarchs. Although Abraham was by all accounts an extraordinary individual who exhibited supreme sacrifice, that fact alone would not qualify him for mention in the Torah.

All the details of our forefathers' lives that are included in the Torah have the purpose of revealing the intrinsic nature of the Jewish people. By mentioning nothing of Abraham's glorious career before he received God's first command, the Torah indicates that the beginning of Abraham *as a Jew* occurred only after God revealed Himself to Abraham and gave him His command. Stated in other words, before his first Divine revelation, Abraham was not yet a Jew, but only a humanitarian. When God spoke to him, however, something inside him changed. And this change was so significant that its occurrence and the changes it wrought warrant mention henceforth in the Bible. What changed within Abraham, and what makes this change so significant?

THE RATIONALIST AND THE REVELATIONIST

To understand this fundamental concept, we must first examine the differences between a philosophical and revelationist approach to belief in, and acceptance of, God. One would think that a belief in God based on intellectual examination and philosophical proof is superior to an experience of Divine revelation. Better, one might think to discover God with one's cognitive and deductive faculties, to see God in the eye of the mind, than to experience Him in the flesh. The rationale for such acceptance can be quite compelling and is as follows.

First, a philosophical approach to the theological mystery of God engages man's highest faculties in discovering and attaching a human dimension to God. By engaging in this approach, one is not merely present as a witness to a revelatory event, such as when God intervened in nature and split the Red Sea. In the case of such an experience, the observer seems no different than a stone upon which the sculptor carves an impression. The stone plays no part in the creation of this beautiful work of art. On the contrary, it is the sculptor who is acting upon the stone. Likewise, when God decides to reveal Himself to man, the human is being acted upon by the Almighty. Human participation in the extraordinary event is very minimal and entirely passive. The Jews who witnessed the splitting of the Red Sea when in flight from their Egyptian oppressors played an entirely passive role in the unfolding of this historic and miraculous drama.

However, in the case of an intellectual apprehension of Godly existence, when man must find God and prove His existence by virtue of his own higher cognitive processes, the individual labors vigorously, using the profundity of man's greatest gift, his mind, to apprehend the Creator. Surely this is far more commendable than seeing or witnessing an occurrence, however inspiring or magical. Moreover, a hard-core intellectual postulate is seldom shaken as one has proven faith to oneself. Philosophical investigation converts the realm of faith into the realm of knowledge and makes one's belief far more tangible and real. There are no doubts, for one has arrived at one's conclusion intellectually and logically.

Faith based purely on revelation can be shaken and denied. Its foundation can be eroded because the believer has never firmly grounded his faith in a foolproof intellectual base. Ah! But what of the revelation? Is that not sufficient proof of the existence and omnipotence of God? Well, even if we do assume that the revelation itself is indeed real and not a hallucination, often the intensity and transcendence of the event can overwhelm the individual to the point where its significance is completely missed by the observer. And even if the individual initially absorbs the sublimity of the event, if it cannot be anchored in intelligible thought and the experience cannot be digested properly or cemented into a rational base, the effect of the revelation will quickly dissipate. Faith can and should be anchored in the mind. It cannot merely hover above one's head. If it does, although it may remain with the individual, its practical effect and influence on the individual's daily life will be minimal if not nonexistent. Revelation may cause wonder and excitement, but when the magic ends it may leave without a trace. As quickly and suddenly as it comes it may go, with little attention being directed its way.

We observe on a daily basis how occurrences that even skeptics refer to as miraculous are completely forgotten a few moments later. Yet, those conclusions arrived at on logical and rational grounds seem to remain forever.

Stated in other words, a miracle, however wondrous, is still an intruder, and people prefer the natural order. Humans become accustomed to the mundane and everyday, and it is those things that are of a repetitive nature that really form and become part of life, and ironically having the most profound effect on the individual.

THE ASCENDANCY OF REVELATION OVER
AND ABOVE COGNITIVE DEDUCTION

In truth, however, a powerful argument for the supremacy of a belief in God based on observation and revelation as opposed to logical deduction can be made easily. As stated above, the philosophical proof of the existence of God seems to be a powerful bulwark against decay caused by doubt and apathy. So why is it that in Judaism we find the opposite to be true? The sudden and immediate belief that resulted from the collective Jewish experience of the Divine revelation at Sinai, the only collective revelation to millions of people ever claimed by any world religion, is always lauded over any philosophical or empirical proofs that may be offered for the existence of the Creator. The Jew who witnessed God's Ten Commandments at Sinai had a far greater apprehension and enjoyed a far closer proximity to the Creator than any of our forefathers, including Abraham, the first intellectual Jew.

Similarly, Maimonides and others go to great lengths to emphasize that the sole basis for the fulfillment of the laws of the Torah in the post-Sinaitic world is not intellectual speculation about the validity of the commandments, but rather God's revelation at Sinai and the simultaneous giving of the Torah to the Jewish people, and His command that they follow its precepts. Even if one finds humanitarian justification for the fulfillments of the Torah's commandments—for example, such rational commandments as the prohibition of removing eggs from a nest while the mother bird is present—although the rationalizations may serve to beautify and enhance one's *performance* of the *mitzvos*, they may never serve as the *criteria* for their fulfillment. The laws are important because *God said so*, not because man feels them to be so. Why then indeed does Judaism reject the indubitable faith of mind in exchange for the instability of revelation?

THE ACQUISITION OF KNOWLEDGE:
TO JOIN MIND WITH MATTER

In answering this question, we must first examine the nature of the acquisition of knowledge. In the acquisition of knowledge, two separate entities are joined: the individual and the object, the person who comes to know and understand and the knowledge or object that becomes known and understood. In order for any knowledge to be acquired, however, one of the two entities must be predominant: either the person examining and understanding the knowledge predominates or the knowledge or object itself predominates.

Suppose an astronaut travels to a distant planet where no human has ever visited. Before his landing, his ship's onboard computers and instrumentation detect no signs of life and even determine that conditions on the planet could not possibly sustain life. As the astronaut exits his spacecraft, however, he is shocked to meet a human being. He radios back to earth about his discovery, but the controllers at base refuse to consider the possibility that human life exists on that planet; they tell him that he is hallucinating. "Get a good night's sleep," they tell him. The highest achievements of human technology have ascertained that he is wrong, but he insists on the truth of his story. Why does he cling to it? Because he has *seen*! An extraterrestrial life form is standing here right in front of him, and he cannot deny what he sees. Unlike the earthbound controllers, the astronaut has not relied on his own intellectual understanding in acquiring this information. His story is not based on his own calculations that, despite the computer's conclusions, the planet is capable of sustaining life. It is not that he has reached any logical or intellectual conclusion at all. Rather, he has seen. Neither the greatest intellectual nor the most advanced machine can ever dissuade him of the truth of what he has witnessed with his own eyes. The phenomenon itself has been revealed to him. It is thus the knowledge itself, the phenomenon that has been revealed to him that predominates, and not the individual who knows. An image is being implanted onto his mind. He is just a passive spectator.

In contrast, when knowledge is based upon intellectual deduction, the knowledge itself is passive and secondary. What predominates is the person who, exercising his intellectual acumen to the best of his ability, has drawn a rational conclusion. Because he has neither seen nor experienced the knowledge himself but has merely drawn a logical conclusion, he must rely on his own limited understanding for his perception. Consequently, that perception can never be fully accurate. The person must use his intellect and imagination to paint a composite picture of what he is trying to grasp. In other words, when a person is shown a picture of a house, for example, it is the image of the house that makes its imprint upon the person, and thus he knows the house perfectly, because it has been shown to him. However, if the person is only told verbally what the house looks like, then he must create the image of the house in his own mind by combining the various descriptions he is being given, and there is no guarantee that the image he creates will be accurate.

Furthermore, because his knowledge is based on his own personal understanding, he can be dissuaded from what he now accepts as a fact. His facts are based only on intellectual argument, and for every argument there is a counterargument. What he accepts today as fact can be intellectually disproved tomorrow and rejected as naive assumption.

The very need on the part of an individual to prove an item of knowledge by the intellectual direction is indicative of the fact that this item is concealed from him. Since he cannot reach it directly by means of direct eyesight, there is no choice but to approach it obliquely, using intellect and logic.

On the other hand, one who actually sees something does not rely on his own understanding of the object he sees. The object itself gives his eye an instantaneous and complete picture, like a photograph. The camera does not give its own interpretation of a scene that it snaps; it merely captures the scene the way it is in reality. In the same way, a viewer's understanding of a scene is totally accurate, for the scene has been directly revealed to him.

For the viewer, it is the knowledge itself that predominates. His own understanding plays little role. Not withstanding the strength of any counterarguments offered, his certainty cannot be shaken. He has seen, while those trying to sway him with logic have not. No intellectual argument nor any empirical proof can change his mind nor weaken his resolve, for it was not his mind that convinced him of the truth of this knowledge; it was the knowledge itself. He has been acted upon by an image, he has not concocted some vague fantasy. This is the meaning of revelation, and these are its implications.

CREATING GOD IN OUR OWN IMAGE

This difference between the philosopher and the revelationist is also apparent in their different approaches to serving God. The philosopher does not have Divine commandments, for God has not informed him through Divine revelation what He requires of him. Even his belief that God exists at all is based only upon his intellectual calculations. Therefore, he bases his worship of God not necessarily on what he *knows* God to desire, but upon what he himself decides will please God, based on his own understanding. Without doubt, this rational approach will lead him to create and conceive God in his own image. Whatsoever is of significance to the philosopher himself will in turn be a priority with the philosopher's God. If the philosopher is an ethicist and feels that murder is wrong, then he will be led to believe that surely in the eyes of God it is also wrong. And if the philosopher believes that compassion is a wonderful trait, then he will speak of a God who is compassionate. Of course, this assumption will extend even into those aspects of human behavior that cannot be applied to God. Because the Greeks were greatly attracted to feminine beauty, they invented gods who chased human women. Theoretically, then, if the philosopher loves chocolate, then the God whose existence comes about by way of the philosopher's mental gymnastics will have a craving for chocolate too.

ALLOWING GOD TO STATE WHAT HE DESIRES

Once a young, best-selling Jewish author, who was taking a course at the University of Oxford, called me to ask whether he could come and spend *Shabbos* with us and witness his first-ever Friday night meal. He made it clear that he was not coming for religious reasons. Why then was he so interested in attending? You see, he was writing a new novel about a Holocaust survivor who emigrates to the United States after losing his entire family in the war. The lead character is a religious Jew, and thus the author must be able to describe how he celebrates *Shabbos* and dons *tefillin*. He came and ate with us and stayed up most of the night with me learning how various Jewish practices are kept. When I told him how we put on *tefillin*, how we take black leather boxes and leather straps and tie them around our arms and head, the author began to laugh. "You can't be serious," he said.

"But why not," I asked. "Why can't you respect this particular precept of the Jewish religion?"

"Look," he said. "To be honest, Rabbi, I don't believe in God. But one thing I know for sure. If there is a God, He couldn't possibly want us to make fools of ourselves by affixing leather boxes on our heads," he said chuckling.

Amazing! He does not believe in God. But my friend the author is sure that if God exists, He would only instruct us to observe those things that *he*, the author, deems important. In other words, what is important to the author is likewise of profound significance to God, and what the author himself finds distasteful must likewise be distasteful to God as well. The Bible says that man was created in the image of God. But of course, this particular author was creating God in *his* own image.

An old joke asks: How do you know when you have finally become old? Answer: When people speak of you while you are sitting in the room as if you were not present. They say things like "My, doesn't he look good today" or "He's looking very tired. I think we better take him home." The same may be said of those who create God in their own image. They may be uncertain as to whether there is a God or incapable of admitting it. But of one thing they are certain. If He *does* exist, He would never want a man to wake up in the morning and wrap leather straps around his arm, as is done in the *mitzvah* of *tefillin*. Surely if God exists He could not possibly be concerned with what kind of meat one consumes. Or He would have much better things to do than sit around waiting to see if one turns on a light on the Sabbath. One of the most common arguments people offer is that surely God is more concerned that we behave like good people and treat our fellow humans decently than whether or not we put a *mezuzah* on our door.

But this attitude, which is highly prevalent in today's society, betrays an incomparable arrogance. Has God become too old or irrelevant to be asked what He wants? The philosopher treats God as if He were not present in the world. He uses humanly engineered ethics and values to create the notion of a God who shares these values. Obviously proceeding in this vein is a far cry from leading a holy life or fulfilling the Divine Will. Holiness does not come about when a human think tank meets on a Wednesday night and decides that God must definitely hate communism, for example, and thus all who combat it or who lead capitalist lives are holy. Rather, holiness comes about when man humbly subjugates himself to God's Will and executes those things that God tells him are virtuous and holy, in the same way that love is shown from a husband to his wife when he asks her what she wants and acts accordingly, rather than guessing at her will. Essentially, the philosopher then serves not God, but himself. The ethics and values he creates may be noble and worthy, but they are not necessarily Godly. Just because man may accept specific goals as being worthy does not necessarily mean that God concurs. Even a strict life of devoting oneself to the ideals that one feels to be the most sublime, and even forfeiting one's life in pursuit of those goals will bring the philosopher closer, not necessarily to the Creator, but to the deity that he has conceived and created.

The revelationist, however bases his worship of God entirely on the Torah, a Divine Law received from Heaven. He does not serve God the way he personally understands and deems fit. He serves him the way God Himself wants to be served, according to God's commands, regardless of how they correlate to society's or his personal set of values. The revelationist excels not at pontificating or waxing lyrical with regard to the heavenly Will. Rather he excels at listening to what God wants and proceeds accordingly.

SUBSTITUTING GOD'S WILL FOR OUR OWN WILL

We may now return and answer our original question concerning why the Torah makes no mention of Abraham's considerable self-sacrifice in his early years but rather begins the account with God's command to Abraham to leave his land and birthplace. The reason is that Abraham's early self-sacrifice had no significance before he experienced his first Divine revelation and fulfilled his first Divine command. Before God revealed to Abraham what it was that He desired of him, Abraham's self-sacrifice to advance and disseminate the awareness of God was done merely to fulfill what he himself considered important, on the basis of his own limited intellectual conclusions, however worthy they were. It was Abraham himself who concluded that there must be a Creator and that this Creator wishes to be known throughout the world. Moreover, he determined by means of his own reasoning that God wishes also to be served, and Abraham set about making himself into the very medium for the propagation of this novel and all-important concept.

However, when the Torah tells us important narratives of the patriarch Abraham's life, it is not doing so as a general history lesson, but only as part of the specific history of the birth of the Jewish nation. The Torah's accounts of Abraham's life are meant to tell us how the first Jew came to be and what this means to those of us living today.

PURPOSE OF THE JEWS

What God desired from the Jewish people was a nation that would reject idol worship and embrace the belief in the one and only omnipotent God. The antithesis of belief in God is not idolatry, but arrogance. Believing in God essentially means taking God seriously, and the more seriously one takes oneself, the less seriously one can take God. The ultimate arrogance is that of a person who takes himself so seriously that he designates Divine commands in accordance with what *he* believes the Supreme Will must be. In other words, the ultimate arrogance is for a human being to create God in his own image, to reject listening to the call of heaven in favor of personal testaments and philosophies.

The exemplary life that Abraham led up to the time of God's bidding, "*Lekh lekha*," may have made him a good person, but it did not make him a good Jew. A Jew is someone who substitutes God's will for his own will, God's set of values and morals for his set of values and morals. A Jew is someone who strives to create himself in God's image, rather than creating God in the image of man. A Jew listens to what God believes is important, rather than lecturing to God about what humans feel is important. And even if the two happen to be the same, the Jew fulfills them because they are important to the Supreme Being, not to himself. The Jew is someone who is prepared to substitute humility and acceptance of the Almighty's Supreme Will for idol worship and arrogance.

ABRAHAM BECOMES A JEW

What defines a proper religious person and that which makes a good Jew is sharing a relationship with God. *Sharing a relationship with God* entails accepting the yoke of heaven, doing what God wants because God wants it done. Incidentally, this is also what makes a good marriage. A couple's life together thrives when they listen to each other and strive their best to fulfill each other's bidding. Therefore, Abraham's intellectual conclusions, regardless of their amazing accuracy and consistency with the Supreme Will, reveal not Abraham the Jew but only Abraham the human being. They show Abraham as a component of creation perfecting his outlook and character, but only on the basis of what he, a finite organism, considered to be correct. The beginning of Abraham the Jew took place when God *revealed* himself to him. Abraham finally experienced the Infinite. He left the confines of created space and was uplifted beyond his own abilities and innate human constraints. He developed an irrevocable bond with the Almighty. He became holy because he was attached to, and in a relationship with, a being of supreme holiness. He became a Jew because the revelation had distinguished him from the amorphous mass of creation and catapulted him to the domain of the Creator, not just the created. He was transformed from Abraham the humanitarian to Abraham the Jew, from Abraham who has his own pet causes, charities, and concerns to Abraham who serves God's cause and enjoys a unique closeness with the Creator of the world. In short, Abraham, by virtue of the fact that he was now executing the Will of the Divine, for all intents and purposes was no longer strictly human. Like the courtier of a king or the adjutant of a field marshal who, in the process of communicating and executing the wishes of his commanders, is thereby uplifted far in excess of his own natural importance, so too was Abraham transformed and uplifted to the realm of the Divine when he received his first Divine command. He suddenly transcended his corporeal being and was lifted higher than the planets and stars to the abode of the Creator. And with this he became the first Jew, the father of a spiritual and Godly nation.

2

THE GODLINESS THAT
IS FOUND IN A JEW

The previous chapter presented the differences between philosophical investigation and Divine revelation, as well as the ascendancy of revelation over rational analysis. The philosopher, who utilizes his own values and intellect in approaching divinity, creates God in his own image, whereas the revelationist accurately apprehends the Creator since the truth of God is revealed to him. By completely subjugating his personal will to that of the Divine Creator, Abraham was transformed from being merely a humanitarian who practices kindness because he concludes that it is worthy, to a Jew who does so because God wills it thus.

To attain an even deeper understanding of this pivotal concept, which serves as the very foundation for defining the Jew and the sublimity of the Jewish nation, this chapter explores the subdivision in the levels of existence in the empirical world that surround us.

DISTINGUISHING BETWEEN CREATOR AND CREATED

Any cursory glance at the empirical world reveals four general categories of creation: mineral, vegetable, animal, and intellectual (human). The *Kuzari*, a profound eleventh-century work of Jewish philosophy by Rabbi Yehudah Halevi, adds a fifth category: the Jewish nation. Nevertheless, Jewish literature generally refers only to the existence of the first four. The reason is that the Jew is not merely a fifth, additional category in creation. The essential nature of the Jew utterly transcends the creation of the universe and its four general categories. This is a curious statement. Like all other created beings, a Jew possesses and is limited by a corporeal body. Surely then, the Jewish people are no different from any other finite being who is a prisoner of his own constitution! Where then does the difference between the Jew and the rest of creation lie? To answer this question, we must begin with another basic assumption: everything in existence must perforce be classified as either Creator or created.

The Creator is the single, infinite God. He alone is in this category. His existence is omnipresent, leaving no room for any other existence. However, being infinite, He has the power to "contract" or restrain His infinite Essence and expanse, thus allowing the existence of other beings. By having done so, He originated the new category of "created."

These created beings did not previously exist within the Creator; they are a new entity other than the Creator, once having been called forth and brought into existence. Every component part of this new entity is inherently limited. These very limitations constitute the created entity. For if this entity is to be classified as a new existence other than the Creator, then it must be defined as such. And if it is capable of being defined, then it is limited. Any definition necessarily connotes limitation.

If something can be defined, it can be understood and explained. In contrast, an infinite existence cannot be understood or explained because it transcends all definition and limitation. The Creator exists outside any kind of limitation. Since He is the Creator of all limitation and definition, He transcends those limitations and exists outside them.

All created existence, being essentially limited, is a secondary entity existing *in addition* and as an auxiliary to God's existence. It is this secondary entity, the creation itself that God constantly sustains and recreates, that is divided into the four categories of inanimate, vegetable, animal, and intellectual. Although qualitatively these four categories differ greatly, they can be classified together because they all have the same common denominator: all are created.

The Creator, however, cannot be placed in the same category as the created or be compared with them, for He transcends all limitation while they are confined to their own meager limitations. What is the difference between infinite and finite? Between one and a million there is a vast gap; between one and a billion is greater yet; and between one and a trillion, the difference can be mind boggling. Yet, all these differences fall within one category, the category of limitation. Between one and two there is but a single unit, and between one and a trillion are a trillion units. We can actually quantify the gulf that divides these two numbers. Yet, both one and a trillion are *equally* of no comparison with infinity. Between one and the infinite and between a trillion and the infinite stands an equally infinite, unidentifiable difference. Every finite number, whether one or a trillion, is in an utterly different category than the infinite.

In the same way, the Creator and the created are utterly different classifications. And despite the vast differences among the categories of created beings, they are all essentially on one plane. An inanimate stone may seem incomparable to the intellect of a human being, yet both are components of the same finite creation. Both are dependent upon God for their existence. The difference between them, vast as it may seem, is therefore only finite and relative. All created existence, then, is a secondary entity distinct from God and is essentially limited. There is, however, one exception to this rule: the Jew. Because Abraham merited a Divine revelation in the form of God's commandment, "*Lekh lekha*," he established a bond with the Creator, thus transcending the domain of the created. Because Abraham was the first member of the category of the created to have contact with the Creator, a contact that continued through ongoing revelation and Divine invitation, he was given access to that domain to the extent that part of it was incorporated into his being. His proximity to God as a result of his execution of the essential Divine Will allowed him to ingest and invest within himself a spark of the Divine.

Stated in other words, the Godly communion between Abraham and the Almighty was internalized within Abraham to the point where it actually became a part of his being. There was a part of God that was integrated into Abraham as a result of his fulfilling God's Divine command. This part became his *neshamah*, or Godly soul. Although every human being, indeed every living entity, has a soul, Abraham's soul was different in that it was a vestige of his constant interaction with the Almighty. It was not merely a "holy" or spiritual entity, as are the souls of all other living things, but it was Godly—an actual part of the Divine. His fulfillment of and attachment to the Divine Will served as an umbilical cord that fastened him to the Almighty, thus ensuring that he was attached, and insofar as classification and category are concerned, virtually indistinguishable, from God Himself.

THE MEANING OF CREATION

Let me elaborate on this important concept. Kabbalah and *Hasidus* speak of three forces in operation in creation, all of which serve as the life force that sustains as well as animates all of creation. These three are known by their acronym, NaRaN: *nefesh* (material life force), *ruah* (spirit or soul), and *neshamah*, which in essence has no translation, but which denotes a holy spark of the Divine One Himself.

Many think of the world before creation as a lifeless, shapeless, unrecognizable mass of material. Others think of a palpable darkness, whereas others simply call the precreated world a primordial mass or chaos. To these thinkers, God's creation of the world involved putting order—life, shape, color, and character—to this mass; in short, putting things in sequence. Yet, this idea is a superficial misrepresentation of the true creation. The Hebrew term for creation is *bara*, which means "to bring into being." "To bring into being" connotes that before that act of creation there was nothing at all. When God "created" the world, He brought into being an existence from something that was nonexistent. In fact, the verb *bara* is used in Scriptures exclusively with reference to Divine activity. By stating, "In the beginning God created Heaven and earth," the Torah wishes to convey that what did not previously exist came to exist. Before God created the world in six days it was nonexistent.

What reigned in its absence was absolute nothingness. The Almighty, through His infinite energy, performed what to man is unfathomable: creation *ex nihilo*.

It should therefore be obvious that the Creation differs greatly from the physical product of human labor. When a carpenter takes a rough block of wood and skillfully cuts, sands, and polishes it into a beautiful table that is sold at a high price, he has not created anything. The block of wood with which he started remains a block of wood, although with a different appearance and form. The carpenter has refashioned, reshaped, and enhanced an existing block of matter, but has introduced no qualitative property into it that it did not previously possess. Had the carpenter never come along and worked on the wood, it would have remained peacefully unmoved in its natural environment. Furthermore, an artist can put paint on canvas or give form to a lump of marble and then walk away, and the work will remain. The marble will not slip back to its original shape, nor will the paint drip off the canvas back onto the palette. Both will retain the shape, form, and character given by the artist. But when one takes nothing and gives it character, what is there that can possibly retain the character given to it? What is the "it" that is going to maintain the shape that one has carved out or the property that one has introduced? The "it" is a nonexistent "it," and therefore there is nothing present that can maintain the shape, character, or properties one introduces. This creation is totally dissimilar to that of the artist, who began with an existing substance.

NEFESH: THE LETTERS OF CREATION

So what is it exactly that retains the existence of all created objects? According to the Kabbalah, it is the very letters of the Ten Utterances with which God created the world, with which He called forth everything that now exists under the sun and beyond: "Let there be light," "Let there be a firmament in the midst of the waters," and so on. These letters, serving as creative channels of consciousness, form the spiritual life force through which the existence of every material object is maintained.

To quote Rabbi Shneur Zalman from the *Tanya*:

These very words and letters stand firmly forever within the firmament of heaven and are forever clothed within all the heavens to give them life, as it is written, "The word of our God shall stand firm forever" (Isaiah 40:8) and "His words live and stand firm forever. . ." (Liturgy, Morning Prayer). For if the letters were to depart [even] for an instant, God forbid, and return to their source, all the heavens would become naught and absolute nothingness, and it would be as though before the utterance. And so it is with all created things, in all the upper and lower worlds, and even this physical earth. . . . If the letters of the Ten Utterances by which the earth was created during the Six Days of Creation were to depart from it but an instant, God forbid, it would revert to naught and absolute nothingness, exactly as before the Six Days of Creation.

This creative life force, in the form of Divine letters and possessed by every single created entity, is known as *nefesh*. Everything from a lofty angel to a stone possesses a *nefesh*, because without it the object simply could not exist. If an object has a name that defines it, then by extension it must have a *nefesh*, because the very name serves as its sustaining life force.

Yet, this *nefesh* does not give the object life. It is not an animating force. It simply sustains its material structure. It is helpful to think of *nefesh* as corresponding to the *body* of a created object. Although it is a purely spiritual entity, it sustains the object's physical dimension, much as a body sustains a soul.

THE SPIRIT OF LIFE

But plants, animals, and humans, being alive, possess something higher than just *nefesh*. They also have an animating, spiritual life force, which in English may be translated liberally as "soul." This animating life force is known in kabbalistic and hasidic literature as *ruah*, which translates literally as "spirit." The *ruah* is the animating, pulsating life force in every living thing. Not every *nefesh* is the same, however: there is a qualitative hierarchy operating among living things. The degree to which the physical object possesses the necessary faculties for the *ruah* to manifest itself determines what kind of *nefesh* and *ruah* enclothe themselves in the object, for not every *ruah* is equal. In a plant, the *ruah* is fairly limited and merely causes the development and growth of the plant. A plant's spiritual life force is therefore referred to as *nefesh hatzomahas,* a soul for growth.

In an animal, the *nefesh* and *ruah* give it the ability to experience vibrant life, to transport itself, and, most important, to experience and act on will and desire. The animal's spiritual life force is known as *nefesh hahiyunis*, a soul of life. And in a human, the *nefesh* and *ruah* further manifest themselves in the unique ability for rational thought, human emotion, and verbal communication. The spirit also manifests itself in the unique ability of a human being to transcend human limitation, which expresses itself in the human capacity for freedom of choice, a capacity unknown to animals, who are ruled by instinct. The natural instincts of an animal will not allow it to jump into a fire, for example, or otherwise negate its existence. But a human can overcome the limitations of the body and forge his own destiny.

The human version, or the embodiment of *nefesh* and *ruah* possessed by human beings, is referred to in the language of *Hasidus*, as the *nefesh hamaskeles,* or rational soul. This soul, far superior to that of any plant or animal, establishes man's spiritual mastery. In this respect, all human beings are equal since they all possess a human soul. No human being, regardless of race, religion, color, or creed, possesses a superior soul to any other. It is vital that this point be kept in mind throughout the book whenever mention is made of a Jew possessing a *neshamah*. This discussion does not in any way imply that a non-Jew does not have a soul, without which he could not live. In fact, it is the belief in the soul, possessed by every human being, irrespective of color, religion, or creed, as set out in the Bible with the words "And God breathed into [Adam] a soul of life" that constitutes the only logical and rational grounds for egalitarian thinking.

To be sure, we who reside in the democratic West live in an egalitarian time in which it is considered that everyone is equal and everyone is free, and the idea of hierarchy is perceived as an arbitrary imposition on the freedom of man. Yet, how realistic is this conception? As the great hasidic scholar Rabbi Adin Steinsaltz has pointed out in *The Strife of the Spirit* (Jason Aronson, 1988, pp. 248–249): "Egalitarian ideas are not supported by any evidence. The inequality of man is bluntly apparent."

How then can we support this most central precept of democracy and freedom? Rabbi Steinsaltz continues:

> The only way one can find any support for the idea of equality is in a very difficult religious concept: the concept that people are born in the image of the Lord and are therefore equal. There is no other argument that I have heard that serves any purpose. All egalitarian movements are an outcome of Judeo-Christian ideas that contain within them the notion of receiving a divine soul that for everyone is more or less the same.
>
> We can speak, in a way, of the equality of souls mostly because we can't see them. But it is very hard to speak about equality in any other way. All forces everywhere, within and without, work against equality. People are so inherently different—not only different, but unequal—that it requires a constant struggle to accept the notion of some kind of equality. The only justification for the idea is what you may call a mystical one; even though people don't appear to be equal, there is something equal in them.

Thus, the belief in a soul serves as the only rational grounds to justify the idea that is at the core of Western liberal thought and that ensures the liberty and freedom of all man, namely the equality of all human beings. This soul is the same in Jew and Gentile alike, and in no way are we implying anything different. All humans are created in the image of God and are thus equal. Jew and Gentile alike are of equal importance in the eyes of God, as evidenced by the fact that both are His handiwork and both are created in His image. In this there can be no argument, and there can be no doubt.

A SPARK OF THE DIVINE

The contention being made here is that, in addition to a soul, a Jew has inherited something else: a *neshamah*. A *neshamah* transcends the idea of a soul as an animating life force. A *neshamah,* which lacks any proper English translation, is a spark of Godliness. A human being who possesses a *neshamah* possesses a part of God within himself. The Jewish people acquired this part of God by virtue of their forefather Abraham's internalization of Godliness. Just as when one eats and drinks and his food and drink become an actual part of him as the saying goes, "You are what you eat," likewise Abraham, by living so meticulously in accordance with God's Will, *ingested* Godliness to the point where it became an actual part of him. At a certain point in his life, Abraham ceased performing Godly acts and became a Godly being. Abraham had merited a *neshamah.*

This *neshamah* was bequeathed by Abraham to his son Isaac, by Isaac to Jacob, and by Jacob to all Jewish people. Thus, the Godly soul earned by Abraham became a genetic inheritance to the Jewish people forever. The same is true of those who convert to Judaism. The celebrated nineteenth-century kabbalist and halakhist, Rabbi Haim Yosef Dovid Azulai, known as Hida, notes that whenever the Torah speaks of someone who has converted to Judaism, it uses the phrase "a *convert* who converts." But surely, he asks, before they convert, they are not converts. It would seem more accurate for the Torah to state, "A Gentile who converts." Hida explains that from this phrase in the Torah we deduce that those who begin their lives as Gentiles and later convert to Judaism are actually born with a "spark" of *neshamah*, a Jewish soul. Even at birth they are destined to be converts. Later, upon conversion, the entirety of that soul enclothes itself within the body. This *neshamah* transmuted to the Jewish people also ensures that the relationship between God and the Jewish people will forever be an intrinsic one, based on Godly communion and revelation, rather than on intellectual speculation.

Thus, although created within the physical world, the Jew has within his limited body a "spark" of God—the *neshamah*, the Divine soul. Unlike the created beings in the various categories, the *neshamah* was not *created*. In other words, it is not a separately created entity that now apparently exists "outside" the unity of God. Rather, it has always been part of God Himself.

The *neshamah* in relation to God is like the flame of a candle that is lit from a fiery torch. Quantitatively, the flame of the candle lacks the intensity and brightness of the torch. Qualitatively, however, the flames of the torch and the candle are identical. Moreover, the flame of the candle in essence remains part of the torch from whence it was drawn. Not only while the flame is still within the torch before the candle is lit, but even after the candle is lit and is a distinct entity removed from its source, the candle is still essentially the same as the original torch. The wick that burns is now different, but the flame is the same. Similarly, although the separate existence of the body would seem to make it different, the soul remains the same entity as its original source. It remains unaffected by its embellishment within the finite body.

Physical distinctions have meaning only in the created world, but in the spiritual realm where the soul exists above the limitations of the body, they are negligible and meaningless. Therefore, despite the fact that the Jew's body is created, he is not separate from God. On the contrary, because his soul is a part of the Divine, he becomes an extension of God, as it were. The fact that the Jew has within him only part of the Infinite does not remove him from the Infinite. He is not newly created, but is like the flame that is an extension of its source. The flame, even though physically separated from its source, retains its source's characteristics. Similarly, the Jew is an extension of his Divine source, and his essence retains the unique characteristics of God Himself. By virtue of the fact that the Jewish patriarchs connected themselves to God and embraced His will, they ensured that their descendants would be as an extended existence of God, not an added one.

The four categories of creation then are limited because they are created and not Divine. But the Creator is only one, and the Jew, as somewhat of an extension of the Creator, just as the candle flame is an extension of the torch, cannot be classified merely as a component of creation. He cannot be considered a fifth category of creation, but rather comes under the classification of Creator, since he constantly remains attached to his source.

BELIEF AS AN INNER EXPERIENCE

Just as God Himself is infinite, meaning that He cannot be limited or understood, so is the *neshamah* of the Jew, for it is part of the Infinite. The sublimity of the soul remains ever elusive; the only factual statement that can be made about it is that it is transcendent and supernatural. More definitive statements about its essence cannot be made.

However, the infinite nature of the Jewish soul finds expression in one area—in the Jew's belief in God, which is radically different from the philosopher's rational approach and acceptance of the existence of a purposeful creator.

Maimonides writes, "The Jewish people are believers, the descendants of believers." Jews believe in God intuitively, not through intellectual proof. For them, lifting their eyes toward the heavens in moments of sorrow or loss is as instinctive as reaching for a crust of bread in time of hunger.

Many inquiring, philosophical minds have succeeded in proving logically the existence of a Creator. Regardless of whether their conclusions are correct, this process is based not on faith but on intellectual speculation. Their belief is based on conclusions arrived at by limited men with limited understanding.

Yet, in his most natural state, before being influenced or persuaded by external schools of thought, the Jew believes instinctively due to the Godliness he experiences from within himself. As a part of God, he naturally experiences the Divine as part of his very being. He believes in God because he experiences himself as an extension of God. And even those Jewish individuals who profess atheism are perforce what we might call "aggressive atheists." They must consciously resist their natural predisposition to theistic affirmation.

LOGIC VERSUS REVELATION

Hasidus emphasizes the magnitude of difference between this intuitive Jewish approach to Divine worship and the rationalist's logical approach.

The Jew, possessing a Divine soul, has a natural, intuitive belief in God. Because he is a part of God, the Jew feels and sees Godliness from within. It is the innate Divine experience that fosters belief. This belief in God is like the love of a child for a parent. Although the child appears as a distinct entity, the child feels intrinsically bound to and inseparable from the parent.

In this attachment of the Jew to his Creator, it is not the believer who is predominant but the Creator in whom he believes. The Jew is being acted upon passively by the supernatural forces that work within him. It is the image of God that is being transposed upon the person, rather than a mere speculative conjecture of an image that he formulates in his own mind. The Jew's faith is founded not on his own intellectual proofs, but on the Godliness revealed in his *neshamah*. For this reason, his belief can never be shaken by intellectual counterproofs or philosophical refutation. Nothing can dissuade him from what he experiences and feels.

The rationalist, by contrast, bases his belief on intellectual proof. Therefore, his grasp of Godliness is limited. If his belief is based on his own personal understanding, it is limited by the boundaries of that understanding. The more intelligent he is and the greater his arguments, the stronger his belief. If he is less intelligent and has weaker arguments, his belief is commensurately weaker. However, even the belief of a great intellectual can falter if a wiser man disproved his convictions. Similarly, a traumatic experience in his life might refute his logical belief in a single moment. One may, for instance believe in God because everything logical points in that direction. But upon making a single trip to Auschwitz and seeing the destruction of human life that took place without God's intervention and protection, one may be led to conclude that indeed God does not exist. This illustration is familiar to many of us and demonstrates, with frightening realism, just how weak intellectual speculation can be.

One of the reasons for this debilitating weakness is that the only bedrock for the intellectual's belief is himself. He has not seen or experienced the revelation. He lacks the internalized Godliness inculcated by Abraham. Rather, he believes in God because he has a brain, and his intelligence points in that direction. The famed MaHaRaL (Rabbi Yehudah Loewe) of Prague expressed this concept aptly *(Gevuras Hashem,* chap. 9): "One whose knowledge of the Creator's existence results from his own probing and intellectual investigation possesses only the knowledge of a mortal, limited man. But one who *believes* in the Almighty, this belief results from this awareness of the presence of God from within, and he is thus drawn to Him immeasurably." Belief is therefore on a much higher spiritual plane than intellectual investigation.

FRIENDSHIP AND THE
PARENT–CHILD RELATIONSHIP

To better appreciate this difference in the connection to and apprehension of God between the rationalist and the revelationist who possesses an internal Godly element, let us contrast the relationship between two friends and between parent and child.

Friends are distinct, identifiable entities who join in sharing good will and companionship. Because the friendship bridges a gap to join two separate entities, friends must share some common interest. One who has a sense of humor, for example, may make friends with others who enjoy a laugh, whereas a profound intellectual may be attracted to friends of a similar academic bent. Their friendship depends on their recognition of their counterpart's attributes, character, and dispositions, as well as their finding something in common that they share.

However, such a bond between friends has an inherent weakness. Since the friendship depends on the perception each has of the other's qualities, and it is in direct proportion to the other's attributes, the bond is limited. How great can a friend's virtues be? How funny can they be, or how intelligent? After all, they are only human. Furthermore, even recognition of these qualities by the other party in the relationship is limited, for the one who perceives them too is only human. Even more important, since the friendship depends on the attributes the two have in common, if one ever loses that attribute, the friendship is dissolved. If he is not funny any more and can no longer make his friend laugh, the friendship dissolves, for the glue binding it has lost its adhesiveness and the common ground on which they once met has now dissipated.

On the other hand, the bond between parent and child is indestructible. It is a relationship that depends upon no tangible quality, such as intelligence or sense of humor, which can disappear and dissolve the relationship with it. In fact, parent and child are halves of one whole, sharing one essence. The proof of this is that no parent who, Heaven forbid, ever lost a child has emerged whole. Something of the parent dies with the child. The two are indivisible. This is also why a parent is willing to do or risk anything for his child, or at least anything that he is willing to do for himself. The child is not an entity divisible from the parent, but an extension of the parent. In effect, they share the same essence.

Therefore, although the greatest of loves is self-love, parents can still love their child as much as they love themselves, for their child *is* a part of themselves. Even if a child lacks all virtue, the parent's love is undiminished. If an outstanding and virtuous stranger were to offer himself to the parent in exchange for the undistinguished child, no normal parent would accept. Although the stranger may be kinder, wiser, more talented, or more respected, he is not this parent's child. The parent's love is not a rational one. These two types of love parallel the difference between the rationalist's and the revelationist's, or Jew's, bond with God. The rationalist's love is an intellectual bond that depends on the conscious commitment of the two parties involved. The Jew's bond, on the other hand, is an intrinsic, intuitive love dependent on no external consideration and therefore strikes far deeper than any love is or bond created by the intellect. We therefore witness the ironic phenomenon that even when a couple divorces, they still remain attached to their children. No one can ever be divorced from their children. Whereas marriage can often be predicated on mutual interests and can therefore break down in the absence of those interests, having children is an extension of one's essence, and in the same way one can never be divorced from onself, one can never be divorced from one's children.

BETWEEN WORSHIPING GOD AND WORSHIPING SELF

The difference between the Jewish *neshamah* and the rationalist's intellect is also apparent in the approach to serving God.

The rationalist does not have Divine commandments, for God has not informed him through Divine revelation what He requires of him. Even his belief that God exists is based solely on his own intellect. Therefore, he decides for himself what he feels will please God. The rationalist creates God in his own image, using the tools of his moral construct and intellect. To this extent, for all intents and purposes, he may not be worshiping the real God. He is worshiping God only as he, a limited human being, perceives Him, in the manner he feels God would favor. Essentially, then, he is serving not God, but himself. His form of worship may have little relation to the true worship of God. And what if he is off the mark completely?

The Jew, on the other hand, bases his worship of God entirely on the Torah, a Divine Law received from Heaven. He does not serve God the way he personally deems fit; he serves Him the way God has told him that He wants to be served. The Jew fulfills the commandments that God gave at Sinai and by subjecting himself to Divine revelation ensures that the God he worships, and whose precepts he follows, is real.

CROSSING THE POINT OF NO RETURN

Surely, as a consequence of all of the above, one of the questions that must be nagging the reader at this point is the fact that throughout the ages, and especially in modern times, there have been many nonobservant Jews, Jews who have abandoned not only their belief in God but also their worship of Him and observance of His commandments. How can we reconcile this fact with everything stated above? How can we maintain that indeed there is an intrinsic bond between the Jew and his Creator that draws him, subliminally and unwittingly, to his Father in heaven when there is such a high number of atheists and agnostics within the Jewish community? The explanation for this seeming inconsistency is as follows: a Jew truly wishes to be connected with his Master in heaven. This desire, which may be an unconscious wish, prevents the Jew from transgressing God's Will and being out of favor with God. The reason that some Jews can lead lives in contradiction to God's Will is that their natural inclination misleads them into believing that God will love them and embrace them, even if they do not keep all the commandments. They talk themselves into believing that in spite of the fact that they may not actively participate in a Jewish community, they are nevertheless Jewish and an indivisible part of the Jewish nation. And although of course this is true and a Jew is always a Jew, irrespective of the level of his or her commitment, they are still deluding themselves into accepting that what is important is merely not to cross the irreversible line that would totally compromise their Jewishness. Thus, the same Jews who profess and practice an aggressive atheism would still never convert to another religion or, in most cases, deny that they are Jews.

Take, for example, a child whose parent asks him to clean up his room every day. The child ignores his parent's bidding, not because he does not love his parents but simply because he believes that in reality ignoring their requests is not a matter of such great importance. In the child's mind he believes sincerely that his failure to listen to his parents is certainly not something that will compromise their love for him. However, if the parent is very sick in the hospital and is calling for his son, the son immediately drops everything and runs to the hospital. The reason: this is something undeniably significant. Refusing the parent's request under such circumstances may indeed compromise the special relationship the son has with his parent, and the son avoids this at all costs.

We observe the same phenomenon in the relationship between Jews and their Judaism. Although many Jews are prepared to eat nonkosher food, even they usually refrain from eating anything at all on Yom Kippur. Or, when Israel is at war, we witness how even Jews who are not affiliated with the Jewish community drop everything they are doing and run to volunteer or raise money for the war effort. Or, when their child tells them that he is about to become engaged to a non-Jewish person, they quickly run to the rabbi for help. The reason: they understand that this is a point of no return. The unconscious desire to remain attached to the Jewish people and the God of Israel emerges, and their desire to retain their link with God is thoroughly manifest.

An excellent contemporary example of this phenomenon is the "Who is a Jew?" controversy that has been raging for a number of years throughout Jewish communities in the Diaspora. The Israeli government's Law of Return stipulates that any Jew who returns to Israel and declares his or her intention to reside in the land is granted automatic citizenship. The question that this law raises, however, is the definition of "Who is a Jew?" When Jews in certain quarters mistakenly perceived that the controversy meant that if they are Reform or Conservative Jews they would be rejected as not being Jewish, they were appalled that someone would remove the title "Jew" from them. They came out fighting. They took out large advertisements in the leading newspapers proclaiming that they are Jewish and no one can dare say they are not. Amid the ugly infighting within the Jewish community, the beauty of this ordeal is that it exposed for all to see how strongly Jews from all sectors of society and at differing levels of observance cling to their Jewish identity. Even Jews who were outside the mainstream of Jewish life were prepared to go to any extreme against those whom they (mistakenly) thought sought to deny their Jewishness. Sometimes this unbreakable bond between the Jew and his God is revealed, and sometimes it is hidden until some experience exposes it.

THE UNIQUENESS OF THE JEWISH MARTYR

Another interesting example of unilateral and undeniable Jewishness, across the entire spectrum of individuals, is the phenomenon of Jewish self-sacrifice throughout history. To be sure, both Jews and non-Jews throughout history have suffered martyrdom for their ideals. Many are the accounts, for example, of Christian martyrs thrown to the lions to entertain Roman masses. The Jewish record, sadly but undeniably, requires no elaboration.

Yet, there is an essential distinction between the sacrifice of the religious revelationist and that of the religious rationalist, a difference that strikes much deeper than dying for one's belief or people. First, the Jew dies for his adherence to the Commandments given him by God; therefore his self-sacrifice fulfills God's Will. The rationalist, however, dies not for God, but for him-

self. The belief for which he lays down his life is no more than
his own personal speculation of what God desires; however
meritorious that may be, it is still his own conclusions for which
he lays down his life. God has not told him that these beliefs
are so precious that they outweigh life itself. The rationalist has
himself determined that this is a belief worth sacrificing one's
life for. Therefore, he dies for what he personally feels is important, not necessarily for what God feels is important. And
even if, by chance they are consistent, the rationalist still gives
up his life for what are essentially his own beliefs. Yet, a more
important distinction between Jewish and non-Jewish martyrs
throughout the ages is the *kind* of Jews who died. In almost
every religion, political system, or other ideological group, the
martyrs have been those who openly followed their religion
(saints and those who adhered to their religion to the best of
their ability). But who ever heard of a nonbelieving Christian
dying for Christianity? And who has ever witnessed a defrocked
communist dying for communism? It has always been those who
strongly held faith in their particular beliefs who died for, or
were prepared to die for, those beliefs. Yet, the Jewish record
is saturated with examples of nonobservant, hellenized, angli-
cized Jews who died, rather than convert and lose the title
"Jew." Throughout Jewish history these Jewish masses have
been ready and willing to forfeit their lives, rather than give up
their Judaism. Why would those who had totally abandoned
Jewish practice suddenly be prepared to die in order that they
might remain Jewish? One explanation might be that the Jew
has a subliminal attachment to his God and to his people, and
that this attachment completely transcends anything rational;
this intrinsic relationship to God is predicated on the possession of a *neshamah*, a spark of God Himself instilled within
every Jewish individual, regardless of observance or lifestyle,
resulting from the revelation of God to our forefathers.

THE FIRST COMMAND: LEAVE YOUR LIMITED SELF

Based on this discussion, we may now appreciate why Abraham's
first encounter with God consisted of a Divine command. After

all, it seems proper that before God actually commands Abraham to perform a specific act, He should first introduce Himself to Abraham as the Creator of the world. Why skip any formal introduction and have the original revelation consist of a commandment, before any salutatory gesture of any kind is made?

The answer is that the great significance of the revelation and how it transformed Abraham is conveyed specifically in the fact that it was a *command*. By virtue of this first command, Abraham was no longer basing his worship of God on his personal, created knowledge. He had received a command from the Infinite above creation and would serve God the way *God* wished to be served. Instead of being a mere mortal who, although a humanitarian, had no real connection with God or His Will, because he was executing his own, and not God's Will, Abraham was now a mortal who was fully in touch with the Divine. It is with this Godly experience of which Abraham became a part that the Torah begins its mention of Abraham, now the Jew, now part of the Infinite. This transformation accounts for the content of the first commandment Abraham received: "Go from your land, from your birthplace, and from your father's house, to the land that I shall show you."

Why does this commandment specify all these actions separately: leaving his land, his birthplace, and father's house and going to the new land? God could simply have told him to go to that new land, and Abraham would have understood that to do so he must leave other places.

Jewish tradition maintains that every word in the Torah is precise and laden with meaning on many levels. *Hasidus* explains that all four expressions allude to basic human faculties:

1. "Your land" refers to the power of will; *eretz*, Hebrew for "land" is etymologically related to *ratzon* "will."
2. "Your birthplace" refers to natural inborn habits.
3. "Your father's house" refers to intellect, which in Kabbalah is called *abba*, "father."
4. "The land that I [God] shall show you" refers to God's Will.

In its deeper spiritual intent, God was telling Abraham in this command to rid himself of his own limited will, inborn habits, and intellect and to start fulfilling the Supreme Will—to discard his own desires and aspirations and to follow the lead of the Divine. But what was wrong with these faculties as they had previously existed within Abraham? Surely his will was to spread Godliness and his habits were noble and benevolent, prompting him to devote his life and fortune to benefit his fellow man by feeding the hungry and the poor and to pursue holiness and spirituality. And certainly his intellect had enabled him to observe the universe and rationally postulate the existence of God. So why God's sudden command to leave them all behind?

Hasidus's answer is that it was the word *you* that preceded each of these faculties that required uprooting. Abraham doubtless had a refined will, noble habits, and a keenly developed intellect. Nevertheless, they were "yours" (human), limited components of creation, not part of the Creator. The essence of the Jewish nation, on the other hand, is to be Godly, veritably part of the Infinite. A Jew should not base his worship of God on limited human logic, but on Divine revelation expressed through commandments. Nor are his habits based merely on a human understanding of the necessity to act nobly. In effect, God was telling Abraham: when you transcend the bounds of a created being and start fulfilling *My* Will, only then will you become transformed into a new being, a Jew.

God's command is followed by a fitting reward: "I will make you into a great nation!" The *Midrash Tanhuma* comments that God did not promise that He will *establish* Abraham as a great nation, but He will *make* you—He is making you, re-creating you, Abraham, into a "new creation." Abraham had long ago risen far above all other creatures in his awareness of God and devotion to Him. Yet, until God's command, he remained a man like other men. However, when he forced himself to submit to the Supreme Will, he was transformed into "a new creation"—a man in accord with God, a man attached to God. And, therefore, a Godly man.

BECOMING A NEW BEING

Making a transition from non-Jew to Jew meant becoming a new entity. This was true for Abraham, and it is true for all genuine proselytes to Judaism, as the Talmud states, "A proselyte converting is like a newborn child" (*Yevamos* 47a; see also *Yad Hahazakah, Hilkhos Issurei Biah,* 14).

One who converts according to all stipulations of *halakhah,* including acceptance of the *mitzvos,* has not undergone any quantitative change, becoming a better person or performing more good deeds. The change is rather a qualitative one, transforming him into a new being infinitely higher than in his previous existence, since now he lives in accord with the Divine Will. The convert is endowed with a *neshamah.* Before the non-Jew converts, he may be most virtuous. Although he is aware that traditionally Jews have been persecuted, oppressed, and afflicted with suffering, his pursuit of truth and purity may be so powerful that it induces him to choose Judaism, exposing himself to these potential hardships in his quest for what he perceives to be a noble and holy life. He may truly be a great human being! But he is *only* a human being. Only when the proselyte actually converts does he merit receiving a new soul, a part of the Divine, since he joins a people who are attached to the Divine.

God also promised Abraham that his descendants, the Jewish people, would become "a great nation." Great and insignificant, large and small, in this world all are relative. To say that someone has only two strands of hair on his head does not sound like much, but to find two strands of hair in one's bowl of soup is quite a bit indeed. Similarly, something is large only in comparison with something smaller. A billion dollars seems vastly greater than one dollar, which in turn seems tiny in comparison. However, the vastness is limited. In fact, without an accumulation of these tiny singles, there can be no billion. Similarly, man may seem great in relation to an insect or a stone, yet he is utterly insignificant in relation to stars and galaxies.

One finds absolute greatness only in God himself. God is intrinsically sublime and transcendent; His greatness is not relative, not dependent upon supremacy over lesser beings. No greatness is like His essential greatness and vastness, which includes all existence. Abraham, by fulfilling God's command, united himself and his descendants with God, elevating them thereby to what may be described as true greatness. The Torah declares, "What other great nation exists to whom God is close?"

(Deuteronomy 4:7). The greatness of the Jews is not that they
are close to God, but that *He is close to them*. Their awareness
of God and attachment to Him are based not on their intelligence
and religious convictions, but on God's revelation and commands in the Torah and *mitzvos*.

GREATER IS HE WHO IS COMMANDED

Having explained the underlying meaning behind God's command to Abraham, we can further elucidate the talmudic dic-
tum "Greater is one who has been commanded and fulfills the
mitzvos, than one not commanded who fulfills them" (*Kiddu-
shin* 31a).

Ostensibly it would seem fair for just the opposite to be true.
One who is not commanded to perform God's command but
who nevertheless fulfills it seems to display a higher degree of
love and devotion. He is fulfilling the command not out of obligation, but purely out of a sincere desire to draw closer to his
Creator. So should he not be greater than one who fulfills God's
command only because he has been commanded to do so?

Hasidus explains that when one who is not commanded
performs a *mitzvah*, he does indeed show that he is perhaps a
righteous person. However, his deed is performed by a limited
being. It does not have the infinite potency of the Almighty.
When, however, one who is commanded by God performs
the exact same *mitzvah*, it becomes a totally different act. The
mitzvah now has within it the potency of God, Who gave the
mitzvah, and it thereby transcends the limitations of creation,
uniting the Jew doing the *mitzvah* with his Creator.

The good deed of a human being, however bold his intention, is still the act of a finite human. But the performance of a
mitzvah Divinely commanded has within it an infinite dimension that elevates the one doing the act, the physical object he
uses in executing the act, and the very act of the *mitzvah* itself.
All are elevated to the realm of the Divine and are thus united
with the source from whence they spring.

3

SYMBOL OF SACRIFICE

As was discussed in the previous chapter, the essence of the Jew is the Divine soul within him. This soul, which is an actual part of Godliness, is a product of Abraham's internalization of his communion with God through the execution of Divine commands revealed to him through direct revelation. This Divine soul is the genetic inheritance of the seed of Abraham, Isaac, and Jacob. The Jew thus experiences Godliness from within, as an integral part of himself. This inheritance shapes his approach to serving God. Although the rationalist bases his service of God on his own intellectual understanding, the Jew serves Him because he has been commanded by God, of whom he is a part and which he feels from within.

This difference in approach began when our forefather Abraham became the first Jew—when he had his first encounter with the Infinite and received his first Divine command. Yet, it was most fully expressed at the *Akeidah*, the well-known biblical narrative of the "binding of Isaac." This narrative in the Torah, in which Abraham is commanded by God to take the son he loves and to offer him up as a sacrifice on a specified mountain, has confounded biblical scholars and moralists throughout the ages and has served as the inspiration for countless discourses and essays on problematic themes. How could the good, benevolent God have commanded Abraham to do such a terrible thing? And if the answer is that it was only a test, it seems even more sadistic. Why would God torment a father with such a horrid commandment only in order to rescind it? These questions indeed require examination.

A TEST TO SUBSTANTIATE ALL PREVIOUS TESTS

Our sages tell us that God tested Abraham with ten trials to prove his devotion to Him. The last and greatest of these trials was the *Akeidah*, the binding of Isaac.

Whenever Jews implore God for Divine compassion and patience we refer to the eternal merit of the *Akeidah*. We include the text of the *Akeidah* (Genesis 22:1-19) in our daily prayers, thus showing its central importance in our religion as the supreme symbol of Jewish sacrifice and devotion.

But surely Abraham showed unprecedented self-sacrifice for religion in *all* ten tests. Why is only the last trial so emphasized? Why do our prayers not mention, for example, Abraham's courage early in life in letting himself be thrown in a fiery furnace for spreading belief in one God, when he could have saved himself by denying his belief? The self-proclaimed god–man Nimrod, who was the ruler of the time, sought to silence Abraham's rejection of his divinity by casting the young boy into a giant fire. Thankfully, the Almighty wrought a miracle on Abraham's behalf that saved his life. Surely this act demonstrated Abraham's true love of God, and although this story is not mentioned directly in the Bible it is nevertheless repeated in several important *midrashim* and is also mentioned in the Talmud.

Furthermore, the *Midrash* says that God appealed to Abraham to withstand the test of the *Akeidah*, for otherwise the nations of the world, to whom He held up Abraham as the paragon of Godly devotion, could claim that all previous trials were of no value. Thus, not only was the *Akeidah* the greatest of Abraham's trials but it was also the testing ground for the substantiation all of the previous trials. What distinguished the *Akeidah* from all the other tests so that only it could prove their value?

We have already discussed the two approaches that lead to belief in God—intellectual or philosophical inquiry and Divine revelation. To achieve love of God, there are, similarly, two paths.

The first is the intellectual route. One who meditates on God's transcendence, understanding it intelligently to the best of one's ability, perforce concludes that God is great beyond description. This person is aroused with a burning desire to become one with God or at least come closer to Him. He grasps that it is only God who is worthy of praise and pursuit.

This process is a natural one within the human mind. The intellect examines a concept or object to ascertain its value. It then relays its conclusion to the emotions, which in turn generate either an attraction or a repulsion to the object. If one's intellect concludes that one can somehow benefit from a given subject, then one automatically harbors a craving for it: a child who sees candy concludes he will enjoy its sweet taste and longs for it.

Similarly, meditation resulting in a yearning for closeness to God is actually no more than an intellectual estimation of how this relationship with God can benefit oneself. It may be a very immature and unsophisticated evaluation of how love for God can bring in its wake material reward. Or it may be a much deeper love in which the worshiper seeks no reward, material or spiritual; realizing God's greatness, he appreciates the exalted value of being close to Him, regardless of other benefits. Take, for example, a philosophy student who is exposed to the greatest intellectual stimulation by his wonderful professor. To him, his professor is the greatest mind on earth and serves as the key to a vast storehouse of knowledge and thought. As a result of this appreciation, the student desires to be close to the professor, to the point where he is willing to follow him to the ends of the earth and do almost anything for him, even at the pain of death. But regardless of how strong his love may be, it is still selfish. The student's desire is to benefit—in mind, wisdom, maturity, and character—from his superior mentor. The student really is manifesting nothing more than his great love for himself and his desire to grow and develop his maximum potential.

MARTYRDOM AS SELF-PRESERVATION

The world's two most widespread religions offer many examples of this first type of love. Christianity bids its faithful to love God and serve Him, for in Him they will find salvation and eternal bliss. Such believers swelled the ranks of the Crusader armies when they were promised that whoever gave his life to wrest the Holy Land from the Islamic infidels would achieve immediate and eternal salvation. Islam too promises all who serve Allah everlasting paradise. At time we even witness fanatical Islamic leaders enticing millions to fight a *jihad*, with the promise of immortality to those who die fighting.

Yet this martyrdom, far from expressing a true yearning to attach oneself to the Creator, is actually no more than self-preservation. Since it is based on material and spiritual considerations, the believer's religious conviction is a one-sided relationship. He wants to be close to God, but on the condition that he receives something from the closeness.

By way of analogy, when a man marries a woman for her wealth alone, then for all practical purposes she plays no real part in the relationship. Her groom has removed her from the picture, replacing her with his considerations of how he will benefit financially from the marriage. His marriage to this woman is a statement of how much he loves himself, certainly not the woman.

Likewise, when religion is practiced solely for personal gain, even spiritual advancement, it borders on idolatry. The idol is the worshiper himself, for God is not a consideration in this relationship. The emphasis is on the *one who loves,* not on the *Loved One.*

Far superior is the second path, the love that emphasizes only the One who is loved, not taking into account at all the one who loves. This love is a complete submission on the part of the religious worshiper who sincerely and devotedly desires to be closer to God. This love is expressed in the scriptural verse "A Godly lamp is the soul of man" (Proverbs 20:27). The soul is compared to the flame of the lamp that naturally burns upward. The soul wishes to cling to its source in heaven.

GRAVITATING TOWARD A SOURCE

Hasidus explains that the nature of every created being is to return to its source. Away from its source, it is independent but alone; in its source it finds security. A young child clings to its mother's dress; a wanderer feels comfortable only when he returns home. Similarly, a stone thrown upward always falls back to the ground, and in the same way, fire burns upward in constant yearning to return to its heavenly, elemental root (as explained in the Kabbalah). Ironically, the flame will lose its existence when it returns to its source, being consumed by the much larger torch. Yet, despite every created being's instinct for self-preservation, the flame longs to return to the place where it will lose its independent identity.

Although returning to its source will negate its existence, as it is engulfed by the intensity of its source, the flame cannot resist its nature. The attraction to become one with its source is not based on the desire to become higher or more perfect or to be totally consumed and cease to exist. The flame does not care. Compared with this urge to return to the source, the flame's own existence is insignificant.

The verse "A Godly lamp is the soul of man" tells us that a Jewish soul has this same instinctive yearning. It naturally longs to be reunited with its God, regardless of its own survival as an independent entity. It is only for Godliness that it longs and that draws it heavenward, and it can do nothing to suppress this longing.

MARTYRDOM OF THE MASSES

As was stated in the previous chapter, this attraction explains the unparalleled self-sacrifice of even noncommitted, uneducated Jews throughout the generations. Many Jewish martyrs knew little Torah. They did not always recognize the importance of bringing God into their everyday lives by studying the Torah and observing its commandments. They may not have even imparted a sense of Jewish identity to their children. Yet, they never hesitated to lay down their lives for God and His Torah. What was it that made them feel they could no longer stay alive if doing so meant denying the truth of God—or abandoning their Judaism?

Rabbi Shneur Zalman of Liadi, founder of *Habad Hasidus*, answers that it was the nature of their Jewish soul to be drawn naturally and instinctively to its source. It is a suprarational longing that makes it impossible for a Jew willfully to deny the Creator and his affinity to Him. Only in this way can he account for the startling phenomenon of nonobservant Jews suddenly being so willing to die for their Judaism.

These simple Jews willingly gave up their lives for God, though often they observed few *mitzvos*. Some may even have claimed to deny God's existence. But when it came to the point of no return, when they could no longer delude themselves but realized that accepting alien gods and beliefs would cut them off from God and that they would lose the title "Jew," they could simply never go through with it. They could not deny the instinctive longing of their souls to be united forever with their Divine source.

Such self-sacrifice of even nonobservant Jews has no rational explanation. It derives from the soul, the very essence of the Jew, where reason, logic, and cognitive deduction can play no role. The Jewish *neshamah*, like God of whom it is part, is infinite.

This love is inborn within every Jew. It is a love that emphasizes the One who is loved, not the one who loves. It is a desire to be totally embraced by Godliness and bask in His glory, not for the sake of reaping benefit for oneself but because one feels irresistibly drawn to God.

The Jew's love of God thus parallels his knowledge of Him. As was explained in chapter 1, his knowledge of God is based not on personal meditation or philosophical inquiry, but on Divine revelation regardless of whether he has intellectual proofs. Despite those who seek to disprove his belief, he will never diminish his faith. When he has seen, he can never doubt what his own eyes have experienced.

Similarly, the Jew's love for God and natural yearning to be united with his Creator do not result from any desire to find fulfilment. They comprise a constant irrepressible attraction to become attached to his source. That is why so many Jews utterly ignorant of the basic tenets of their faith have been ready to die for their Creator.

LEVELS OF MARTYRDOM

Martyrs throughout the ages have had widely varying motives for their self-sacrifice. Some become martyrs just to achieve a place in history, so they would be remembered as saints who gave up their lives for their cause. This is not self-sacrifice at all; self-sacrifice means self-denial and humility, whereas this category of martyr seeks self-preservation and self-aggrandizement.

A more exalted but still imperfect level of sacrifice is one in which an individual is ready to give up his life not to advance his own name but out of a sincere belief that the cause is worth dying for. His intellectual deduction brings him to the conclusion that this cause is so precious that it is to his benefit to die for it. Since his own spiritual benefit is the motive, this belief too contains some pride and self-aggrandizement.

Even Abraham's exalted self-sacrifice of letting himself be thrown into the fiery furnace could be construed as embodying elements of selfishness and pride. As the first human to realize independently the falsehood of idolatry and the existence of the true Creator, Abraham had decided to disseminate the knowledge of the one, true God. His campaign brought him into conflict with the authorities, who condemned him for sacrilege. They gave him a choice: deny God's existence or die for your beliefs. To choose the former would have cast serious doubts on Abraham's original sincerity. It would be claimed that his public preaching of his own beliefs could not hold up when the price became too high. Any hesitation to give up his life would have been taken as denial of the ideal he had always sought to affirm and promote. This consideration could have been so strong that Abraham might have felt he could not afford even to imply any denial of his lifelong campaign. How could he destroy in a single moment what had taken a lifetime to build? Better to die a terrible death now at the culmination of his campaign for his beliefs than to admit defeat of all he had worked for. This sacrifice, noble as it might be, is still far from the burning desire of true love for God Himself, above all personal considerations.

MARTYRDOM AS AN UTTER DENIAL OF SELF

The *Akeidah*, however, was different from all previous trials. Abraham could not be suspected of sacrificing his son for the sake of publicity or to show that his belief was worth dying for,

for no observers were present. Even the two servants accompanying him on his journey stayed behind when he ascended the mountain with his son. It was an affair between him, Isaac, and God alone.

Furthermore, if Abraham's motive in agreeing to sacrifice Isaac was to promote his cause, then the last thing he would want was to take that son's life, for doing so would mean the end of his cause. Isaac, the son born to Abraham in his old age, was raised to pursue the same ideals for which Abraham had striven all his life, the only one on earth capable of propagating belief in one God. Although Abraham had another son, Ishmael, born of his Egyptian concubine wife, Hagar, this son abandoned Abraham's monotheistic way of life and embraced idolatry (although later in his life he repented of his ways). It was Abraham's second son, the son born of Sarah, who was groomed as Abraham's spiritual successor and ultimately the only conduit through whom monotheistic belief would be carried forth. To sacrifice this son would destroy Abraham's hope for continuing his life's work. The *Akeidah* could bring only harm for Abraham's cause. In essence, what Abraham was asked to do was sacrifice the entire edifice of monotheism that he had so carefully constructed.

Nevertheless, Abraham did not hesitate. He disregarded all rational considerations of these consequences as his selfless love impelled him to fulfill God's command. And he fulfilled it eagerly and joyfully, elated at this further opportunity to become united with God in this way, regardless of its personal cost.

This was true self-sacrifice, the ability to give oneself totally to God, even if logic dictates that doing so can impede one's personal advancement in spiritual service to God. This supreme level of self-sacrifice Abraham reached only at the *Akeidah*. His previous trials had been based on rational considerations, involving his intellect. They may have been noble efforts, but they smacked of personal motivation and fulfillment. They were attempts on the part of a mortal man to die for those things that he felt to be truly sublime and worthy. But when he withstood the ordeal of the *Akeidah*, God told him, "Now I know that you really fear God." His selfless devotion and burning desire to be attached to God had become manifest.

It is this degree of self-sacrifice that every Jew possesses. It is an integral part of his being, inherited from his forefather

Abraham. His connection with God utterly transcends intellect. He cannot deny it or fight it, just as the flame cannot prevent itself from burning upward. This suprarational, irrepressible love has been manifested by Jews the world over, through all generations, in their consistent readiness to die for God and His commandments, in order to maintain their unbreakable bond with Him.

May their memory inspire us forever!

We conclude this chapter with a more recent symbol of total sacrifice as described by the third Rebbe of Lubavitch. In 1843 the Czarist government of Russia called a rabbinical conference to discuss various matters affecting the religious life of the Jews. The delegates chosen were Reb Menachem Mendel of Lubavitch (known as the Tzemach Tzedek), the renowned scholar Reb Yitzchak of Volozhin, a magnate from Berdichev by the name of Reb Yisrael Heilprin, and Betzalel Stern, the headmaster of the school in Odessa. When Reb Menachem Mendel returned to Lubavitch, he heard that *hasidim* were saying he had sacrificed himself at St. Petersburg for the sake of the House of Israel. He wept bitterly and said,

> Woe is him concerning whom the world errs! Is this self-sacrifice, that a man sacrifices himself for the sake of the House of Israel; perhaps even with a motive of self-interest, for he knows that he is thereby increasing his reward in the World to Come? There is nothing worthy about that kind of self-sacrifice. True self-sacrifice is the kind of action I heard was exemplified by Reb Baruch of Mezhibezh, who sacrificed his life and his share in the World to Come for a solitary Jew—not for the life of that solitary individual—but for saving his property.

Reb Menachem Mendel then told his *hasidim* what happened to Reb Baruch:

> It so happened that one of Reb Baruch's close disciples, a God-fearing *hasid*, was a merchant who used to deliver wine to distant towns. He did not possess the capital needed to pay for his wares at the outset, but because he was known to be a trustworthy man, the wholesalers used to give him wine on account. One night, while he was staying at some wayside inn, the thought entered his mind that there was a certain matter for which he

had not yet repented as fully as he should have. So eager was he to set this right that he left his wagons loaded with wine at the inn and set out at once to see his rebbe at Mezhibezh.

When he arrived, Reb Baruch asked him about his business affairs, so he told his whole story. Hearing that he had left his whole stock of wine unattended at the inn, Reb Baruch surprised him with an avalanche of scolding and abuse: "Fool that you are! How did the thought ever enter your head that you should abandon the property of others over a matter of no consequence?" This encounter took place on Friday afternoon, before the approach of *Shabbos*. But later in the evening, and again by day, there was no end to the same kind of rebuke, which was even carried on in the presence of others.

One of Reb Baruch's guests that *Shabbos* was his relative by marriage, Reb Avraham of Chmielnik, who could not refrain from protesting: "Mechutan! Does the Talmud not say something about he who shames his fellow in public?"

Replied Reb Baruch,"Don't I know that he who shames his fellow in public has no share in the World to Come? But I decided to abandon my share in the World to Come in order to do this poor fellow a favor. You see, his Gentile wagon drivers had already conspired to rob him of all his wine and leave him penniless. But the distress that I put him through with my abuse will save him, for the anguish of publish shame has been reckoned in the Heavenly Court as an ample substitute for the anguish of monetary loss which had been ordained for him."

"This," concluded Reb Menachem Mendel, "is an example of true self-sacrifice: that a person should be prepared to abandon his share in the World to Come in order to spare a fellow Jew some monetary loss!"

4

THE DEBATE BETWEEN ISAAC AND ISHMAEL

In the first three chapters we examined the unique Godly quality instilled within the Jew thanks to our forefather Abraham. We shall now examine an added dimension of spirituality infused within the Jew as a result of the birth and life of the patriarch Isaac.

Abraham waited eighty-six years before he saw the birth of his first child, Ishmael, born of his concubine wife, Hagar. One can appreciate what ecstasy he experienced upon finally being granted an heir. Thus, when God later told Abraham not to despair because his wife Sarah would also provide him a son, Abraham's immediate reaction was "*Lu Yishmael yihyeh lefoneha*," that he would be sufficiently satisfied if his son Ishmael lived on to inherit him. Commenting on this verse, Rashi adds that Abraham meant that he would be satisfied if Ishmael lived on *in the fear of God* all of his days.

But in the midst of Abraham's protest, God interjected, "Still, your wife Sarah will give birth to a son. You must name him Isaac. I will keep My covenant with him as an eternal treaty, for his descendant after him." The Almighty's response established irrevocably the fact that Abraham's mission could be realized only through Isaac, not Ishmael, and that only Isaac would carry on the fathering of the Jewish nation. But why the sudden rejection of Ishmael? It could not be attributed merely to the fact that Isaac was more righteous than his brother, for the implication was that even had Ishmael remained righteous and God-fearing, he still could not have fathered or served as patriarch to the Jewish people. There was something in his very constitution that was un-Jewish. Conversely, there was something inherent in Isaac's nature that was Jewish, and so he was chosen. What advantage did Isaac possess over Ishmael?

THE FIRST TO BE BORN A JEW

The birth of Isaac was a landmark in the formation of the Jewish people. Isaac was not the first Jew. He was preceded by his father, Abraham, as we have already seen. But he was the first to be *born* a Jew. Abraham had been born a heathen and later, after receiving and fulfilling Divine instruction, acquired the characteristics of a Jew, namely a Godly soul. Isaac, however, as the first individual to be born in holiness, embodied a new degree of Jewish sanctity that superseded even that acquired by his father. By first examining the differences between Isaac, the prototype Jew, and Ishmael, the prototype Gentile, who is still a monotheist, we gain an insight into the unique spiritual dimension of our forefather Isaac. We focus on two of the most important events in each of their lives: their birth and their circumcision.

ISHMAEL: A NATURAL, UNCIRCUMCISED BIRTH

Ishmael was born in a totally natural manner. His birth was the intended outcome of Abraham's union with Sarah's handmaid, Hagar, a young Egyptian princess of childbearing age. Isaac, on the other hand, was born to parents well beyond the age of fertility, as Scripture itself testifies: "Abraham and Sarah were old, well on in years, and Sarah no longer had a female cycle." Isaac's birth was thus a miracle. Furthermore, his birth was foretold by God, again demonstrating its miraculous nature.

Although Ishmael's circumcision took place when he was thirteen years old, Isaac was circumcised at the tender age of eight days. The significance of this seemingly trivial detail can be better appreciated through an examination of a dialogue between Isaac and Ishmael found in the *Midrash*. "Ishmael taunted Isaac saying, 'I am dearer [to God] than you, for I was circumcised at thirteen years old.' Isaac replied, 'No. I am dearer than you, for my circumcision took place when I was eight days old.'"

Isaac's reply is baffling. Ishmael seems to have a powerful argument. He is dearer to God since he displayed a greater measure of self-sacrifice for the service of his Creator. Ishmael, at age thirteen, had the choice of whether or not to proceed with the circumcision, and he made a conscious decision to endure the pain and suffering that it would entail. Fulfilling God's command was of more importance to him than avoiding physical pain.

Isaac, on the other hand, was given no choice in the matter. As an infant of eight days he was hardly able to appreciate what was taking place, much less voice dissent. In addition, he was barely aware of the pain. Thus, there was no conscious consent or self-sacrifice to fulfill the Will of his Creator. How then could Isaac, by virtue of his circumcision, be closer and more precious to God than Ishmael? Moreover, how can a *bris*, a covenant, a profound metaphysical connection between the Infinite Creator and man be made with an infant of eight days? Can an infant really appreciate the magnitude or sublimity of such Divine contact? Ishmael, who had forged his covenant as a young adult with the mental capacity to appreciate the magnitude of a heavenly covenant, seems to be more worthy on this point. To understand the virtue of Isaac's *bris* over that of Ishmael, we must return to our earlier discussion of human interrelationships.

THE LOVE BETWEEN RELATIVES AND FRIENDS

In chapter 3 we discussed two kinds of love that take place between humans: a love between friends, *ahavah sichlis* (intellectual attraction), and a love brought about by blood relation, *ahavah atzmis* (intrinsic love). Friends are not born with an intuitive or natural fondness for one another. In fact, at birth they are not even remotely aware of each other's existence. Yet, as they come into contact with one another and share experiences, an affinity between them develops. What is the cause of this attraction? Often love and admiration are aroused through the appreciation of one another's character and talents and virtue. One person's charismatic personality or dedicated leadership may attract others to him. Or a favor rendered may initiate a friendship. In any case, since the two friends or acquaintances are not related by blood, the love must be constantly nurtured and developed if it is to last. One way of doing so is to create a covenant, a binding agreement made between two discrete parties in order to bridge the gap between them and establish a more permanent bond. It is an assurance that although the two may drift apart and find that their interests conflict so that emotional attraction diminishes, they will nevertheless remain loyal and committed to one another.

An example of this first type of love, which does not come naturally and must be aroused, may be taken from a contemporary event. Over the past decade or so the world was exposed to an international media campaign depicting the horrific sight of emaciated mothers and young children in Ethiopa and Somalia. There were also appalling scenes showing how insects and rodents ate from the decaying skin of the forsaken African children. The publicity campaign was tremendously effective and generated a universal outcry to save them. Many countries used their vast resources to provide food and medication for the victims. Rock stars and other celebrities the world over donated their time and talent to organizing concerts and other fund raisers to relieve the plight of the starving Africans. Rescue workers, doctors, and nurses poured into Ethiopia and Somalia from all corners of the globe in an attempt to end the rampant disease and suffering.

Indeed, it is to the credit of humanity that these rescue efforts were launched at all and that they were successful to an extent, notwithstanding the difficulties involved in distributing food in that turbulent part of the world. Yet, although its significance is not minimized, the help arrived only after the publicity campaign. The compassion of the world had to be aroused. Had the original reports of the agony of starving Ethiopians and Somalians been confined to a small column on the last page of some daily newspaper, without any gory picture, the world's reaction might have been less extensive and swift and much more subdued. This phenomenon demonstrates the inherent short-comings of an "artificial" affection. It is not instinctive and therefore must be aroused and thereafter sustained constantly.

WHEN LOVE COMES NATURALLY

Conversely, there exists a higher form of love, congenital and intrinsic, like the love between parent and child. There is no need for this love to be fostered or developed. At the moment of birth, a child is unpresentable and unclean and, having just begun its life, could not possess worthy social or intellectual qualities that would make it appealing to its parent. Yet, at that moment of birth, the parents of the child are overjoyed and love their child as much as, or maybe more, than they ever will. A newborn babe need not arouse the mercy or pity of its mother in order for the parent to feed and care for it. What is the cause of this love?

The answer is as simple as it is mysterious. It is *her* child, her own flesh and blood. Just as self-love may be described as the greatest of all loves, so too is the love for a child an extension of self-love above all others. The love is obvious, instinctive, and natural and requires no attractive qualities. In the event of life-threatening danger, although the natural human reaction is to preserve oneself before others, a parent instinctively puts himself in danger in order to save his own child.

LOVE THAT IS ALL-ENCOMPASSING

If we consider the inherent differences between the two forms of love, the advantages of the latter type become readily apparent. First, when one is attracted to or learns to respect another person by virtue of his or her qualities and character, in effect the love is directed to those particular qualities, rather than to the person himself. The love from parent to child, however, is directed to the very essence of the child, and not to positive personality traits or virtues.

This factor of only one element of the person being admired exists reciprocally as well. If a person's love for another is evoked by virtue of the latter's intellectual faculties, the basis for this love is the fact that the intellect of the former is able to appreciate the intellect of the latter. Thus, the former loves the other only from his own intellect, not from his entire being. His whole being is not permeated with love for the other, but rather his mind is attracted to only one aspect of his colleague.

By contrast, a parent's entire being, not merely a solitary aspect of himself, is bound up with his child. His love does not stem from some isolated intellectual faculty or external arousal. He loves the entire being of the child. The supremacy of loving a person in his entirety is expressed beautifully in the hasidic explanation of why people hug each other when they desire to show affection. For example, when two people who love each other greet at the airport after not having seen one another for a long time, why is it that the first thing they do is hug? Why not talk? Is it not better to exploit each other's higher faculties, such as thinking and communicating? Or why not at least sit and stare at each other, appreciating each other's beauty? Why immediately grab the other person's back and embrace him or her? The hasidic answer is that these two lovers are making a profound statement. They are saying, "I love all of you, not just the part of you that is funny, or your beautiful face, or the fact that you are smart or speak elegantly. Rather, I will grab all of you, even hold on to your back, to show that I love even the back of you. Even that part of you that doesn't *earn* my love, I will specifically hold you so that you may know it is *you* that I love, and not just your higher faculties."

In summary, a relationship between two people whose love is generated by an external cause is inherently limited to that cause, as well as the depth of apprehension of the cause, whereas the love between parent and child has no limits or bounds.

There is another significant flaw in the first type of love. If the loved one ceases to excel in the quality for which he is loved, the love will wane. The love is commensurate with the sublimity of the attribute. Furthermore, even if the attribute and the parallel love remain steady, because the person loving is only relating to a singular facet of the other, when an issue affecting his entire being comes into conflict with his love, the relationship will falter. The consistency and intensity of the parent–child relationship, however, are completely unaffected by variations in either parent or child or by any alien circumstance.

SHARING ONE ESSENCE

It is written, "You [the Jewish people] are children unto the Lord your God." Surely, the Jewish people possess and have manifested throughout the ages transcendent spiritual and physical qualities, but it is not on account of these qualities that the Jew enjoys an intimacy with God. The relationship between the Jews and God, unlike that between friends, is not founded on any external quality that could cause it to flourish or diminish. Rather, the love God harbors for the Jewish people is an intrinsic one, *ahavah atzmis*, like that of parent and child, and is therefore not subject to any outside influence or fluctuation.

The nature of this Divinely oriented parental love is expressed aptly in the Talmud, "For better or worse, they are My children." The *Midrash* continues this thought: "I thus cannot exchange them for a different people." No parent would agree to exchange his child for another, even if the proposed object of exchange is far more intelligent or gifted. The reason: this one is my child, the other is not. Likewise, for God to exchange His people for another is simply absurd. The Jewish people are His children. And this argument serves as the definitive response to those theologians of other religions who have argued that once the Jews forsook the covenant of the Lord, they were in turn forsaken by God as well and replaced by another people and Judaism by another religion. The love that God has for His people is immutable, since it is like that of a father to his children.

Conversely, a Jew's love for God parallels a child's love for a parent. There is really no need to expound on this love inasmuch as it has been demonstrated throughout Jewish history. As was discussed earlier, martyrdom has been commonplace to the Jew, a basic fact of life, yet in itself it does not constitute proof of this love. Thousands of martyrs have died for other religions and beliefs, and even if Jews have a quantitative advantage in the field, this leadership may not be qualitative. What is unique to Judaism is not martyrdom itself, but who the martyrs were. Whereas the martyrs of the Gentile religions were largely the leaders, teachers, and spiritual masters, the great majority of Jewish martyrs were the unlearned, simple masses, people who not only were religiously uncommitted but in many cases never had any exposure to anything Jewish. Yet, even they laid down their lives rather than converting or worshiping idols and thereby being cut off from their Father in Heaven. But why? If they were illiterate in the fundamentals of spirituality and Godliness, why nevertheless were these values dearer to them than life itself? Because God is their Father in Heaven. Just as a child cannot renounce or accept a substitute for his father, a Jew dare not be dissociated from God. This is especially so in times of trouble. As the Talmud proclaims, "As an olive, when pressed, yields its oil," so when the Jews are torn and stricken, their inner love for God is "pressed" into being and is revealed for all to see.

The Jew's identification with God has also never been throttled by the vast number of obstacles that have been thrown in its way. Through all the challenges of history, from attempted intellectual refutation to physical coercion and torture, the Jew has emerged victorious in his steadfast adherence to God's covenant. The recurrent choice between the cross or the sword has always been the sword. At the cost of his life, the Jew cannot be severed from God, his Father in Heaven.

APPLICATIONS OF THIS INTRINSIC LOVE IN *HALAKHAH*

These reciprocal loves find expression in applications of *halakhah.* God's unalterable love for the Jewish people is typified in the laws concerning *tumat ohel*—impurity transferred through tent or roof. This impurity is caused only by the corpse of a Jew and not by the corpse of a Gentile. But what of a *mumar,* a self-proclaimed heretic who had willingly dissociated himself from his Jewish brethren? The *halakhah* states that even a heretic renders a tent unclean. So although this individual may never have lived as a Jew and may even have scorned and insulted the Jewish religion while alive, he remains a Jew. In connection with this ruling, the celebrated talmudic commentator Rashba quotes Rabbi Meir: "For better or for worse they are My children," and concludes that even a heretic is referred to by the Almighty as "My son." Thus, this *halakhah* illustrates that God's love for the Jewish people is not dependent on merit or virtue, but is like the immutable love of father to son.

Conversely, the Jewish people's innate love for their Creator and the impossibility of their being severed from Him are also reflected in various halakhic rulings. Since there exists within the Jew a natural love for God and a desire to fulfill His commands, why is it that we find disobedience so rampant not only among the Jews of today but also throughout the annals of Jewish history? Because, like any human, a Jew also has an inclination toward selfishness, an inborn disposition to wrongdoing that receives its vitality from man's animal soul (*nefesh habehamis*). How can the two coexist: a natural love for God on the one hand and an inherent attraction for evil, the negation of God's Will, on the other?

Although seemingly contradictory, the truth is that even at the moment when a Jew sins and thus defies the Will of his Creator, his love for God is still as great as it is in the performance of a *mitzvah,* only it is being obscured and hidden. His overbearing attraction to personal indulgence conceals his love for God, so that he is not consciously aware of this love at this moment. It would be ludicrous to infer that a child who disobeys the instruction of a parent not to eat candy does so because he loves the candy more than he does his parents! Rather, the child finds justification for his action by thinking to himself that his parents will forgive and love him anyway, or that the parent was not completely serious about the prohibition. He thus mentally minimizes the severity of the action and its repercussions. Similarly, the Jew sins only because he does not realize that by sinning he is cutting himself off from his Father in Heaven. His *yetzer hara* leads him to believe that God will completely overlook, or at the very least forgive, the infraction.

Thus minimizing the gravity of his sin, he puts his love for God "on hold."

STATING ONE'S SUBCONSCIOUS INTENTION

This principle not only finds expression in theory but is also used as an actual application in *halakhah*. Jewish law requires that a divorce be given willingly by a husband. Thus, if a husband is physically coerced into giving a divorce, it becomes null and void. Yet, what if a husband is obligated by Jewish law, a *Beth Din*, to divorce his wife and yet is unwilling to do so? Maimonides, the great medieval Jewish philosopher and codifier, citing the talmudic solution, writes, "He who is required by the *halakhah* to divorce his wife and yet is unwilling to do so, every Jewish court in every place and at every time is required to beat him until he proclaims, 'I am willing [to deliver the *get*].' The court shall then write out the *get*, which is then valid."

Now what is the status of the *get* (divorce decree) if later it is proven that this verdict of the court was incorrect and in truth he was not required by *halakhah* to divorce his wife? The Rambam continues, "If the law indeed did not require that the husband be compelled to give the divorce and the court erred in their decision, the *get* is retroactively invalid."

First, in light of the fact that the *get* must be given willingly, how may we compel the husband to grant the divorce? Does the statement of willingness that is extorted from him alter the reality of his unwillingness to divorce his wife? Can physical coercion bring a Jew to fulfill God's law?

On the other hand, if the husband's willingness need only be expressed verbally and his heart does not have to be in agreement with his mouth, why then in the latter case is the divorce invalid? True, the judges erred, and by law the man would be permitted to remain with his wife. Nevertheless, he has already declared his willingness for the *get* to be given, albeit after being compelled to do so!

In explanation, Maimonides responds, "Since this person desires to be a Jew and wishes to fulfill all the *mitzvos* and distance himself from wrongdoing, [and the reason for his present improper behavior is due to the fact that] his *yetzer* has over-powered him, since now he is beaten as a result of which his *yetzer* has been weakened to the point where he pronounced, 'I wish to give the *get*,' he has banished his [evil will]."

Thus, Maimonides, in an original halakhic ruling and declaration, states that the real inner desire of every Jew is to fulfill God's Will, but at times one's evil inclination can thwart that aspiration. In this instance, since the *halakhah*, that is the Will of God, requires him to divorce his wife, then to do so is the husband's innate desire as well. The coercive force serves to weaken the obstinate evil inclination and allow the Jew's true desire to be manifest.

CIRCUMCISION MANIFESTS AN INNATE BOND

This demonstration of the innermost yearning of a Jew to unite with God enhances our understanding of the idea that a covenant made with an eight-day-old infant has greater significance than one made with an adult. A covenant made with an infant emphasizes the true nature of the relationship between the Jews and God, a relationship that is based not on the qualitative appreciation by the one of the other, but rather is the expression of an innate bond that exists between the two. The nature of the relationship is such that there is no room for doubt about its intensity and continuity. It cannot be obscured by ulterior motives.

Although a non-Jewish rationalist desires to come closer to God on the basis of an intellectual appreciation of God's sublimity, the Jew has an inborn desire to be attached, just as a son wishes to have a warm and intimate relationship with his father. Our earlier description of the contradistinction between these two different ideologies allows us to posit three basic differences between the religious affiliation of the Jew and of such non-Jews who approach religion by logic alone.

First, because a rationalist, or one who lacks an intrinsic bond, relates to God on the basis of intellectual apprehension, his love will be commensurate with the limits of his mortal, therefore limited, understanding. Moreover, his love will be directed only to certain aspects of God—namely, to the manner in which God manifests Himself in this world—rather than to the hidden essence of God, which is not revealed and so cannot be apprehended intellectually. For instance, he may learn to apprehend Godliness merely by means of the wonders of nature. He may even go so far as to ascribe divinity to nature, not recognizing it for the "veil" it is, and may subsequently align himself with a pantheistic philosophy, such as was postulated by the Jewish philosopher Baruch de Spinoza. But the Jew, possessing a *neshamah,* is intimately bound to the quintessence of God, rather than only to specific manifestations of Him. Thus, he cannot err in his apprehension of God, for it goes far beyond the superficial.

Second, the rationalist, whose Godly relationship thrives on intellectual appreciation, is a testament to the fact that in essence there is no real relationship but rather a mutual appreciation of similar qualities. His intellect or emotions have come closer to God, but certainly not his whole being. In contrast, a Jew is bound to God in his entirety.

Finally, the Jew's Godly love is not subject to variation, whereas the rationalist's commitment is eternally challenged and fluctuates. This fluctuation has two causes: (1) If his intellectual arguments for the existence and greatness of God are refuted or even challenged, once his basis for belief has been shaken or removed, his attraction to Godliness will slowly erode; (2) Even if his intellectual proofs remain secure, should something of greater personal concern come into conflict with this Godly devotion, such as financial risk, family disapproval, or the need to sacrifice his life for his beliefs, these considerations may take precedence because his relationship with God has not penetrated to his essence.

THE REAL ISSUES OF ISAAC AND ISHMAEL'S DEBATE

Returning now to our original debate between Isaac and Ishmael as to who was more beloved unto God, Ishmael for being circumcised at thirteen or Isaac at eight days, this was not merely a question as to what age is the most suitable for the performance of a *bris*. Rather, it was a debate about the embryonic nature of the covenant, a debate between two conflicting philosophies concerning Godly service and spiritual virtue.

Ishmael, who as a son of Hagar lacked the Jewish bond with God and adopted that of the rationalist, related to God on an intellectual and emotional plane, born of Godly understanding, appreciation, and subsequent commitment. After arriving at certain conclusions about the greatness of God, with his attraction to the Almighty aroused, Ishmael was ready to enter His covenant and commit himself, much like a friend whose love stems from an appreciation of another's attributes. Since his love was born of what was at most a superficial intellectual appreciation, once Sarah instructed Abraham to "drive away this slave together with her son; the son of this slave will not share the inheritance with my son Isaac," Ishmael strayed from the path of righteousness. The issue of inheritance struck deeper than his relationship with God.

Isaac's philosophy of Divine covenant was more esoteric. To Isaac a covenant with God was a total expression of the intrinsic bond and intimacy between father and son. As such, it could not be confined to something as superficial as an intellectual apprehension of the greatness of God. It was rather something that enveloped the essence of the Jew and the whole of his Father, the Almighty, of which he is a part. In the face of such a comprehensive attachment, intellectual comprehension and emotional maturity are insignificant. This covenant is therefore made with an infant who cannot relate to God in any way other than as a son does to his father.

Thus, the establishment of a covenant between the Almighty and Isaac (and thenceforth with every Jewish male) at the tender age of eight days was in perfect order. As a newborn, Isaac obviously did not have the intellectual depth to comprehend or cherish the sublimity of the covenant he was entering, nor was he in possession of any personal characteristic that would make him worthy of such a covenant. Nevertheless, it is precisely through this poverty that the transcendence of the covenant could be expressed. The establishment of a covenant with an eight-day-old infant expresses the fact that the love of God

for a Jew is an elemental one, one not born of spiritual qualities, virtue, religious commitment, or character superlatives.
This covenant testifies to the fact that God's love for the Jewish people is like the love of a father for his son, and even greater,
as we shall see.

This is the meaning of Isaac's proclamation to Ishmael, "I am
dearer [to God] than you." That is to say, "My relationship with
the Almighty is innate, and from the womb." Ishmael, whose
bris took place when he was intellectually conscious of the
covenant and in possession of noteworthy spiritual attributes,
represents an external love between friends. He bragged to Isaac
that more honor was due him, since he had undertaken the *bris*
with great bravery and anguish, and he felt he was more beloved
to God on the basis of his righteousness. Yet, this type of worthy love by no means emulates the intrinsic love of father and
son. A son does not have to be worthy of his father's love. What
Ishmael thought would reflect his proximity to God actually
indicated his distance.

Moreover, had Isaac's *bris* actually taken place when he was
older and capable of intellectual insight, the nature of his covenant with God would not have been known. But because that
covenant took place when he was an infant, it was manifest to
all that the covenant was an intrinsic one, that the association
between a Jew and God is entrenched deep within the soul of
a Jew, in his blood, in his genes, and in his very being. This bond
is manifest with every male Jew when he enters God's covenant
and is circumcised as a tiny infant. The same is true of a female
Jewess; the Talmud says that a girl is born as if circumcised. A
Jewish woman is born into God's covenant.

A LAMB AMONG WOLVES

The very existence of *Am Yisroel* is miraculous. That the one
nation that has repeatedly been the target of mass extermina-
tion should outlive its attackers defies every law of nature. A
well-known midrashic saying expresses this aptly: "One small
lamb among seventy wolves and yet she survives." There is no

other such comparable phenomenon in the annals of human existence. According to the laws of nature, a lamb surrounded by seventy hungry wolves ought to be immediately torn apart; it should not survive even a fraction of a second. But the Jews have endured for well over three millennia. The only explanation that can be offered for the endurance of the Jewish people is that God breaks through the bonds of nature and guards His vulnerable children.

It follows therefore that Isaac, the first person to be born a Jew, would be born in a miraculous fashion accompanied by many kinds of supernatural phenomena. Not only is the continued existence of the Jewish people miraculous but the very inception of the nation is also miraculous, a miraculous indication that the Jewish people, although living within the creation, are above and beyond the creation. They are part of the Creator, just as a child is an extension of his father.

In the Passover *Haggadah* we read, "In every generation they rise against us to annihilate us!" How do the Jews survive these insurmountable odds? Therefore, the prayer continues and answers, ". . . And the Almighty delivers us from their hands." Because of our intimate association with the Creator, the existence of the Jewish people transcends the laws of nature, and we manage to endure against all odds.

Concerning what Abraham said regarding Ishmael, "*Lu Ishmael yihyeh lefoneha*," that he would be satisfied if his son Ishmael lived on to inherit him, the Almighty answered Abraham, "Concerning Ishmael I have listened to you." Ishmael would indeed grow to be a God-fearing person, a productive citizen as epitomized by *hasidei umos ha'olam*—the righteous Gentile. (Sure enough, the Talmud notes that although Ishmael lived a less than exemplary early life, he subsequently repented and returned to the path of righteousness. The Talmud deduces this fact from the Torah's description of Ishmael's death, where it uses the word *vayigvah,* "and he was elevated," an expression used only in reference to the righteous.) Ishmael would further grow and prosper, and mighty nations would stem from him. But this was not Abraham's concern. Notwithstanding Ishmael's righteousness, Abraham's purpose was to establish the Jewish nation, the nation that stands above the whole of creation, the nation whose very existence is connected with the Infinite Creator and whose association with God transcends mere intellectual or emotional bonding. This objective could be realized only through Isaac, the first Jew who was born in miraculous circumstances and was circumcised as an infant of eight days.

5

LOVE OF GOD
FOUND IN A GENE

The formation of the unique character of the Jewish nation had two significant stages. The first stage came about through our forefathers, Abraham, Isaac, and Jacob. Their personal conduct in serving God was transmitted to their descendants in the form of spiritual qualities that became intrinsic to the Jewish people's nature. The stage of the patriarchs actually comprised three different stages, each patriarch bequeathing to his descendants a trait that was unique to that forefather and his mode of Godly service. We have thus far discussed the natural love for God and the Jewish soul attained by Abraham, and the added dimension of spirituality attained by Isaac, who infused the soul within the body, causing the natural love of Abraham to be ingrained within the Jewish psyche. In chapter 7, the contribution of Jacob is explored.

The second fundamental stage in the formation of the Jewish people was the giving of the Torah at Sinai, when the essence of the Jew was raised to unimaginable heights.

In the preceding chapters we discussed the inherent qualities of the Jewish people as bestowed upon them by Abraham. Before we turn to the traits that were handed down by the other forefathers, we must first examine the very notion that character traits may be passed down from the patriarchs to every Jewish man, woman, and child. Indeed, are we suggesting some Lamarckian variation on acquired characteristics? Is it indeed possible to impart a spiritual trait that will be transmitted to offspring through the generations as if it were a genetic trait? Can love of God really be transmuted into, and then transmitted via, a gene?

The Alter Rebbe, Rabbi Shneur Zalman of Liadi, writes in chapter 18 of his celebrated work, the *Tanya*, that in every Jewish heart there beats a hidden love for God that was "passed down to us from our forefathers." Even though a Jew may not be conscious of this love, he nonetheless harbors this natural attraction to God in the innermost recesses of his heart.

As was mentioned earlier, this point was first elucidated by the great Jewish sage Maimonides in his halakhic compendium, *Mishneh Torah*, in the section on the laws of divorce. He writes that even though a *get*, a Jewish divorce, to be kosher, must be given willingly by the husband, the court of law may physically coerce the husband into saying that he is delivering the *get* willingly. The question arises, of course, as to how the husband may be coerced into *wanting* to give the *get*. Maimonides explains that inwardly the husband is not being forced against his will. Since the Torah requires this of him, it is God's Will that he divorce his wife, and, like every Jew, he subliminally wishes to perform God's Will, although he may not be conscious of this fact. The point is that every Jew, as a result of that hidden love for God that was bequeathed to us by our forefathers, wishes to live in accordance with God's Will. The Alter Rebbe simply added to this concept the fact that this love, codified by Maimondes as law, was pioneered by the forefathers and was subsequently passed on to their descendants.

WHAT A GENETIC INHERITANCE MAY COMPRISE

The fact that an individual receives a love for God as a result of inheritance requires explanation. When we speak of things transmitted genetically from father to son, it is important to differentiate among personality traits, opinions, and feelings. Only character traits may be inherited. If a father is by nature a merciful person with a good heart, it is likely that his son will be the same. Similarly, if the father is hot-tempered and aggressive, then there is a likelihood that his son will be born with the same aggressive disposition. If the father is an outstanding intellectual, then he may pass his intellect to his son, whereas if he is a fool, he might have a son who enshrines his father's foolishness. It is the deeply rooted character traits, be they of the body or of the soul, that are transmitted to the offspring. Even modern-day geneticists will agree that certain emotional traits are genetically inherited and that such traits as anger are genetic character dispositions, and chances are that if one had a very angry father, one would more than likely be angry too.

Opinions, feelings, and knowledge, in contrast, cannot be transmitted from father to son. If a father is an expert in the entire Talmud and knows it all by heart, of course this does not mean that his son will be born a talmudic scholar. If the son does not exert himself and study vigorously on his own, he will remain an ignoramus. Similarly, a father does not pass on to his son his affinities or affections for particular things. A son will not be born with an outpouring of affection for a particular individual merely because the father is fond of this person and considers him his closest friend. Moreover, as the son grows, he may even treat his father's closest friend with contempt.

A philosophy, or *weltanschauung*, of life is also genetically untransmittable. A philosophical outlook is evolved through the various events one witnesses through life and more specifically through the influence of various teachers, politicians, and thinkers.

The rule is that the ability to transmit inherited character traits within the genes totally excludes external quality traits. Only inner character attributes may be transmitted. If a given individual possesses certain character or personality traits, we may assume that his children will possess the same features, but there is no reason to assume that his offspring will perpetuate his particular persuasions or convictions. A father may be a firm believer in democracy and even risk his life for the preservation of democratic government, but his son is not thereby precluded from becoming a rabid fascist or communist.

As a matter of interest, this is also the reason why Abraham instructed his servant Eliezer to take a wife for his son Isaac only from his own family. Seemingly, Abraham's family, from whose stock Rebecca came, were idol worshipers, as opposed to Abraham himself, who originated the belief in the One God. Rebecca's own father and brother, Besuel and Lavan, sacrificed and bowed to stone and the dust of their feet. Why then was Abraham so set on taking a wife from his family?

The explanation is rooted in this all-important concept of what may be genetically transmitted. Lavan and Besuel's tendency toward worshiping idols was derived not from their character per se but from their convictions and beliefs. Within this family were positive personality traits that may have been misdirected through external causes, such as the sociological influences to which they were exposed. Their acquired beliefs were faulty, but their inherited character traits and temperaments were not. Therefore, it was possible to find a member of the family who had not adopted their ancestral religious perversions.

On the other hand, the Canaanites, the people from whom Abraham had specifically commanded Eliezer not to take a wife, were said to be morally corrupt in their very essence. Their personalities were essentially base and immoral, and these negative traits within them could not be readily redirected. Hence, Abraham commanded Eliezer to take a wife only from his own family, who by nature were benevolent and generous people.

HOW CAN LOVE BE INHERITED?

If we accept this understanding of what is and what is not inheritable from one's ancestors, amid the firm conviction that emotions cannot be genetically transmitted, we meet with difficulty in qualifying our claim that every Jew inherits a love for God. How is it possible for this love to be inherited? As has been emphasized, Abraham, at a young age, recognized the Creator and as a result aroused himself to love God and to consecrate his very being to His service. Why should this love have been inherited by his children? Did they have the intuition and depth to be able to discover a Creator amid universal idolatry and paganism? Did they display the same willingness to die on behalf of that Creator, even to sacrifice their own sons at His behest, as Abraham had done? Did his children, like Abraham, strive to find God, fostering in the process an immense love for Him that they might earn this prodigious longing for the Creator?

When we say that the *nature* of the Jewish people is to be compassionate and merciful, as Maimonides expressly asserts in the *Mishneh Torah*, we can understand how such virtues were inherited from and instilled within the Jewish character by Abraham, our father, who himself was a model of compassion and kindness. These are qualities of character and emotion and so may be transmitted to subsequent generations. But how may we say that the love for God that Abraham nourished in his heart was transmitted to his seed? Why does *Hasidus* continually insist that because Abraham loved God, his children love Him too?

In truth, even the inheritance of mercy and compassion is not completely comprehensible. For even the character traits discussed earlier that are said to be transmitted from father to son need not necessarily be transmitted. It may be fair to say that in the majority of cases, the inherent character traits of the son are similar or identical to those of the father, but certainly this is not always the case. A single parent may father a variety of children with altogether different propensities. Furthermore, even if such characteristics were always handed down, they would occur only in the first or perhaps second generation at most. To assume that an attribute will be inherited by descendants fifty or a hundred generations down the line is unreasonable.

Yet here we are implying that every Jew, to the end of all generations, will inherit the same qualities possessed by the patriarchs of old, that not only will they inherit the attributes of compassion and mercy, but even an inborn love for God!

DISTINGUISHING BETWEEN VIRTUE AND ESSENCE

With regard to one's essential character, we may subdivide a man into three categories. First are the attributes that are not genetic and are thus not transmitted at all to subsequent generations. Second are those that are generally, but not necessarily, handed down. Finally, there is the inner core, the inner essence of man that must be, and always is, transmitted from one generation to the next. By this we mean those elements that are intrinsic human properties and character traits. These, perforce, will be transmitted from one generation to the next.

Opinions, dispositions, and a philosophical outlook are not bequeathed to subsequent generations because they are external facets of an individual. They in no way constitute the integral part of man. The convictions and persuasions of an individual do not contribute to the definition of a man as such. It would, of course, be absurd to say that how a man feels politically, how he votes, or what his opinion of a certain individual or idea is determines whether or not he is human. Rather, it is more logical to presume that after a person comes into possession of whatever components are necessary for being human, this man has *in addition* certain persuasions, convictions, and positions on given issues that form an ancillary part of his charter. So, it is a man who has these opinions, not the opinions that make the man. Therefore, these convictions and persuasions may best be regarded as an appendage of the human, but not part of his essence. They are things that a man may feel, but they are not essential or intrinsic to the definition of our humanity.

The evidence for this fact is how often these feelings and convictions change. Today an individual may feel like this and be in favor of that, and tomorrow, after maturing or becoming more informed he may change his entire outlook. That which he likes today, tomorrow he may despise; that which repulses him today may attract him tomorrow. This volatility and the ephemerality of the emotions are attributable to the fact that these attitudes and sentiments are not part of one's actual being. They are thus subject to fluctuation.

Since they are not intrinsic, these convictions and persuasions are not hereditary either. Those things that are not an integral part of the father are not inherited by his offspring.

On the other hand, character traits and attributes, such as kindness or sharpness of mind, emanate from a deeper source in man. They are not strictly external, as are convictions or character disposition. One individual, by his very nature, may be good and generous, and another evil and vengeful. One may be naturally inclined toward magnanimity, and the other toward selfishness. These character features are deeply rooted, and it is evident that they do not change so suddenly. Any individual who is inherently selfish must exert herculean efforts to become good. Those who have a natural bent to think first for themselves must work hard to reverse their inward orientation and think first about their fellow man.

Nevertheless, although coming from a deeper source, character traits are also not part of man's essence. It is possible for a man to change them, although doing so requires a more concerted effort. When a person wills strongly enough to change his nature and his inclinations and makes the necessary effort to do so, he will succeed. Without this belief in the essential ability for man to reorient his nature, there would be no basis for any religious, moral, or ethical code. Nevertheless, because such characteristics are entrenched more deeply in the bedrock of man, they *may* by passed down from one generation to the next.

WHERE THE ESSENCE OF MAN LIES

What is the quintessence, the very definition and composition of man? The fact that man is human and not an ape or other animal life form is obviously not merely a *characteristic* of man, such as being good or bad. Nor is it an ancillary or added entity of man, such as an opinion. Rather, being human is his very *essence.* This essence is unalterable and indestructible. A human may employ all the means available to try to change his humanity, to no avail. He will forever remain human. He can act like a wild ape, swing like a monkey, think like an ass, but will still forever remain a human.

There is a popular fable told by Rabbi Nachman of Braslav about this inability to change one's humanity. There was a king whose eldest son, the crown prince, thought he was a turkey. This situation was a terrible embarrassment to the king since at all the state dinners, in the presence of foreign dignitaries and heads of state, the crown prince would frolic under the banquet tables squawking, "Gobble, gobble," and eating scraps from the floor. The king tried everything to help his deranged son; he even hired psychologists and therapists, but when they tried to persuade his son that he was a human and not a turkey, his only response was "Gobble, gobble."

Finally the king brought a famous wise man who promised to cure the crown prince. The sage dressed up like a turkey, got down on the floor with the crown prince, and started muttering, "Gobble, gobble. " The crown prince was surprised and asked the sage whether he also was a turkey, to which the sage responded in the affirmative. "Good," said the Prince. "Now I have someone to keep me company," and together they licked up all the scraps on the floor.

The next day the sage, still acting like a turkey, used a fork to eat up the scraps. The prince was surprised. "I thought you said you were a turkey," he exclaimed. "I am," replied the sage, "but who says that a turkey can't use a fork?" The prince was convinced, and he too began using a fork.

The next day the sage brought a plate. Again the prince was puzzled, but the sage assured him it was normal for a turkey to use a plate.

The next day the sage wore a suit and ate at the table. Encouraged by the sage, the prince did the same, all the time believing that he was a turkey. Finally, after a period of time, the prince was acting like a perfectly normal human being, and the king was more than satisfied, although the prince was sure that everything he did was common for a turkey. Of course, it did not really matter what the prince thought, because that would never change the fact that he was human and not a turkey.

The moral of the story is that no matter how you behave, whether like a turkey or any other animal, the fact remains that a human is always a human.

Many people are in the habit of saying that Hitler, may his name be erased, and others like him were monsters, beasts, animals. Although this is only a figure of speech, it is a severely pernicious one because it lessens the enormity of their crimes. The reason Hitler's crimes were so heinous was precisely *because* he was a human being. And how could a human being have committed the atrocities he did?

Man may change everything about himself except this fact of being human. This being so, it is inevitable that this quintessential facet of man is channeled down throughout all generations. External facets may or may not be transmitted, but this human essence must be handed down. All species breed true to type. Humans will give birth only to humans.

A RELATIONSHIP THAT BECOMES PART
OF ONE'S ESSENCE

The bond that Abraham our forefather achieved with the Almighty was not in the form of conviction and sentiment. It was also not merely in the form of a psychological bond. Rather, as has been discussed throughout this work, Abraham's connection to God was developed to the point where it became an integral part of his being. This connection with God entered his genes! Stated in other words, in much the same way that Abraham *Avinu* was human, so too was he, by his very essence, connected with God. His affiliation with, and attachment to, God entered his being as a veritable genetic construct.

We previously examined from different perspectives the scale of difference between the knowledge, worship, and love for God, exhibited by Abraham and the nations of the world. Our major objective was to demonstrate that with Abraham all of these things—his commitment, devotion, and passion about all things Godly—were basic to his very being and not simply incidental, arbitrary, or ancillary.

The advantage of being bound to God in essence rather than by intellectual choice is manifested at four different levels:

1. *In relation to the Almighty.* When a person loves God because he comprehends God's sublimity and excellence, he is not connected to God's Essence, but rather to God's external powers that are expressed through His visible attributes. Therefore, he is not attached to God at all. He is not even attached to God's true greatness, but merely appreciates the greatness that he, a mortal man, understands. It goes without saying that God's true greatness transcends by far what an inadequate human can comprehend. So this love reaches only the superficialities of the beloved, and even this only to the extent that the individual is capable of comprehending. To be sure, therefore, loving God because of His greatness alone leaves much to be desired.

In an essential relationship, in contrast, the love is to *the beloved*, God Himself. This love is not the result of contemplating God's qualities, but derives from the fact that the Jews are children of the Almighty and are connected with Him in their blood. The love that emanates from this affinity is directed to God's Essence, not His external powers.

2. *In relation to man.* An intellectual connection encompasses only the external aspects of man. Unlike man's essence, his intellect is only an external faculty, and the love that results from this faculty will not be any more essential than the faculty itself. Such a love is strictly an external love. The individual who achieves this love is not essentially connected with God. It is only his intellect and his other external faculties that have been connected.

On the other hand, the love that personifies that of a father and son, an essential love brought about by the biological symbiosis of the lover and beloved, is a love that encompasses the very essence and the entire being of the person. This love is not an isolated expression of the individual's intellect or other faculty, but arises from the deepest, darkest, and most sublime recesses of the person, from his essence. The essence of the lover becomes united with the essence of the beloved.

3. *Possibility of change.* An intellectual bond is not permanent. It may easily be modified since its foundation, the intellect, is itself susceptible to modification. Frequently, what an individual accepts as fact today will tomorrow seem to him to be complete nonsense. Similarly, a theologian who has affirmed intellectually the greatness of God, and who hears arguments from a greater intellectual maintaining there is no God and that all of existence may be explained as the evolution of cosmic primal matter over billions of years, may suddenly transfer his loyalties to evolutionary theory. Under such circumstances, not only is the Godly love produced by the intellect likely to wane but it is also even more likely to revert to outright contempt for the very notion of a deity.

An essential bond, on the other hand, is not susceptible to any degree of modification or compromise. Since it does not derive from any external factor, no outside considerations affect it. The essential bond between father and son can never change because it springs from the very essence of each individual.

4. *The ability to withstand a test.* An intellectual bond, even at its peak of power, cannot prevail against things that are dearer to the individual. As ardent and compelling as the intellectual bond may be, it is as external as the intellect itself. Yet, there are matters that are anchored more deeply within the soul. It is to be expected that the matters that are more crucial to the individual would take precedence over those that are not. When there is a conflict of interest between a Godly love born of intellect and some more intimate matter, the more intimate matter would prevail and might even completely dissolve the Godly love.

ISHMAEL FAVORS A MATERIAL EXISTENCE

An example may be found in the life of Ishmael. The *midrashim* explain, and Rashi makes mention of this in his commentary on the Torah, that Ishmael's departure from Godly worship began with his hearing the dark prediction of Sarah that "this maid's son will not inherit with my son Isaac." Ishmael thereupon decided that, if he was not going to benefit from serving God, he would abandon such service. So, although he had possessed a love for God that had induced him to worship and serve the Almighty and even to withstand the pain of circumcision in order to enter God's covenant, nevertheless when something more meaningful to him came into direct conflict with that love, he discarded his religious convictions.

An essential love, on the other hand, is the most formidable of all emotional attachments. There is nothing that can override it. It is no less intense than the love one has for oneself. The Jew's connection with God is of the same pivotal importance as his very life. He is willing to sacrifice everything so as not to sever his connection with the Almighty. This connection is lodged within his very essence. When a Jew does sin and thereby forsakes this cherished connection with God he does so, Maimonides has explained, only because his (evil) inclination misleads him and obscures his great thirst to be one with the Almighty. But if the deceit of the evil inclination is removed and the essence of the Jew is allowed free range, there is nothing that can obstruct or frustrate the inherent connection that the Jew seeks to maintain with his Creator. His Jewish soul naturally desires to reunite with its source, the Almighty.

AN EMOTION INDISTINGUISHABLE FROM ESSENCE

With this in mind, it may be appreciated to what extent this character trait of love for God became embedded within the very being of our forefathers. Their love for God became a rudimentary facet of their character. Just as the ability to grow is an essential element of plant life, as the ability to move is an integral part of animal life, and as the ability to think and cogitate is an essential aspect of human life, so the love for God became a permanent part of our forefathers' lives. It was ingrained into their souls and became an actual part of them. Their love for God became an essential and intrinsic part of their character, indistinguishable from their very essence.

Seen in this light, we may appreciate why it is impossible for a descendant of theirs, a Jew, to be born without a love for God. Chapter 1 discussed the four categories in the hierarchy of creation: mineral, vegetable, animal, and intellectual. Each is possessed of a life force, *chayus*, in ascending order corresponding to its particular needs, the highest life force being the intellectual (human) soul. All are inherently different: a plant can never give rise to an animal. This rule applies not only vertically but horizontally as well. A bird will never descend from an ox, a lion will never give rise to a giraffe, and a human will never give birth to an ape, even after thousands of generations. All will breed true to type only, as dictated by the DNA code in their genes. Yet, all of these examples represent categories within the creation only.

But the Jew has a *neshamah*; internalized Godliness sets him apart from the remainder of creation. Just as a giraffe must give birth only to a giraffe, a Jew must be born with a *neshamah*. And just as it is impossible that from the seed of a tree shall spring forth a horse, so too it is impossible for our forefathers to give rise to an individual who does not have a natural love for God ingrained into his very fabric and construct. If an individual is of the progeny of Abraham, Isaac, and Jacob, he must be possessed of a Godly soul with a love for God pulsating in his heart.

Furthermore, this certainty that every descendant of Abraham, Isaac, and Jacob inherits a love for God is even firmer than the fact that an ox will not give birth to a bird, a bird to a tree, and a human to an ape. After all, these categories are subject to the limitations of the creation. And if the finite physical entities within creation are not subject to change and breed true to type only, how much more so that no such deviation would take place with something eternal, such as the *neshamah* of the Jew, an intrinsic part of the Creator.

ESAU AND ISHMAEL DISINHERITED

The question now arises as to why Ishmael and Esau did not inherit this love, since their fathers were Abraham and Isaac, respectively. The answer is to be found in God's reply to Abraham concerning Isaac: "For *in* Isaac will children be called unto you," that is, in Isaac, part of Isaac, but not all of Isaac. The verse thus excludes Esau.

In a similar fashion, in describing how Ishmael was Abraham's son, the Talmud states, "Abraham from whom Ishamel went out, Isaac from whom Esau went out" (*Pesahim* 56a). Note that the Talmud uses the expression "went out" instead of a more suitable term, such as "descended." The implication of these expressions is that Ishmael and Esau were not sons in the true sense of the word. Rather, they "went out" from their fathers. Abraham and Isaac were their biological progenitors only, for rather than "extending" from them or emulating them, Ishmael and Esau "went forth" as if detached and removed. Furthermore, in their own lifetime they "went out" from them with respect to walking in their father's way. They abandoned their fathers' worship and the principles of monotheism their fathers had worked so hard to establish. In essence, they left their fathers' fold and reentered that of the pagan multitude.

HOW CONVERTS MAY ENTER

Another question may arise here with regard to converts. If the Jew is a sublime entity far removed from the creation, how may converts join the ranks of the Jewish people? If a plant cannot become an animal and an animal cannot transform into a human, how can a non-Jewish human become a Jew, when being a Jew involves a priceless genetic inheritance of an internal divine spark?

The answer to this question may also be obtained from the Talmud: "A convert is equivalent to an infant newly born." When someone converts, he is said to be divested of his previous existence and character and to reenter the world in a completely different manner. In the transformation, he assumes the unique identity of a Jew.

Just as the Almighty transformed Terach's son Abraham into the first Jew and introduced a new entity far beyond the created reality, so too does the Almighty take each individual who converts according to the stipulations of Jewish law and instills within him or her part of Himself, the Jewish soul. This soul is in turn inherited by all of their descendants so that they too are part of the Jewish nation.

This principle allows us to appreciate why conversion is taken so seriously in Judaism and why rabbis are always watchful that the motives of the candidate for conversion be sincere. Conversion to Judaism involves a fundamental transformation of self, not just a change in name or affiliation only. Such a transformation must transcend man and imbue a Godly *neshamah* within the prospective candidate. What is needed is the active participation of the Almighty in the process, which is engendered by following the principles and guidelines of the Torah, since the Torah is God's communique to man of how he might rise to, approach, and apprehend the Divine.

6

THE BODY
ASSUMES HOLINESS

In the previous chapters we discussed the supernatural aspects of the birth of Isaac, the first person to be born a Jew. This virtue was highlighted by the fact that his *bris*, his covenant with the Almighty, took place at the tender age of eight days. In examining the possibility of an infant's forming a spiritual bond whose significance completely eludes him, we began with a discussion of two types of love: first, *ahavah sh'al pi taam ve'daas*, a love dependent on external qualities such as one's intelligence or charm as exemplified by the love between friends, and second, *ahavah atzmis*, an elementary love unalterable and independent of any external factor as exemplified by the love between a parent and child. The former type of love becomes highly unpredictable, as one's appreciation for another's attributes tends to fluctuate. An essential love, on the other hand, not being based on the virtue of the beloved, transcends any changes within the relationship. This is why even a rebellious son will always be cherished by his parents.

As the Jewish people are children of the Almighty, they enjoy an intimacy with God that is not duplicated in other spheres. Thus, although Isaac as an infant did not himself attain any virtue, he still was able to enter a loving covenant with God. Even today, as we perform the *bris*, we are expressing this relationship between the Jews and God, one of total devotion and unconditional affection. As the prophet so eloquently expresses it, *Ahavas olam ahavtanu*, with "an everlasting love have You loved us," one that does not fluctuate with changing external conditions. Even at times when the Jews are disobedient and the relationship between God and them is strained, the Almighty declares, "For better or for worse they are my children and I cannot exchange them for another people." The Almighty's love for His children, Israel, is immutable.

The Jews, in turn, harbor an identical unconditional love as displayed throughout the ages by even the most ignorant of Jews who, although unlearned and even sometimes guilty of misdeeds, laid down their lives in sanctification of God's holy name. The Jew cannot be severed from God. This love is inherited by every Jew at birth as part of his birthright.

JEWISHNESS IS NOT EXTERNAL

The Jew embodies within himself a part of the Creator and is therefore in a different category from the elements of creation. This understanding is essential to an appreciation of the value of being Jewish, and it must be communicated to our children if they are to remain passionate about their Jewishness. It teaches us that being Jewish is not some ancillary or external virtue that one acquires through good deeds, thoughts, or feeling; then adds to his existing person; and subsequently emerges a Jew. The extent of one's Jewishness is in no way determined by religious commitment and affiliation. Action and deed cannot make a non-Jew Jewish. Even if a Gentile were to keep the entire Torah with all its commandments, he would still not become a Jew. Rather, it takes an *act of conversion* to instill a Godly soul into the nethermost reaches of the heart of man, and to be transformed.

Conversely, we learn from this principle that a Jew cannot disaffiliate himself from Judaism by virtue of improper thought, speech, or action. With this concept in mind we see more clearly the significance of the great spectrum of Jewish martyrs. From the most saintly to the *most unworthy*, Jews have forever been prepared to forfeit their lives, rather than renounce, even verbally, their Jewishness, because their Judaism was embedded deep within their soul. Just as one's intellect is intrinsic to being human, Judaism and Godliness are intrinsic to being Jewish. They form a Jew's most basic identity.

As we learned earlier, Abraham became a Jew when God revealed himself with His first Divine command. In reward for Abraham's fulfillment of that command, the Almighty promised Abraham, "I shall make you into a great nation," or in the words of the *Midrash*, "I will make you into a new [previously non-existent] being." At this point the Jew as a distinct and meta-physical being was born. The intrinsic bond between the Jews and God was later strengthened with God's command to Abraham that he and his descendants observe circumcision, a formal Divine covenant. Although Abraham himself was circumcized at age ninety-nine, Isaac and all his other descendants have entered the covenant at eight days, demonstrating that the Jew's intimacy with God is a closeness from the cradle, independent of any external, intellectual, or emotional virtue.

HOLINESS THAT PERMEATES THE BODY

What is incumbent upon us to understand at this point is the added dimension brought about by the *bris* after God had already "re-created" Abraham and his descendants into a new entity. If it is true that the Jew enjoys an essential connection with the Almighty that exists even before birth, since the Jewish soul, a part of God, is already existent, what can the *bris* possibly add to the relationship that is not already there?

The answer to this question may be found in the *Shulhan Orukh HaRav*, the code of Jewish Law, authored by Rabbi Shneur Zalman of Liadi (*Orah Haim* 4). In it the *Alter Rebbe* writes that the beginning of the *neshamah*'s (soul's) entry into the body occurs at the *bris*. This statement implies that, although the soul is already existent and in unison with God, the connection remains only temporal and spiritual. The soul does not yet permeate the body. What the *bris* does is cause the soul to enter and permeate the body completely so that the body too becomes elevated and connected with the Almighty. It brings about a truly sublime fusion between the physical and spiritual, as the Almighty Himself expressed to Abraham, "This shall be My covenant *in your flesh*, an eternal covenant" (*Bereishis* 17:13). This is quite an achievement: not only can a Jew be connected to God through his *neshamah* and spiritual faculties, but his very flesh, which is seemingly diametrically opposed to Godliness, can serve as a medium for interaction with the Divine.

At first this phenomenon seems strange. What kind of association is there between flesh and blood and God? The two seem to be diametrically opposed and inversely proportional; the greater the ascendancy of the body, the greater the descent of the soul. That there of course exists an inherent bond between the soul and God requires no elaboration. However, to claim that an all-powerful, all-spiritual, omnipresent Being has a connection with a limited, confined, physical body seems inappropriate and even sacrilegious. It seems insulting to God to believe that He even takes an interest in our temporal flesh, let alone harbors a capacity to join with it.

The answer to this question is identical to the answer to the question of how God can establish a covenant with an eight-day-old infant. Although within the confines of human comprehension these disparate entities cannot coexist, let alone coalesce as one, nevertheless here the emphasis is on the fact that the Almighty is doing the impossible: "This shall be My covenant." Precisely because He is infinite and not bounded in any way, He is also not confined to the spiritual realm. He can communicate with the body of man just as well as with the soul.

In fact, if God is infinite, why should there be any difference to Him between the body and the soul? Differences are recognizable only in the face of something finite. For example, an entrepreneur who has untold millions of dollars will still recognize the value of one thousand dollars and of one hundred dollars and will therefore become very irate if that money is lost or squandered. His wealth does not cancel out the calculated worth of two things subordinate to it. But, if the same entrepreneur had an infinite supply of money, then a hundred and a thousand and a million dollars would all be equal to him, and he would not care if he lost a hundred or a thousand dollars. In the face of infinity all finite things lose their distinguishing features.

Another illustration might be the case of a great professor who must teach obtuse philosophical principles to his disciples. If he has a truly great mind, he will be able to teach not only people who are more knowledgeable than he but even people who are far inferior to himself. And the smarter he is, the more he will be able to cause his transcendent thought to descend to the level of his students. And if he is truly brilliant he should be able to teach the most difficult subjects even to kindergarten children. In other words, the greater he is, the smaller he should be able to make himself, because the loftiest thoughts and the lowliest nursery rhymes are equally trivial to a sage of infinite intelligence. It is just as difficult to build a complex transistor as it is to build an enormous stadium. And conversely, if one is empowered with the ability to do both, then it is just as easy to build a stadium as it is to build a transistor.

The point of this discussion is that limitation extends in two directions and the lack of limitation also extends in two directions. If one is very limited, then it is difficult to ascend and difficult to descend. So if an individual is not a fantastic teacher or does not understand his subject well, then he cannot condescend to teach schoolchildren just as he cannot teach university professors.

In the same way, from God's perspective there is no difference between the spiritual and the physical. Just as He is able to connect Himself with man's soul, so is it possible for Him to introduce that connection into the flesh and introduce Godliness into man's body. Just as it is possible to establish a covenant with an adult, so is it possible with an infant. In the face of God's infinite knowledge, the intellectual ability of both adult and child is equally deficient. Whereas the limitations of a human being's covenant are commensurate with the limitations of the human himself, God is unlimited and so is His covenant.

The verse thus states, "This shall be My covenant in your flesh, an eternal covenant." Because it is God's covenant, it is also an eternal covenant. A covenant constructed between two friends, no matter how strong, cannot be guaranteed to last forever. Just as the actions of a man are limited, so are his pacts limited. Since God is limitless, however, His covenant is not affected by any time element.

Thus, the transcendence and sublimity of God's covenant are underlined by three pivotal aspects: first, it permeates the very flesh of the Jew (physical space is not a limitation); second, it is made with an infant (intellectual understanding or lack thereof is not a limitation); and third, it is eternal (it is not limited temporally).

From this vantage point the covenant of circumcision is greater even than the covenant God made with the Jewish people when He gave them the Torah at the foot of Sinai, which was itself outstanding. It is written in the Torah concerning the establishment of the covenant at Sinai, "Those who are here [at this time] and those who are not here," which the *Midrash* explains to mean that all souls of the Jewish people throughout all generations were present at Sinai. Nevertheless, it is apparent from that very virtue that this covenant was made with only the *souls* of the Jewish people, for not all the bodies were yet in existence or present. Thus, it touched only the spiritual dimension of the Jew. Yet, the covenant of circumcision made with an eight-day-old Jewish child connects God with the Jewish body. This point emphasizes the fact that the relationship of God with the Jew is not by virtue of, or limited to, the lofty spiritual status of the Jew, but extends to the Jew as a human being, and an unworthy human being, an infant, at that.

PREPARATION FOR THE BIRTH OF ISAAC

Only after Abraham attained a new spiritual level made possible by the *bris milah* in which his body also achieved holiness, was he able to father Isaac. The Almighty had previously told him, "Walk before Me and be perfect" (*Bereishis* 17: 1), regarding which the *Midrash* says that the circumcision was necessary before the birth of Isaac "so that he be born of holy seed."

The essential harmonization of the Almighty with the Jewish body was accomplished through Isaac. To facilitate this synthesis, Isaac's body itself had to be a paragon of holiness and purity, so his birth had to be from holy seed. Abraham had brought about the spiritual connection with God, the transformation into "a new entity" caused by the acquisition of a Godly soul. Later he was also circumcised, becoming attached bodily to his Creator. Nevertheless, this event took place a hundred years after his birth. Because he had been without physical perfection for so many years, his bodily holiness lacked the potency to be a paradigm to subsequent generations. Isaac, on the other hand, was holy flesh born of holy seed. Therefore, in him was manifest the principle that bodily attachment to God is not an external dimension added to the Jew's holy soul, but, rather a Jew's entire being is permeated with holiness.

Because Isaac was the first person to be born a Jew, in him were manifest all the attributes intrinsic to the Jew. It was blindingly clear that his entire being, physical and spiritual, was connected with God. He was biologically of holy seed. His very birth was miraculous and heralded by God. He was embraced by God with fatherly love while still an undeserving infant, and later he was brought up as a holy sacrifice upon God's altar (even though it did not finally occur).

ISAAC'S HOLINESS BEQUEATHED TO SUBSEQUENT GENERATIONS

It is this treasure of physical holiness and spirituality that Isaac transmits to all his descendants. The Jew's Godly soul was acquired through our forefather Abraham, and the holy body was acquired through Isaac, Although Abraham was circumcised before Isaac, he was not born a Jew, and consequently his holiness was an added dimension to his already existing flesh; it was not intrinsic to his being. Abraham was not born a Jew, but became a Jew.

Just as the "body" (physical dimension) of a plant is dissimilar to that of an animal, so too was Isaac's body born as a new physical entity that was in turn passed down to the Jews of all generations. His physical body was different from those who had preceded him because he was born in holiness.

The total union with God is a fundamental part of the birthright of the Jew, existing from the moment of birth, but it is the *bris* that translates this intimacy from the potential to the actual, thus signaling the relationship.

The fact that this integral intimate relationship exists before (or without) the performance of the *bris* is demonstrated by two talmudic statements:

1. "A woman is as if circumcised." As was stated earlier, God's covenant with the Jewish people is obviously inclusive of Jewish women, and thus, although they do not actually undergo circumcision, their entry into the covenant begins from the moment of birth and without the physical performance of the circumcision.

2. The Talmud declares that he who makes a *neder*, vow, that he will not derive benefit from a circumcised Israelite is also forbidden to derive benefit from an uncircumcised Jew. The reason: even without the *bris*, he is still part of the covenant.

Thus, it is clear that from the moment of birth the Jew is one with God.

7

JACOB:
AN UNBLEMISHED BED

I n our discussion of the unique spiritual and physical character of the Jewish people, we have so far witnessed the gradual evolution of the Jews as a product of the lives and actions
of our forefathers Abraham, Isaac, and Jacob. Each one instilled
within the Jew a different inherent quality that forms the
makeup of the Jew and defines his sublimity.

We have seen how originally there was God, the Creator, and
the world, the created. With the fulfillment of Abraham's first
Divine command of *Lekh lekha*, he was transformed into a new
being who defied the boundaries of created and Creator. The
Almighty granted him a Godly soul, thus distinguishing him as
a "new species," a being who because of his Divine soul was
essentially bonded with His Master and raised above the created world. Yet, the innate spirituality that was granted him did
not yet permeate his physical existence. Abraham had transcended human limitation and become closer to God, but only
in soul. The holiness conferred upon him by his *neshamah* did
not permeate nor directly affect his body.

It remained for Isaac, the first individual to be born a Jew, to
accomplish this transformation. His circumcision at eight days
old, whereby his body became holy, merged the infinite into
the finite. Now even the Jewish body was united with God. The
sublimation of the body is made possible by the fact that the
bris is "My [God's] covenant." Since God is infinite and tran-

scends all boundaries, all is as naught before Him. Therefore, a covenant with flesh and blood is equally within His capabilities as is a covenant with the soul. The spiritual is no more virtuous or distinguished before God than the physical.

Parenthetically, this understanding of the attachment between God and man created by virtue of circumcision enables us to elucidate a well-known question of the Torah commentators. The Talmud states, "Abraham fulfilled all the *mitzvos* of the Torah even before they were commanded." If so, why did he wait for God to command him before he circumcised himself? The Talmud maintains that he observed all the other commandments that were in his power to perform. So why did he not circumcise himself?

The explanation, however, is simple: The purpose of the *mitzvah* of circumcision was to cause a supernatural bond with the body by drawing Godliness into it. For this to occur, the specific command of the Almighty was necessary, for it is only within *His* ability to transcend the laws of nature, which clearly distinguish between the holy and mundane, between the soul and body. The sublimation of the body could not have been accomplished by Abraham alone. So circumcision on his own initiative would have been useless.

In summation, these two central episodes in the lives of Abraham and Isaac relate to two distinct qualities of the Jew. The command of *Lekh lekha* sublimated the metaphysical component of the Jew, and the commandment of circumcision sublimated the physical element. The common denominator, however, was that these virtues were not attained through human effort (thereby limiting their potency), but through the power (command) of the Almighty, and thus they transformed the essence of the Jew.

In addition, the initiation and participation of God in these processes took place not only in a supernatural context, insofar as it was His covenant, but in a concrete manner as well. The *Midrash* comments that when Abraham went to circumcise himself, his hand shook, whereupon "God sent forth His hand (as it were) and held [the knife] with him and etched the covenant with him." Thus, the physical act of circumcision also came about with Divine assistance.

UNITY BETWEEN GOD AND MAN IS COMPLETE

The culmination of the process of sublimation of the Jew and the solidification of his bond with the Almighty was reached with Jacob, the last of the forefathers. In him was completed the unification of the Jew with the Almighty, both spiritually and physically. In order to understand the excellence of Jewish character attained by Jacob, we must first examine more closely the difference between the circumcision of Abraham and that of Isaac.

The *midrash Shir Hashirim Rabbah* comments that the verse "He [the Almighty] shall caress me with the kisses of His lips" refers to Isaac at the time of his circumcision. Isaac's circumcision surpassed in its spirituality and transcendence even that of Abraham, and thus he enjoyed an exceedingly intimate relationship with God. The reason was that Isaac's circumcision was essentially untainted by human involvement. As an infant, he could not actively participate in or appreciate the significance of the occurrence. Neither his intellect nor his emotion played a role in his entering the covenant of God. He was lovingly embraced by God as a newborn son is lifted by his father. With the human effort thus minimized, the Divine effort was commensurately enhanced. Human limitation could not restrain the outpouring of Divine love at the circumcision for it was not present. As was pointed out, this was the essential distinction between the religious philosophies of Ishmael, the prototype rationalist Gentile, and Isaac, the prototype Jew. Ishmael, circumcised at age thirteen, represented human effort and intellectual appreciation in the service of God. Isaac maintained that a Godly bond is more sublime. When there is a Divine connection, factors of age, understanding, and affiliation are negligible. Isaac was the first Jew in whom an unlimited and unrestrained association with God was achieved.

Abraham could not develop his intrinsic relation to God to this extent. Circumcised at age ninety-nine, he was fully aware of the gravity and magnitude of his undertaking. With conscious premeditation he had performed the circumcision and apprehended its spiritual repercussions. He knew what it meant for Godliness to be synthesized with the flesh. Abraham's circumcision thus involved a measure of human participation, hence limitation. It could not pervade his being to the extent it did Isaac's. To be sure, Abraham's covenant was more internal than that of Ishmael, for whom human calculation and involvement were the essential ingredients. Ishmael did not possess a Jewish soul and was unable to appreciate the transcendence of an intrinsic bond. Abraham, the first to receive this Godly soul, was inherently bound to the Almighty through that soul, but because his intellect participated in the formation of the Divine relationship, that relationship was not as pure, nor as transcendent, as that of Isaac.

CIRCUMCISION AS A GIFT

Hasidus clarifies the difference between the circumcisions of Abraham and Isaac by comparing the former to a present. A present is not an exchange between giver and recipient. It is not, for example, a sale, which requires the involvement of both sides, the buyer providing money and the seller providing the article. A gift is given entirely on the initiative of the benefactor, with nothing expected in return. Yet, the Talmud states a general rule regarding gifts: "If the recipient had not caused the giver a good feeling [at some point], he would not have given him the gift in the first place." At some point, then, the recipient did a favor, however small, or brought pleasure, however minute, to the benefactor, and the benefactor now wishes to compensate the giver as part of an exchange. Thus, there is active, albeit indirect, participation on the part of the recipient. How may we resolve this inherent paradox: on the one hand a gift is a uni-directional undertaking from giver to recipient; and on the other hand, the recipient must have previously engendered some goodwill with the giver.

The explanation is that the "good feeling" generated by the recipient is less than the emotional or even financial value of the gift. Although it served as a catalyst for the feelings of the benefactor, it still does not measure up to a gift that is given freely and generously. Therefore, it may be said that a gift involves only the benefactor, and the "good feeling" is necessary only as a prerequisite and is not a part of the gift itself. To be sure, we seek to bestow gifts upon those we love and admire. Yet, the actual presentation is done freely and without recourse to thoughts of recompense. A gift is mostly unidirectional.

Abraham's circumcision, then, was analogous to a gift. Abraham served God with great self-sacrifice and loyalty throughout his life. No obstacle was too great, no mountain too high to prevent Abraham from selflessly executing the wishes of his beloved Master. By disseminating the knowledge of God to the earth's inhabitants, he generated a great deal of "good feeling" with the Almighty. As a result, God gave him the command and privilege of circumcising himself, thereby enabling him to enter God's covenant and become intrinsically connected with God. Needless to say, God's gift to Abraham was infinitely higher than the connection he had already achieved and anything he might have aspired to by virtue of his own efforts. The intrinsic bond achieved through the circumcision surpassed by far the intellectual and emotional one he had so far developed, and the love that God showed him was far greater than any love he could have shown God. Still, the gift was not gratis, and Abraham's devotion was not an insignificant factor. Rather, it served as a catalyst to his being granted an intrinsic connection to God. In the words of the daily morning prayer, "You [the Almighty] found his [Abraham's] heart faithful before You; and You made with him a covenant." The making of the covenant was thus preceded by "finding Abraham faithful."

IMPERFECTION IN THE CIRCUMCISION
OF ABRAHAM AND ISAAC

Herein lies the fundamental difference between the *bris* of Abraham and that of Isaac. Both were the result of a Divine command to be circumcised, but Abraham's *bris* involved a degree of human effort in service to God. It was not completely removed from the limits of human ability and so was not the pure Divinely oriented covenant that is by definition infinite. Abraham's active participation in the performance of the circumcision, and his keenness in joining God's covenant in the first instance, in a sense served to diminish, or blemish, the holiness of the covenant.

But Isaac, on the other hand, in the eight days of his existence, had not yet been given the opportunity of producing a "good feeling" or such displays of loyalty that might make him worthy of entering God's covenant. His covenant with God was free of all human effort and hence of limitation. It was a Divine covenant in its purest sense. It was an outpouring of Godly love resembling the unconditional natural affection a father has for his newborn son. Isaac's passive role in the formation of the covenant emphasized that this was truly and totally "My [God's] covenant."

The very intensity of this relationship permeated Isaac's very flesh and remains ingrained within his children and children's children until this very day, "in the flesh, for an eternal covenant." Its ramifications extended far beyond those of Abraham.

Yet, notwithstanding the spiritual heights that Isaac attained, in one important respect he was still deficient. Although he himself had been born of a "holy seminal drop," he was not born of the holy seed of one who had been circumcised at eight days. He enjoyed a definite advantage over his father Abraham who had been born to the never-circumcised pagan Terach. When Isaac was born, Abraham had already circumcised himself, but the fact that Abraham had not been circumcised at eight days retroactively caused a deficiency in Isaac. We have already seen why the holiness, added late in Abraham's life, although permeating his physical body, did not strike as deep as it did in Isaac who was *born* holy. But even Isaac started off on the wrong foot, so to speak, for the seed he was born from was not completely permeated with holiness.

JACOB: THE PROCESS IS COMPLETE

Complete fulfillment of the attachment of God was realized in Jacob, who was the first Jew to be born of the "holy seed" of a Jew who was circumcised at eight days. He had the capacity to be completely saturated with holiness and Divine connection. He brought the fusion of holiness with the body of the Jew to its peak. There was not a single aspect of his physical body that had not become impregnated with holiness. The preliminary stages of this impregnation, the acquisition of a holy soul and the penetration of holiness into the body, had been accomplished by Abraham and Isaac before his birth. When he subsequently underwent circumcision, there was nothing preventing the bond with God from penetrating deeper than it had ever done with his father Isaac, overtaking him to the core of his existence and even to his every external faculty.

Beginning with Jacob the essence of the Jew became saturated with Godliness and holiness, free of all external human encumbrances. This was the intrinsic element of the Jew added by the last of our forefathers. The sublimation of the physical and metaphysical properties of the Jew was thus consummated. All who descend from Jacob's seed inherit this supreme essence of the Jew: a Godly soul and a holy body, both unified with God.

UNWORTHY OFFSPRING

This distinction between the nature of the respective Jewish patriarchs enables us to understand how it was possible for Abraham and Isaac to have begotten such children as Ishmael and Esau. "Abraham from whom Ishmael went out, and Isaac from whom Esau went out." What was it in the nature of these two patriarchs that granted latitude for these unworthy descendants to "go out" from them? Were Abraham and Isaac so ineffective with their offspring that although the two of them together served as the fathers of monotheism their own sons were pagans?

Since Abraham was not born of holy seed and was not circumcised at eight days, he had not been completely permeated with Godliness. His external faculties were not imbued with divinity. There existed the possibility of his "external seed" not being pure, and thus arose Ishmael. Similarly with Isaac, the process of sublimation, although it had achieved a higher level, was not yet completed, and thus there existed the possibility for blemished offspring such as Esau.

Regarding Jacob, however, the Talmud says, "His bed [offspring] was unblemished." Because his entire being was permeated with holiness, including the external elements of his physical body, there was no room for unholy seed and unworthy descendants to emanate from him. There was no spiritual imperfection in his loins that might be translated into, or give rise to, children without profound spiritual virtue.

Further, we may witness how, since the sublimation process was more thorough with Isaac than with Abraham, Isaac's offspring, Esau, was of higher standing than Ishmael, who emanated from Abraham. Concerning Ishmael, God informed Abraham, "For in Isaac children shall be called unto you," thus excluding Ishmael from any connection to the holiness of the Jewish people. He "went out" completely from Abraham. On the other hand, some halakhic authorities maintain that Esau is considered the seed of Isaac and that he did not "go out" completely. Furthermore, the Talmud states, "Esau was a Jewish heretic (*mumar*)." Even as a heretic, he was still a Jew, for he was born to a Jewish mother, Rebecca, and from a Jewish father who was circumcised at eight days old.

Abraham who was not born of holy seed gave rise to Ishmael, who was not called after his father's name and shared nothing of his spiritual inheritance. Isaac, who was born of holy seed, though not the holy seed of one who was circumcised at eight days, gave birth to Esau, who possessed more of a connection with Isaac than did Ishmael with Abraham. And Jacob, who was born of the holy seed of one who was circumcised at eight days, had seed that was perfect. No spiritual defect was found in his descendants. And all of his seed, every Jewish individual through every generation, contains within him or her all of Jacob's celebrated intrinsic attributes, both physical and spiritual.

8

Spiritual Contrast of the First and Second Temples: Fire and Water

Abraham, Isaac, and Jacob are the fathers of the Jewish nation. Other great sages and exalted righteous men assumed the mantle of leadership after them, yet however great they may have been, these people are not the patriarchs of the nation. As the Talmud declares, "Only three are referred to as fathers." Even Moses, who delivered the Jews from the slavery of Egypt, received the Torah, and led the Jews to the threshold of the Land of Israel, is not credited with being a father of the Jewish nation.

The virtue of fathering the Jewish nation is ascribed only to these three because they fathered the Jewish body, as well as the Jewish psyche. Through their lives and experiences they cumulatively evolved the essential character of the Jew, each passing down what he had acquired so as to ingrain it within his descendants for all generations. The Jew of today as well as the Jew of medieval times contains all the attributes of the three patriarchs, which in turn serves as the defining rubric of the Jewish people.

The birthright transmitted by the forefathers has two parts. First is the intrinsic nature of the Jew, which is the sum total of the individual aspects that each patriarch contributed, namely, the Jew as a holy being connected with God. In the earlier chapters we saw how this intrinsic nature evolved. First, Abraham acquired a Godly soul; then with Isaac that soul became infused within the body; finally, with the birth of Jacob, that Godly soul possessed the body and permeated it throughout.

Thus, all the forefathers participated, in their own capacity and through different actions, in the formation of the Jew as a Godly entity, which in turn became the genetic blueprint of the Jew that distinguishes him from other creatures in the empirical world.

The other aspect of the Jew that was transmitted by the forefathers incorporates the individual facets of each, the highly personal manner in which each expressed his Divine service. Each patriarch, by his individual disposition, actions, emotions, and mode of service and Divine worship, had his own personal *midah*, or attribute. Each one communicated and expressed his commitment to God through his own distinctive channel.

The unique attribute of Abraham was *hesed*, loving-kindness in a sense of absolute, gratuitous benevolence. The verse "Abraham my beloved" emphasizes Abraham's relationship to God in a manner of love. The distinctive attribute of Isaac was *gevurah* and *yirah*, might or power in the sense of severity, awe, and fear. It is written, "The God of my fathers, the God of Abraham and the *Dread* of Isaac," showing how Isaac related to God in a manner of awe, trepidation, and reverence. Finally, the distinctive attribute of Jacob was *tiferes* and *emes*, beauty and truth, as it is written, "Deliver truth unto Jacob."

A profound study of all the stories in the Scripture concerning each forefather brings to light the particular attribute that is special to him. We briefly mention here only one story relating to each.

ABRAHAM'S GENEROSITY AND GOODESS OF HEART

Abraham was the paragon of altruism. The Book of Genesis relates how he sat outside in the blistering heat while still suffering from the excruciating pain of circumcision, awaiting the passage of travelers whom he could invite into his tent as guests.

[Abraham] lifted his eyes and he saw three strangers standing a short distance from him. When he saw [them] from the entrance of his tent, he ran to them, bowing down to the ground.

He said, "Sir, if you would, do not go on without stopping by me. Let some water be brought, and wash your feet. Rest under the tree. I will get a morsel of bread for you to refresh yourselves. . . . After all, you are passing by my house." Abraham rushed to Sarah's tent and said, "Hurry! Three measures of the finest flour! Knead it and make rolls." Abraham ran to the cattle and chose a tender choice calf. . . . [Abraham] fetched some cottage cheese and milk, and the calf that he prepared, and he placed it before [his guests]. He stood over them as they ate under a tree (*Bereishis* 18: 1-8).

This is but one example of his great generosity and kindness.

ISAAC'S SEVERITY

Isaac's digging of wells as related in the Torah reflects the attribute *gevurah*, severity and stringency. Rainwater is an act of kindness by the benevolent Creator. It falls from the heaven without any preliminary effort on the part of man. Extracting water from a well, on the other hand, requires diligent effort, first in digging the actual well and subsequently in drawing the water to the top. Thus, by relating these seemingly trivial and oblique stories about well digging, the Torah conveys that Isaac's life was dominated by awe, might, and severity, which he came to symbolize. Rainwater reflects Divine grace and benevolence, whereas well water describes the opposite: a need to invoke, engender and discover, in short, judgment and stringency. Well water reflects the need to exert strenuous effort in order to sustain life. It is the antithesis of rain water, which is a gift and a blessing.

JACOB'S HONESTY

Concerning Jacob, the Torah tells how, even after being cheated by his uncle Laban after working seven years for the sake of Rachel and then by being given Leah as a wife instead, he did not hesitate to work another seven years. Furthermore, he was swindled again as Laban changed his salary and terms of work time and time again. And through all of this Jacob never dreamed of cheating Laban in return. On the contrary, he continued to work with the greatest vigor and devotion, to the point where Maimonides cites Jacob's diligence in executing his duties as an employee as the basis for the halakhic requirements concerning the extent to which a worker is obligated to serve his employer. Jacob himself testifies:

> Twenty years I worked for you! All that time, your sheep and goats never lost their young. Never once did I take a ram from your flocks as food. I never brought you an animal that had been attacked; I took the blame myself. You made me make it good whether it was carried off by day or by night. By day I was consumed by the scorching heat, and at night by the frost, when sleep was snatched from my eyes. Twenty years now I have worked for you in your estate; fourteen years for your two daughters, and six years for some of your flocks. You changed my wages ten times.

Notwithstanding the above circumstances, Jacob remained loyal and honest in his service to Laban, thus demonstrating love and pursuit of truth. Thus, truth is what Jacob came to symbolize.

The fact that each patriarch had a unique approach to serving his Creator and that these were genetically transmitted to their descendants may also explain Maimonides' celebrated declaration, "The activities of the forefathers are a symbol for their children." All the biblical narratives of our forefathers constitute a sign, that is, a symbol of strength for their children that they may receive and employ these same virtues in their service of God. So the kindness, severity, and fidelity to truth of our forefathers gave rise to the ability of the Jewish people to be caring, courageous, and sincere in their devotion and worship.

Now, to demonstrate more openly the workings of this principle in terms of Jewish history and achievement. As we are standing at "the heels of the Messiah" and believe ourselves to be the last generation before redemption who will, in fact, witness the Messianic Era, we begin our exposition with something applicable to the third *Beis Hamikdosh* (Temple), may it be built speedily in our days.

"THE GLORY OF THE LATTER SHALL BE GREATER THAN THE FORMER"

In hasidic philosophy the three Temples are said to correspond to each of the forefathers: the first to Abraham, the second to Isaac, and the third to Jacob. We refer to this later.

Concerning the second Temple, we find an enigmatic prophetic proclamation and an accompanying explanation. After the destruction of the first Temple, the prophet Chaggai stated that "the glory of this latter (second) house shall be greater than the first." What property of the second Temple was he referring to that would be greater than the first?

The Talmud cites a dispute (*Bava Basra* 3a) between the celebrated sages Rav and Shmuel. Rav contended that the second Temple was greater in physical structure, since the first Temple building was 30 cubits (15 meters) high, whereas the second reached the extraordinary height of 100 cubits (50 meters); Shmuel, on the other hand, maintains that the second Temple outdid the former in duration, having existed for 420 years as opposed to the first Temple, whose duration was but 410 years. Thus, although Rav and Shmuel disagreed as to the exact nature of the supremacy enjoyed by the second Temple over the first, they both agree that it was of a spatial-temporal nature, and not (just) spiritual. The talmudic dispute about the superiority of the second Temple over the first thus revolves around its existence in one of the two physical components of the empirical world, time or space.

The fact that this dispute concerned physical matters requires immediate explanation. The *Beis Hamikdosh* (Temple) housed the presence of God on earth. Its preeminence over all other physical structures was due to its spiritual transcendence. It was famous not for being the most beautiful, spacious, or decorative dwelling (although in many respects it was), but for being the Almighty's dwelling. Many kings of that era may have owned palaces that were bigger and far more beautiful and had stood for thousands of years, but the *Beis Hamikdosh* was the residence of the King of kings. Is it then reasonable to assume that the "glory of the house" foretold by the prophet would not denote merely an additional few cubits or years! Is it in these seemingly trivial aspects that the glory of God's home is measured? If the Temple is truly a dwelling of outstanding spirituality, then its greatness should lie in a spiritual plane and not ordinary physical height or temporal longevity.

Furthermore, from the perspective of spiritual rankings, the second Temple existed on a much lower plane than the first, for it lacked the five essential elements that comprised the very sublimity of the Temple and its holiest vessels: the Ark (*Aron*); the heavenly fire, which descended and consumed the burnt offerings; the Divine presence (*Shekhinah*; Divine inspiration (*Ruah Hakodesh*); and the *urim vetumin* of the breastplate of the High Priest (used as a medium for Divine inspiration and communication). Yet, it is proposed that the second Temple nevertheless was greater than the first because of simple, material properties, namely, a larger structure and having endured ten more years.

It is therefore logical to conclude that the eminence of the second Temple rested in a spiritual quality, but that quality, although metaphysical, was manifest in the physical elements of the Temple: its height and duration.

FIRE AND WATER: PATHS BY WHICH TO UNITE THE PHYSICAL WITH THE DIVINE

As was expounded in the earlier chapters, there exists the Creator (the Almighty and the spiritual reality) and the created (our earth and the physical reality). God willed to unite the two. He wished His Presence to be manifest not only in the spiritual but also in the physical realm. The principal earthly location chosen for the synthesis of the spiritual and physical, the place where it was to reach its apogee, was the *Beis Hamikdosh*, a material structure that housed the Presence of God, fulfilling that which is written, "They shall make Me a sanctuary, and I will dwell among them." Our earlier description of the first Temple as corresponding to Abraham and the second to Isaac was intended to indicate that there are two disparate ways in which the Divine Presence can merge with the physical world (the *Beis Hamikdosh*). It can settle in a manner of *hesed*, the instinctive attribute of Abraham, as it did in the first Temple, and it can settle in a manner of *gevurah*, the attribute of Isaac, as it did in the second Temple. Both have their advantages. Thus, from one perspective the first *Beis Hamikdosh* was greater than the second, and from a second the reverse becomes true.

To understand the underlying difference between *hesed* and *gevurah* and how they connote two respective paths of achieving closer proximity with the Divine Creator, we may use the analogy of water and fire. The nature of water is to descend from higher to lower. It does not take any particular effort to cause water to descend. Furthermore, what the water flows into is not a significant factor in determining the direction of flow. It will flow regardless of whether there is something to receive it or not. To this extent, water exemplifies *hesed*, kindness, which is the tendency to give to another without any particular effort on the part of the recipient, as mentioned in the previous chapter. Even the virtue or worth of the recipient is insignificant. The giving is on the basis of sheer generosity, not meritorious standing. In the case of *hesed*, then, God descends from higher to lower, thereby consecrating and hallowing the world. Even though the recipient of this holiness, the world, plays no active role, it still becomes holy because Godliness has enclothed itself within it. God has come down to earth, and the earth is so much the better because of it.

The alternative manner for the physical to unite with the spiritual is symbolized by fire. Fire does not descend but rises, constantly burning upward from lower to higher. It thus represents an ascent of the recipient, a steady energetic effort to remain aloof and transcendent. This amalgamation of the world and Godliness is in a manner antithetical to that of *hesed*. Although *hesed* connotes the sanctification of the world by means of the descent of Godliness and its integration into the world, *gevurah* indicates the ascent of the world to Godliness, thereby achieving the same result. *Hesed* represents God coming down into man's world, and *gevurah* represents man ascending to God and thereby achieving a closer proximity.

If we examine the kind of divinity represented by *hesed*, we see that the world essentially has not changed, refined, or elevated itself, but has merely become a receptacle for the Divine Presence. Godliness descends to the world *in spite of the world*, not because of it. In this instance, in which the Holy Presence descends and envelops the physical, the physical is left just as it was before the descent.

In contrast, in the case of *gevurah*, represented by fire, Divine transcendence involves the physical elevation of the finite world. This creates a residence fit for spirituality, which draws the Divine Presence into it. The physical not only has been overtaken by Godliness but has also changed to become Godly and has raised itself to a metaphysical plane.

ONE MASTER AND TWO TYPES OF STUDENTS

Hasidic thought clarifies these antithetical approaches by means of an analogy of the teacher–student relationship.

The instruction a teacher gives to his student, regardless of the method used, has one of two objectives: (1) the teacher can transmit his knowledge to the student, in which case the student remains strictly a recipient, or (2) the teacher can implant within the student a capacity to learn, understand, and acquire knowledge on his own. In the latter scenario, the student learns to become like the teacher himself; he not only acquires wisdom or knowledge, but masters the art of its acquisition.

In the first case, the student thrives on the great wealth of knowledge transmitted to him by his educator. He takes notes and reviews repeatedly until he has understood the material the teacher wishes to impart and memorizes it, transforming himself into a "walking encyclopedia." He has obtained "real" knowledge, as opposed to "potential" knowledge. Thus, everything he knows belongs originally to his teacher. However, he is not able to intellectualize on his own, nor has he truly developed his analytical or higher cognitive or deductive processes. If, in the course of his studies, he comes across something that was never covered by his teacher he will not know how to tackle it, somewhat like a blind man who knows how to walk but must be led by someone who possesses the capacity to see. He is similarly blind when it comes to obtaining knowledge without an instructor. And yet no one can deny that from his teacher he has learned a great deal and can thus impress everyone with his range and breadth of knowledge.

In the second case, however, the student is not dependent on the teacher for instruction, but possesses the ability to investigate and research on his own. He received not "actual" knowledge, but the "potential" to acquire knowledge. Thus, when he encounters a new field of study, he will not be as disadvantaged as will the first student, for he has been given the means to analyze and deliberate on his own. He may not have as much raw information as his colleague, but then he is now empowered with the capacity to acquire so much more on his own.

If we are to ask, "Which student is greater?" the answer is dependent on the angle from which the question is asked. In terms of depth of knowledge, the former pupil is superior. Since he acts as a sponge for the ideas of his master, his knowledge is profound and refined, because it is the wisdom of a teacher with a higher intellectual grasp than a mere student.

The latter student is laden not with the knowledge of a teacher, but only with his own wisdom, which is that of a student. With his newly gained skills for the acquisition of knowledge and deductive thought, he may discover powerful intellectual insights into many an obscure field, but he is still only a novice. Thus, no matter how acute and penetrating his insights and intuition may be, it will come nowhere near that of his professor, a proven intellectual master.

However, in terms of individual elevation, the latter student is undoubtedly superior to the former. He has transcended the limitation of being only a recipient and has developed his own intellectual prowess to the point where he is capable of intellectual innovation. In other words, the knowledge he has acquired has not been added to him, so that he now knows more than he did before, but it has been forged deep into his essence. His ability has been synthesized with a higher aptitude, and he has emerged a new person. The tutelage he received has transformed and elevated his mind to the point where it emulates that of his teacher.

The former pupil lacks the ability to think on his own and to create; he is only a "receiving station." In essence, he has not changed at all; he merely has more information. Indeed, he may possess an enormous amount of knowledge, but it is the teacher's, not his. When confronted with new material, he is unable to systematize or sift through it without the assistance of his master. Thus, this student has not been changed by his master's teachings. Although his thoughts are more profound than those of his colleague, they are not his own. He is completely dependent on an intellectual guide and master.

THE CISTERN AND THE SPRING

The differences between these two students helps explain the comments in *Pirkei Avos* (Ethics of the Fathers) concerning Rabbi Eliezer ben Hyrkanos and Rabbi Elazar ben Arah made by their teacher, Rabbi Yohanan ben Zakkai. On the one hand he used to say, "If all the sages of Israel [commentators explain that this includes Rabbi Elazar ben Arah] were on the pan of a balance scale, and Eliezer ben Hyrkanos were on the other, he would outweigh them all." Yet, there is also a contradictory statement in Rabbi Yohanan's name: "If all the sages of Israel, with even Rabbi Eliezer ben Hyrkanos among them, were on one pan of the balance scale, and Rabbi Elazar ben Arah were on the other, he would outweigh them all." The explanation offered by the commentator to alleviate the contradiction in statements is that each one had a certain virtue in which he surpassed his fellow.

Just one *mishnah* before this one, Rabbi Yohanan praises Rabbi Eliezer as a "cemented cistern that loses not a drop," while he describes Rabbi Elazar as a "spring flowing stronger and stronger." Rabbi Eliezer's greatness lay in his absorption and retention of the wisdom and teaching of his celebrated master, Rabbi Yohanan. Because, like a cistern he "lost not a drop" of his master's Torah, he outweighed all the sages of Israel. Like the first student described above, he was the most outstanding in terms of depth of knowledge. It was as if his great teacher, Rabbi Yohanan, had entered into him. From a perspective of development, however, Rabbi Elazar ben Arah was the greater. Like the second student, he developed his own intellectual capabilities and became a "spring flowing stronger and stronger," that is, one who formulated his own ideas. From the perspective of he who had risen higher as an individual and who had become more developed, Rabbi Elazar ben Arah exceeded all the sages of Israel.

SPIRITUAL INFUSION VERSUS TRANSFORMATION

Following this analogy, we can better understand the differences between the revelation of Godliness brought about by the descent of spirituality into the physical, and the ascent of the physical to the spiritual—higher to lower and lower to higher. In the first mode, the metaphysical incorporates itself into the physical, but the world is not refined or elevated. The quality of that spirituality is very lofty, since the physical neither facilitates nor hinders the descent of holiness, but simply remains open to the spiritual infusion. Precisely for this reason, however, the physical never actually improves. It is similar to the former student, who accumulates an immense amount of knowledge but never actually changes. The physical construct of this world is only temporarily transformed and ultimately remains unaffected by the spiritual. If the spirituality is subsequently removed, the site loses its holiness. Without a proper vessel, there is no Godly light. Stated in other words, then, in this scenario the world becomes holy but only so long as God's spiritual light shines upon it.

In this latter case, however, the physical itself is elevated and has become spiritual. It is perfected and purified to the point where it becomes holy. Just as the second student has enhanced his intellectual profundity to the point where he is capable of creating new ideas, so too the mundane world has raised itself to the point where it becomes holy. Of course, the level of spirituality attained will be much lower than in the first scheme, for this is not pure spirituality, but rather the physical that has become spiritual, analogous to a student who begins teaching and whose ideas do not compare with those of his master. Nevertheless, this is a much truer metaphysical transcendence, for the physical object has become completely united with Godliness. Instead of being a passive receptacle, the world acts as a conduit to holiness. The physical has elevated itself to the point where spirituality has become its very nature and character. Or stated in other words, in this scenario the world itself has changed and has acquired an independent spiritual character that is not due to any higher source enclosing itself within it. A more thorough explanation of this sublime distinction is found in the next chapter. For now we concentrate on the way in which this difference affected the first and second Temples.

ANTITHETICAL SPIRITUAL ORIENTATION
OF THE FIRST AND SECOND TEMPLES

The fact that the Temple is God's House implies that Godliness radiates and dwells within its physical structure. But does it only radiate or dwell within the structure, or is the structure itself holy? Are the holiness and the structure of the Temple one and the same or two different things?

The first Temple corresponded to Abraham. The divinity invested within it was of the type that descended into it from higher to lower. It therefore enjoyed a loftier degree of spirituality than the second Temple. Accordingly, it possessed the five spiritual elements: the Ark, the heavenly fire, the Divine Presence, Divine inspiration, and the *urim vetumin*. Godly illumination descended and took hold of the house, but it did not transform it, rendering the house itself as holy. The Temple was a receptacle for the *Shekhinah*, holy Presence, but it did not become fused with it. The physical structure and the spirituality it housed remained two distinct entities that were never truly orchestrated as one.

Conversely, the spirituality of the second Temple was an ascent from lower to higher. Accordingly, it lacked the high degree of spirituality contained in the first Temple since its holiness was self-induced, with the physical acting as a catalyst. It lacked the five fundamental divine objects present in the first, but it had the tremendous advantage of being more greatly permeated with Godliness. Its material structure itself was elevated to the point where it became transfused with holiness, albeit in a lower form. The second Temple reached the pinnacle of integration of the physical and metaphysical. Godliness did not merely reside in the second Temple, but became an actual and integral part of it. Even its geographic location became infused with holiness. Therefore, the site remains holy today, although there is no actual Temple standing. The reason—the site is wholly independent of any Godly activities that would have taken place there if the Temple were still standing.

This, then, is the reasoning behind the dispute of Rav and Shmuel; both sages recognized the prophet's statement that the second Temple would be greater than the first in respect to the unparalleled integration of the spiritual and the mundane. This is what the Talmud means when it says that its greatness was manifest in endurance and structure. These represent the elemental components of the physical world, namely, time and space. The empirical world in which we reside is governed primarily by a spatial-temporal reality that serves as the most basic units of its definition. The spiritual realm is void of these limitations, and thus they constitute the two basic ingredients of the physical world and serve as the very limitations, and hence, the definition of created existence.

THE MANIFESTATION IN TIME AND SPACE

Because the greatness of the second Temple lay in its integration of spiritual and physical with the physical playing an active role, this transcendent quality was displayed in one of the two physical properties of time and space. Rav held that it was displayed in space, and therefore the second Temple's structure was higher that that of the first; Shmuel held that it was displayed in time, and therefore the second Temple outlasted the first by ten years. It was not that the Temple's greatness lay in its structure or endurance, but rather that Godliness had become more deeply infused in the physical than ever before. And the manifestation of this synthesis between the spiritual and the physical was through the spatial–temporal increase in the second Temple, which was both higher and endured longer.

9

THE RIGHTEOUS MAN AND THE PENITENT

EMULATION VERSUS ASSIMILATION

In the previous chapters we introduced new elements in the character matrix of the Jewish people as laid down by our forefathers Abraham, Isaac, and Jacob. We first explained how the birthright transmitted by the forefathers is composed of two parts—the intrinsic holy nature of the Jew, which is the sum total of the patriarchs' individual contributions, and the personal *midah*, or attribute, by which each of the three communicated and expressed his commitment to God. Abraham's *midah* was *hesed*, kindness and love; Isaac's was severity, awe, and fear; and Jacob's was *tiferes* and *emes*—compassion, benevolence, and truth. We also explained that Abraham's *hesed* corresponds to Godly devotion, an expression emanating "from higher to lower." Compassion is a downward effusion from provider to recipient, like a gift. Ultimately, it signifies an actualization in this world of a specific form of energy in the spiritual realm. Isaac's *gevurah*, on the other hand, connotes a process of sublimation by which the mundane, un-Godly world elevates itself to a spiritual plane and thereby is consecrated by the spirituality that suffuses it.

We compared these two attributes using an analogy of two students. One plays a passive role in absorbing the information and ideas of his teacher but is not empowered to intellectual-

ize on one's own. He represents the higher to lower process.
The ascent from lower to higher is analogous to the student
whose teacher guides him in cognitive deduction and speculation, thereby enhancing his aptitude. This student is elevated
to a new level where he can think along the lines of the teacher.
The first student has retained more actual knowledge, but the
second has received the ability to develop his own awareness
and rational deductive processes. In short, he has *learned how
to learn*.

Each approach has its advantages. The first student undoubtedly has more depth of understanding of the Torah and a deeper,
more penetrating analysis. He possesses the wisdom of a teacher,
not of a mere student. The supreme Torah understanding of his
master is alive within him. Conversely, the second student possesses his own understanding, derived from his personal perception and intellect, yet it is obviously inferior in caliber to that
of his teacher. Yet, in terms of which student has advanced and
developed more fully, it is obvious that the second is a quan-
tum leap ahead of the first. The first student has himself undergone no change. He acts merely as a receptacle to wisdom.
When confronted with a new area of information, he is dependent on the guidance of his master. For all intents and purposes,
his master has merely entered into him and planted his knowledge within him. The second student, who may not possess the
depth and scope of knowledge of the former, has nevertheless
been elevated intellectually. In him is manifested the lofty ability of his master to uplift his students and transform their intellectual lives.

In reality, however, the differences are not absolute: each student possesses elements of the other. The latter student, although primarily intellectually self-sufficient, has obtained gifts
as a result of an effusion from above, that is, the tutelage of his
master. Had his teacher not taught him, he would never have
advanced. In the same way, to imply that this student's achievement is solely dependent on his individual effort would likewise
be untrue. His ability to be intellectually original is a product
not only of an innate aptitude, but of his master's guidance and
thought. He bore within him seminal ideas that the teacher
helped mature, an inherent potential that the teacher translated

into actuality. After all, intellect cannot be created, and a teacher cannot possibly work with someone who is not somewhat mentally gifted. Similarly, the first student, although primarily a receptacle, had to exert a substantial degree of self-motivation and effort to obtain, comprehend, and retain the knowledge of his teacher.

Both systems of thought require strenuous effort, the difference between them being one of direction. Both students must labor to retain the teachings of their respective masters, but the effort of the first is vastly different from that of the second. The first student must exert strenuous effort to *digest* all the material from his teacher. His principal objective is to *receive* the wisdom being transmitted from above to below. Thus, his effort is being exerted in a way of *absorption and assimilation*. Conversely, the second student seeks to enhance his own personal ability, refining and elevating it to the same standard as his teacher. His effort is directed at revealing and enhancing his latent talent for creative thought. Thus, his effort is directed in a way of *progression and emulation*

DESCENT OF TORAH AND ASCENT OF *TESHUVAH*

These two models in the student–teacher relationship provide a working model for the different facets of the relationship between God and man. They can also help us understand the two forms of Divine service, the movement from higher to lower and the movement from lower to higher. We consider here but one of the many examples that exist in *Hasidus*. The Divine service, which is regarded as coming from above to below, is represented by the fulfillment of the Torah and *mitzvos*, whereas the Divine service regarded as going from below to above is represented by *teshuvah*, the art of repentance.

The Torah is God's Torah, as are the *mitzvos*. The object of man in his study of Torah and the performance of *mitzvos* is to incorporate into his being as much of the inherent holiness found in them as possible. It is not incumbent upon man to produce his own holiness when engaging himself in Torah study, for Torah and *mitzvos* are themselves holy. Thus, the action of man in his fulfillment of Torah and *mitzvos* is a progression from higher to lower—bringing the inherent holiness of the Torah from the sublime spiritual domain to the lowly physical reality. He seeks to imbue the holiness of the Torah within himself, by fulfilling its commandments.

Teshuvah, on the other hand, involves not man's apprehension of holiness from the lofty spiritual realm, but rather a cultivation of the latent holiness that lurks within man and the physical world. Unlike an ordinary *mitzvah, teshuvah* is not a commandment from God. What then is the nature of *teshuvah?* Man has cast off the yoke of heaven and acted in a sinful manner. He has willfully violated the Will of the Supreme Judge whom he has blatantly forsaken. Suddenly a complete reversal of this rebellion takes place. Regretting his estrangement from his beloved Creator, he sheds tears and becomes a penitent. He vows never again to transgress the Almighty's commandments, but to serve God with increased fervor and devotion. True to his pledge, he summons forth his strength and fulfills the Torah and *mitzvos* with added zest and zeal, intent on refraining from stumbling as before.

What caused this sudden reversal? Was it due to a Godly command that man must repent upon sinning? This cannot be, for a moment ago this very person completely forsook God and His Will! So although he may indeed be aware of the fact that God wishes him to return from his evildoing, this knowledge is in itself insufficient to redirect his actions to righteousness. The very fact that he has acted wickedly testifies to his insubordination to God's desires. Why then has he suddenly become a penitent with tears streaming down his cheeks who comes begging not only to be forgiven but also to be reinstated in a close attachment to God, his Creator? Because deep inside him, in his hearts of hearts and in the innermost recesses of his soul, he has always remained one with God, and he possesses intrinsic holiness. Even in the midst of his insurrection he has remained a Jew. As the renowned talmudic maxim declares, "A Jew, although he has sinned, is still a Jew." He shares an unbreakable bond with God, like that between father and son. Now that this latent bond has been restored he feels it anew, and the Jew longs to be consciously and openly reunited with his Father in Heaven.

It follows, therefore, that the fundamental aspect of *teshuvah* is the cultivation and development of the innate holiness of the Jew. Whereas the fulfillment of Torah and *mitzvos* involves the Jew's drawing holiness and enveloping it into himself from above to below, with his primary effort being to make himself a proper receptacle, *teshuvah* involves the manifestation of man's latent holiness from below to above, his primary effort being to make himself an actual luminary radiating with holiness. In the performance of Torah and *mitzvos*, the functioning of spirituality has not necessarily made a lasting impact on the individual. Yet, in the performance of *teshuvah*, the individual himself is elevated to a higher plane: he has become a living source of holiness. Conversely, it may be appreciated that the level of spirituality apprehended through the fulfillment of Torah and *mitzvos* is far loftier than that of *teshuvah*, for the holiness of Torah descends from above, whereas *teshuvah* is a cultivation of the spirituality in man, which is of a lower degree.

CULTIVATING LATENT HUMAN HOLINESS

To explain this point in another manner, the goal of man in the study of Torah and the performance of *mitzvos* is not to reveal the intrinsic holiness contained within oneself, but to absorb the holiness contained within the Torah and have it permeate one's being. This objective is like that of the first student described above, whose ambition is to apprehend the wisdom of his teacher, not to pursue new insights of his own.

On the other hand, the purpose of *teshuvah* is to expose and bring to the fore the inner latent holiness inherent within the Jew that has heretofore been concealed in the depths of his soul. In the *teshuvah* process, the Jew is required to manifest and translate his dormant ability from the potential to the actual. This phenomenon evokes comparison with the second student, who cultivates his hidden potential for new intellectual insight, rather than basking in the acquisition of his teacher's insights. His is an art of innovation, not passive reception, just as *teshuvah* is a procedure of individual breakthrough and development and not mere absorption.

And just as each of the methods of the two students possesses advantages and disadvantages, so too with the service of Torah and *mitzvos* vis-à-vis *teshuvah*. When looked upon from the perspective of personal elevation, *teshuvah* is greater. When a person, by virtue of his study of Torah and performance of *mitzvos*, is uplifted spiritually, he himself has not been elevated. Rather, he has remained stationary while holiness has rained down upon him. It is not his personal holiness that has brought him to his higher plane; rather, it is the sublimity of the Torah and *mitzvos* found within him. This again is comparable to the first student, who has become knowledgeable but not by virtue of his own knowledge. With the performance of *teshuvah*, on the other hand, the individual elevates himself by way of his own capacity for spiritual elevation and redemption. He taps the vast storehouse of holiness found deep within himself, thus upgrading his very being. His progress emulates that of the second student, who has labored with his own intellectual fertility to the point where he can function in an imaginative and creative way, independent of his master's assistance.

But, in regard to which kind of holiness is loftier, of course the holiness brought about by Torah and *mitzvos* is superior to that of *teshuvah*. The holiness mined from within man as a result of his performance of *teshuvah* is limited, since man himself is fundamentally limited. The holiness inherent in Torah and *mitzvos*, by comparison, is of an infinite nature. Torah and *mitzvos* are the "supreme Wisdom and the supreme Will of the Almighty." The scale of their holiness is immeasurable. This difference is comparable to the supremacy of the wisdom and knowledge possessed by the first student over the second, since the former's ideas are those of the teacher and the latter's only those of a student.

ELEVATING THE SPARKS OF MATERIAL EXISTENCE

Just as these differences between the holiness wrought by *teshuvah* and by Torah and *mitzvos* exist in relation to man, the microcosm, so too do they exist in relation to the world, the macrocosm. In *Koheles* (Ecclesiastes) it is written, "The world as well was given unto their hearts." From this statement we infer that everything that transpires in the world is a reflection of "their hearts," that is, that which occurs within the heart of the Jews. Thus, the random, private acts of the Jew have universal repercussions. The macrocosm of the world is acted upon and influenced by the microcosm of the Jew.

Through the study of Torah and observance of *mitzvos* the Jew causes holiness to descend into the physical world from above to below. This light of "Godly wisdom and Godly will" is the purest form of holiness. Conversely, *teshuvah*, the nature of which is to elicit the natural holiness inherent within man, induces a spiritual elevation of the world, raising it from below to above by extracting and refining the individual sparks of holiness submerged within the coarse, material fiber of the world. A well-known kabbalistic doctrine teaches that within every crevice of this created world are Divine sparks of holiness that await redemption from that solitary confinement in which their true nature is hidden. The Jew, given mastery over the empirical world, possesses the ability to release these sparks through the performance of *teshuvah*. Through a cultivation and manifestation of his intrinsic holiness, the Jew causes a chain reaction. Reflecting this outwardly directed revelation of holiness, the sparks of divinity within the world raise themselves above their material shell, thus raising the entire world along with them.

Once again, each approach possesses its own virtues. With regard to the level of holiness, it is clear that Godly light resulting from Torah and *mitzvos* is superior. Yet, with respect to the degree of change within the world, the elevation of the Godly sparks, which pull the world along with them to sublime spiritual heights, is far greater. In this case, it is the world itself that is transformed into a spiritual entity, and in this sense *teshuvah* may be said to be superior to first-time acts of Torah and *mitzvos*.

INHERITED ABILITY TO PERFECT THE WORLD

Thus, there are two modes in the sublimation process and hallowing of this world—the descent of Godliness from above to below and the ascent of the world to a more Godly plane from below to above. The ability to create spiritual changes in the cosmos in these ways stems from our forefathers. The Jew's ability to cause holiness to descend into this world is inherited from Abraham, whose principal attribute in the service of God was *hesed*. And the potential for elevating the world from itself is inherited from Isaac, who exercised the attribute of *gevurah* in his worship of God.

Regarding Abraham, the Torah relates, "*Vayikra*"—"And he called in God's name, Lord of the world." Commenting on this passage, the Talmud adds: "Do not say *Vayikra*, he called, but rather *Vayakri, he caused others to call.* This teaches that Abraham caused the name of the Almighty to be heard in the mouths of all who passed by him." Through his considerable powers of persuasion Abraham was able to cause even the basest idol worshipers to proclaim the glory of God.

The great Jewish medieval philosopher Maimonides, in his codification of Jewish Law, the *Mishneh Torah*, elaborates greatly on the all-encompassing campaign launched by Abraham for the dissemination of Godly knowledge in the midst of the heathens. Other authorities as well note that Abraham had an immense capacity for verbal communication and explanation that enabled him to expound upon profound concepts of divinity even to the most ignoble of pagans and the lowliest nomads who would worship "the dust of their feet." Thus, through his vast efforts he caused Godly recognition and awareness to descend into the palpable ignorance and pagan tendencies of the masses.

However, given the nature of this method of influence—above to below—Abraham may have imbued his listeners with more knowledge, but he did not alter their state. He was able to instill within them spiritual ideas, but they remained lowly and degenerate. Abraham had not transformed or elevated them. The belief he communicated to them did not permeate their person, and so with the passing of time it diminished until ultimately many returned to their idolatrous ways. The stamp that Abraham made upon his listeners and converts was largely ephemeral, coming as it did from above to below. Isaac, however, employed the second form of service. The Torah narrative focuses on Isaac's building of wells. This physical act was a reflection of his approach to religious ritual. In the digging of a well, one does not fill the newly formed pit with water from another source, nor does one await rainfall to accumulate and fill it. Rather one digs a well in order to tap the water below the surface—water that has always been in that location, but has been hidden beneath the soil.

POURING WATER AND CREATING A LIVING SPRING

A rabbinic maxim as found in the Talmud declares, "There is no water save that of Torah." Water connotes Torah and Godliness. When an area is devoid of water or devoid of Godliness and spirituality, there are two ways to remedy the situation. Godliness can be brought from another location, just as water may be transferred into an arid or parched area. That is, the Godliness can descend from above and fill the void and make it holy. But in that case the spirituality is not really a product of the location. An alternative method is to dig and uncover the possibly vast underground water resources within the location—in other words, to mine and elevate the Divine sparks of holiness enclothed within the physical world. Thus, the service of Isaac reflects the holiness inherent within the world and man.

It was Abraham who opened the channel and invested his descendants with the ability to draw holiness downward from the celestial spheres to the mundane world. Isaac continued that process by reversing it, enriching the Jewish people with the potential of disclosing the dormant holiness of creation.

With this in mind we may appreciate why the first Temple corresponds to Abraham and the second Temple to Isaac. History records that the Jews of the first Temple era were generally righteous people. They learned Torah, observed the *mitzvos*, and caused spirituality to descend into the world. The standing *Beis Hamikdosh* reflected this output of spirituality, and therefore its holiness by far surpassed that of the second Temple, which lacked the five fundamental properties of the first. In addition, its Godliness was far more obvious and revealed and of a far more transcendent quality than that of the second Temple.

Conversely, the second Temple was built by *baalei teshuvah*, penitents. The Jews, who had begun deviating from the path of righteousness near the end of the first Temple period, were expelled by God from their land and the Temple was destroyed. While in exile in Bavel, the Jews repented of their sins and returned to the Land of Israel, where they built the second Temple. Thus, the second Temple itself was a product and a symbol of *teshuvah*–repentance. The primary mode of Divine service was the consecration of the world by means of uncovering its own innate holiness and raising it from "below to above." This method of sublimation, as we have seen, is inferior to the former in the degree of holiness, but it penetrates deeper and becomes more deeply rooted and orchestrated with the material world since its holiness is a product in and of itself. Thus we explained the talmudic proclamation that the second Temple was greater than the first in terms of height (structure) and years (duration). The principal elements of the empirical world, time and place, had been forged more into the holiness of the second Temple, and it therefore stood for a far longer time and occupied more space. Yet, it lacked five integral properties of holiness, conforming with the fact that the light of *teshuvah* is lower.

Parenthetically, with this we can explain why the enthusiasm and driving force behind the building of the second Temple and its primary builder was the Persian king, Cyrus, a non-Jew. Since the second Temple reflected the elevation of the mundane to holiness, it was constructed by a non-Jew who begins on a more earthy plane on the spiritual hierarchy.

SYNTHESIZING THE FIRST AND SECOND TEMPLES

The third and final *Beis Hamikdosh* corresponds to Jacob, who was the synthesis of the positive aspects of each of these modes of Divine service, as it is written, "The God of my father Abraham, and the Dread of Isaac has been with me." Jacob is representative of a third type of student, who incorporates within himself the virtues of the other two. He has the ability to think on his own and be intellectually creative, like the second student, but he also resembles the first student in that his ideas are so profound that they partake of the caliber of the teacher. Thus, he represents perfection in the formation of the student: he has uplifted and transformed himself to the point where his created ideas meet the standard of the teacher.

In microcosmic and macrocosmic terms this means that Jacob personifies a sublimation process in which man and the world effect an outward effusion of holiness that, although originating from themselves, is not limited to themselves. The holiness they generate is identical with the high degree of holiness that descends from the spiritual realm above.

Therefore, the Temple corresponding to Jacob will incorporate the attributes of the two Temples that preceded it. The Godly light that will shine in it will be caused by the service of the "lower" physical world, and yet this light will parallel the Godly illumination that is brought about by the spiritual realm.

The comforting expression used by the prophet Isaiah concerning the third Temple is *"Nahamu, nahamu Ami"*—"Be comforted, be comforted, my people." Commenting on the seemingly needless repetition, the *Midrash* explains that the first word corresponds to the first *Beis Hamikdosh* and the latter to the second *Beis Hamikdosh*. The comfort that will be wrought with the coming of the third Temple will represent the synthesis of the inherent qualities of the first two. The world will then be uplifted to the level of holiness that previously could be attained only through an effusion from above.

This unique ability to evoke the latent Godliness from within the creation and to raise it to the loftiest spiritual heights is a part of the birthright of the Jew transmitted to him by the third and most select of our forefathers, Jacob.

10

CATAPULTING FROM THE HEIGHTS OF SINAI

In the previous chapters we traced the gradual evolution of the Jewish people. We saw how their inherent holiness was initiated with Abraham, who acquired a Godly soul; continued with Isaac, who brought about the integration of the soul with the body; and culminated with Jacob, whose body was completely permeated with holiness. In this chapter we continue to expound upon the unique attributes of the Jewish people by examining the second fundamental and preeminent stage of Jewish sublimation, the receiving of the Torah at Sinai.

A HOLY AND CHOSEN NATION

The Jewish people possess two transcendent virtues as a nation: first, they are a holy nation, and second, they are God's chosen people. That they are a holy nation we have already seen. However, a people or object may be holy without necessarily being the chosen of God.

These two intrinsic character traits that are the birthright of every Jewish individual stem from two sources. The holiness of the Jewish people was established and developed by our forefathers, who dedicated their lives to the pursuit and internalization of holiness, divesting themselves of independent personal will. This holiness they instilled within their im-

119

mediate offspring and subsequently transmitted it in the fiber and construct of the Jew from generation to generation, until it became an actual part of the Jew's being. Thus, notwithstanding religious commitment and virtue, the Jew himself is holy.

In addition to being a holy nation, the Jews were chosen by God to become His people. No matter how great the potency for Godliness inherited by the Jew from his forefathers, it does not parallel the magnitude of holiness associated with being the chosen of God. The forefathers may have had the ability to implant holiness within their offspring, but only the Almighty could elevate them to the plane of becoming His chosen people.

This greatest attribute possessed by the Jewish people was accomplished at the giving of the Torah at Mount Sinai. It was there that the one and only God delivered His one and only Torah to His one and only nation, selecting them from all other nations of the earth. The Divine manifestation that the Jews experienced at Sinai was of an intimate and personal nature. No other nation enjoyed this degree of personal association with the Almighty. This closeness was established both with the Jewish people as a whole, and specifically with every Jewish individual. Each Jew enjoyed a proximity to God that was to continue throughout the generations. No other nation in history has ever had the effrontery to even claim that they experienced a collective revelation to millions of people. God chose and showed Himself only to the Jewish nation.

This concentration of Jewish attributes—the holiness imbued by the forefathers and the subsequent selection of the Jewish people at Sinai—is expressly declared by a verse of the Torah. In his lengthy rebuke of the Jewish people found in the Book of Deuteronomy, Moses tells them: "You are a nation consecrated to God your Lord. God has chosen you from all nations on the face of the earth to be His own special nation." Commenting on the verse, Rashi, the classical biblical commentator, explains, "Your own holiness [is derived] from your forefathers, and in addition, 'God had chosen you.'" So it may be clearly seen that these are two distinct attributes: subliminal holiness and chosenness by God.

It is of interest here to note that only on *Yom Tov*, that is, the Jewish festivals, and not on the Sabbath, do we recite the prayer of *"Attah Behartanu"*—"You have chosen us from all nations of the world." This is so because the observance of *Shabbos* is one of the few commandments that preceded the giving of the Torah at Sinai. The commandment to keep the Sabbath holy was given at *Marrah*, before the Jews received the Torah at Sinai and became chosen. Therefore, in the prayers commemorating the commandment to observe the *Shabbos*, we do not mention having been chosen, for the commandment of sanctifying the *Shabbos* came before the Jewish people were actually chosen.

The recognition that the status of the Jews as a chosen people originated at Sinai is again expressed in Jewish law, wherein the Magen Abraham states that in the blessings preceding the *Shema* prayer, upon reciting the words "You have chosen us from all other nations and tongues" one must contemplate the giving of the Torah at Sinai, for it was then that the Jewish people became God's chosen nation.

Notwithstanding the fact that the holiness of the Jewish nation is lofty indeed, it is dwarfed by the virtue of being God's chosen people. By first achieving a deeper understanding of the quality of holiness, we can better appreciate the quality of being chosen.

QUALITATIVE DISTINCTIONS WITHIN CREATION

Earlier we observed that the empirical world comprises four levels of existence: mineral (inanimate, lifeless objects), vegetable (plant life), animal, and intellectual (human). In addition a fifth category exists: the Jew. According to this categorization, the Jew is not a mere division of the intellectual species, but is actually a classification unto himself

To explain: each of the four categories includes different levels of existence. For instance, in the realm of the inanimate there is dust, and higher than dust is silver, and still higher is gold. Each element is an inanimate object with its own properties.

At times their characteristics differ so greatly that it is difficult even to make comparisons between them, much less classify them in the same category. Nevertheless, their classification is justified on the basis of a single common denominator: they are inanimate.

Thus, it would be misguided to make a comparison between gold and plant life by saying that one is higher or more valuable than the other, for the primary difference between them is so great that it precludes any possibility of comparison. One has life; the other does not. Thus, a tree is not merely a rock with the power of growth and development; it is a creation that completely transcends the concept of unchanging lifelessness. Any resemblances between a plant and a rock are trivial when seen against the basic difference that one has life whereas the other does not.

Similarly, no association may be made between a vegetable and an animal. An animal is not merely a mobile plant; it is a totally different being. Although both are alive, the life of the vegetable affects only the ability of the plant to grow, whereas the life of the animal is far loftier and more intense: the animal possesses sensory perception and instinctual tendencies, and it can move about freely. Most important, the animal possesses *will*. It feels its needs and pursues them accordingly. All these facets make for a complexity of life completely different and qualitatively superior to that of the plant.

The same rule applies when one draws comparisons between the animal and the human. Man is not (as some anthropologists would have us believe) merely an animal with the capacity for thought and speech. To be sure, there are animals that display a high degree of intelligence. For example, the fox is said to be clever. Nevertheless, the superiority of the fox over, say, an ox, could in no way serve as an analogy for understanding the degree of intelligence of the human in comparison with an animal. The intelligence of an animal is in no way comparable to the intelligence and cognitive power of a human. Man is not simply a more complex organism in the hierarchy of animals; he is endowed with a different form of liveliness that gives rise to a novel intellectual capacity, namely, *nefesh hasihlis*, an intellectual soul. Animal intelligence is acquired solely from and is completely dependent upon sensory perception, whereas a human is endowed with the capacity for cognitive and deductive thought, as well as verbal communication.

THE JEW: A CATEGORY TRANSCENDING CREATION

It follows then that this rule applies with equal force when the Jew is compared with all other components of creation. The Jew is not merely a human being with an added dimension; the Jew constitutes a separate category. Within the Jew the Almighty deposited a part of Himself, the *neshamah*, or the Godly soul. Unlike the components of the creation, the *neshamah* was not created outside the unity of God, but is a part of the benevolent Creator.

The *neshamah* in relation to God is analogous to the flame of a candle drawn from a torch. The candle lacks the quantitative intensity of the torch, yet qualitatively the fire emitted by both is identical. Moreover, the candle flame is in essence a part of the torch from which it was drawn, even though it exists as a detached entity, removed from its source. So it is with the Godly soul. Corporeality marks differences only in the created world, but in the spiritual realm it is negligible. In the spiritual realm the soul exists above the distinctions of the body and is said to be in constant communion with God.

Therefore, the Jew, notwithstanding his created body, possesses a part of the Almighty and is not a separate entity from God, but rather is an extension of Him.

The creation, therefore, rightfully possesses only four limited categories. The Jew is not a fifth category, since the Godly soul he possesses lifts him above the creation and makes him an extension of the Infinite. He cannot be classified as merely a physical detail of the creation any more than can the Creator Himself, since he is one with Him.

We have seen how the Jew's Godly soul, his *neshamah*, became a part of the Jewish birthright because of our forefathers. Yet, the transcendental quality of this holiness was only a preliminary step in the formation of the Jewish nation. It does not parallel the great virtue that came later when at the foot of

Mount Sinai the Jews were chosen by God to be His people. It was there and then that the association of the Jewish people with the Almighty reached its apogee.

AT SINAI THE BODY WAS CHOSEN

It is incumbent upon us at this point to examine the significance of the added quality of being chosen. What did it add to the quality of holiness already instilled within the Jew, and what were its ramifications? *Hasidus* offers two general explanations, which in practical terms become one.

In his *magnum opus*, *Tanya*, Rabbi Shneur Zalman of Liadi offers a novel insight: "This is the meaning of . . . 'and You have chosen us from every people and tongue,' which refers to the material body which, in its corporeal aspects, is similar to the bodies of the Gentiles of the world." This doctrine seems somewhat fantastic, and rightfully so. It revolutionizes the stereotypical concept about what aspect of the Jew was chosen by God. Amazingly, the feature of the Jew that was chosen was not the soul, with its unsurpassed holiness, but the Jewish body, a part of the Jew that is identical to that of the non-Jew and that seems to be lacking in any kind of uniqueness. Yet, it is precisely because of this equality and lack of transcendence that the body of the Jew was selected.

CHOICE APPLIES ONLY WHEN
THINGS ARE IDENTICAL

To understand this phenomenon, let us briefly explore the nature of choice. A real choice may be made only between two objects that are identical in all aspects. If one is told to choose between two things, and one is far superior to the other, how can one help but select the superior one? Is there a sane man alive who, if given a choice between five dollars and a million dollars, would choose the former? This rule applies even when the worth of one is only minimally greater than the other; say, if the choice were between ninety-nine and a hundred dollars.

Similarly, if a person is instructed to "choose" between two objects and told that if he chooses the first one he will have his head blown off, would a sane person even dream of choosing the first item? To any rational individual, human logic and intelligent dictate are just as strong, and in many cases far stronger, than physical coercion. So given a choice between ninety-nine and a hundred dollars, even if one is not forced at gunpoint to choose the hundred, in every instance every person confronted with the choice would choose it. If the intellect dictates that one item is more valuable than the other, the individual is "forced" to choose the superior one. He basically has no choice in the matter.

Authentic, objective choice can exist only when two things are identical in every way. There can be no intellectual or emotional partiality. When two things are equivalent, and an individual chooses with his own free will the one that he wants, only then is the choice not intellectually impelled but rather transcends reason. Such a choice is not a biased or subjective selection of mind and heart, but emanates from the nethermost reaches of human existence.

This type of choice emanates from a totally intangible part of man that can only be described as "intrinsic will." At this level, what we want and what we are cannot be distinguished from one another. Without our intrinsic will we can have no identity. And it is only at this embryonic level that true choice exists and enables us to select one thing over another, even when there is no tangible, logical justification for the choice. (A common example of intrinsic will is the desire to be and remain alive, but there are others as well, such as the ambition to succeed and to search for meaning in life.) The same guideline applies to God's selection of the Jewish people. Since the Jew possesses a Godly soul, it is illogical to say that God would have chosen the Jewish people from among the nations of the earth. After all, what would attract God more than a Godly soul? What choice could there be? It seems fair to assume that God in His choosing would naturally gravitate to Godliness and holiness. The Jews were already holy. The past few chapters have described how they acquired their spiritual holiness through the sublimation and internalization of Godliness by the Jewish patriarchs. So what was there to choose? Only in the material body of the Jew, "which, in its corporeal aspects, is similar to the bodies of other nations of the world," could there be a choice. Even though the external body of the Jew does not possess any virtue that would make it worthier than other human bodies of the nations of the world, God nevertheless chose it. This is the nature of the immortal selection made at Sinai. God chose the Jewish body from among all others of the world.

Bearing this in mind, we can appreciate the magnitude of elevation that the Jews experienced upon being chosen at the giving of the Torah. Until that time, the Jews were distinct only spiritually; they were holy only in terms of their Godly soul. The Godliness had not yet permeated deeply enough to transcend the still un-Godly physical constitution of the Jew.

But God's selection of the Jewish people at Sinai was directed to the body, now sanctifying the physical element of the Jew. The eternal effect of this landmark event was that it caused the Jewish body to become holy and Godly, irrespective of the soul. No longer would the holiness of the body be dependent on the *neshamah* resting within it.

BEING CHOSEN DIFFERS FROM THE EXISTING HOLINESS OF THE BODY

The timeliness of this milestone becomes all the more pertinent in light of our earlier discussion that as a result of *bris milah*, the covenant of circumcision, the Jewish body was infused with Godliness. We saw how originally the soul encompassed but did not enter the body on a material level and how, beginning with the circumcision of Abraham and culminating with that of Isaac, the Jewish soul permeated the body with Godliness from head to toe. Are we not now contradicting that earlier discussion? We refer to this again later, but for now offer a brief clarification. The holiness of the body that resulted from the act of circumcision was due to the fact that the *neshamah*, the soul, had entered the body, consecrating it in the process. Thus, the holiness was not that of the body, but of the soul that permeated it. Conversely, the holiness of the Jewish body that emanated from God's selection of it was a product not of the soul, but of the material body itself. In other words, once God chose the Jewish body at Sinai, it achieved a lasting and unique sublimity that was source-independent. It was not due to the infusion of the soul.

In the next chapter we continue our study of the implications and repercussions of God's selection of the Jewish people. We observe how it was that this selection, born of the fact that the Jews were similar to all other peoples, distinguished the Jewish people from all other nations of the world and brought them closest to the Almighty.

11

WHAT IT MEANS TO BE
THE CHOSEN PEOPLE

In the preceding chapter we introduced a new ingredient of the Jews that we characterized as their most prized attribute: God's selection of the Jews as His chosen people. This Divine selection was directed at the Jewish body—that aspect of the Jew that is externally similar to that of the other nations of the world—since a true choice can be made only between two completely equal things. God's choice of the Jewish body established a direct association with the body, thus consecrating and sanctifying it. The holiness of the body was no longer dependent on the permeation of soul, but was attributable to its own devices. When God chose the Jewish body, He lent it eternal holiness independent of the overtly spiritual *neshamah*.

Before the stand at Mount Sinai, then, the sublimation of the Jewish personality had been only "soul deep." Now the body was holy in its own right. From this it would seem that the only accomplishment of God's selection was the sublimation of the material body. Although the significance of such an attainment should not be minimized, the true prominence of the event was not that it extended the association of God to the Jew's mundane feature, but rather that it established the closest and most intimate relationship imaginable between God and Jews. It did not merely connect another part of the Jew to God, but brought the Jew in his totality, both physical and metaphysical elements combined, closer to God. To appreciate this statement fully, we

129

must once again explore the original connection inaugurated by our forefathers.

LOVE OF CHILD APPROACHES LOVE OF SELF

As was mentioned earlier, the Jew, because of his *neshamah*, is best classified as an extension of God. Therefore, the descendants of the forefathers (who instilled the "Jewish" soul within their offspring) are referred to in the Torah as God's "children," and properly so. Just as a son is a mere extension of his father—that is, intrinsically they may be looked upon as a single entity occupying two separate bodies—similarly the Jew is an extension of his Father in heaven, his soul being an actual part of the Divine but occupying an unattached body. The separation between God and the Jew, therefore, is only a corporeal one.

It follows then that the love that existed between God and the Jewish people before the giving of the Torah was like that of a parent and child, a congenital, intrinsic love. This love contrasted with an external, unnatural love based on the loved one's attributes and characterized by an intellectual understanding. The love a parent fosters for a child, insofar as depth is concerned, is far superior to that intellectual love. In fact, it may be said that a parent loves his child as much as, if not more than, himself.

We therefore observe how, when anything tragic happens to a child, God forbid, the parent's reaction immeasurably exceeds someone's reaction to the news of a disaster befalling a close associate. The extent of a friend's reaction ranges from a slight sigh to shock and depression that will slowly subside. The pain of a friend's misfortune does not reach the depths of the soul, because it is not oneself or one's own flesh and blood that was affected. But any mishap to a child, God forbid, will anguish a parent to the depths of his or her soul, and the misery will last until the day he or she dies. It is simply irrevocable. Essentially, the parent him/herself has been hurt.

These same rules apply in the relationship between God and the Jews. The Jews enjoy an intrinsic, eternal love relationship with their Creator. Thus, a significant amount of *midrashim* record statements by the Almighty that expose His great remorse over the pain and suffering of the Jewish people. For example, the Talmud states that when the Temple was destroyed and the Jews exiled from their land, the Almighty went into exile with them. The remainder of creation has an external relationship with God, but the Jew's woes are God's woes.

This unique intimacy, notwithstanding its sublimity, still does not rival the closeness the Jews established with God upon receiving the Torah.

CHOICE: A UNIQUELY HUMAN ACTIVITY

To understand this closeness, let us delve more deeply into the nature of choice. Maimonides, the great medieval Jewish thinker, explains in his halakhic compendium *Mishneh Torah,* and at greater length in his theological treatise known as *The Eight Chapters*, that the potential for choice is exclusive to man, and it is this virtue more than any other that places man above all other creatures.

Every created being is limited by its anatomical composition and the nature intrinsic to it. The very existence of the creature acts as a limiting force upon it that it cannot transcend. A rock will forever remain nonresponsive and unfeeling, and it will never assume flight like a bird. A plant will never be able to roam, converse, or think. An animal, lacking the ability for long-range premeditation, will always act on impulse and on instinct, which guides while also limiting it.

We have observed how sheer instinct prevents an animal from approaching fire. In fact, man universally uses fire as a protection from wild beasts, entrusting his very life to a simple torch, knowing that an animal cannot help but flee from fire.

Man too has an instinct to flee for his life when threatened with fire. Nevertheless, we know that throughout history individuals have thrown themselves into scorching infernos for the sake of their beliefs. In fact, this practice was originated by Abraham, our forefather, who allowed himself to be thrown into a smoldering cauldron in a blatant refusal to relinquish his monotheistic faith (*Bereishis Rabbah, Midrash Rabbah*).

Unlike other creations, then, man was endowed with the ability to transcend his natural limitations. All of animated existence is a ladder, with the angels standing on the top rungs of the continuum, the animals at the bottom, and man in the middle faced with the choice to rise and personify an angel or fall and become a beast. Even those born with a genetic predisposition for selfishness possess the ability to redirect their inclinations toward altruism and righteousness. The wicked man cannot justify his actions by saying that he was born with a wicked heart, because that heart was given the power to defy that predisposition to evil or violence. He could have chosen to become the most righteous of all men. Conversely, even one born with a good and humble nature has no guarantee of becoming a saint. He can choose to degrade himself to ugliness and corruption. All men were imbued with the capacity to defy their limitations and act according to their desires, for better or worse. Man is the arbitor of his destiny and is uniquely endowed with the capability of choosing to be either good or evil.

In reality, this unique ability should be surprising. How does man, a created being, possess this uncommon ability to transcend his inborn inclination and nature? It is in response to this query that Maimonides cites the verse, "Behold, man has become as one (ke'ahad) of us" upon which Hasidus, following the midrashic interpretation, elucidates that ke'ahad, which stems from the word ehod, meaning "one," refers to the One and Only, the Almighty. Thus, "man has become as the One."

IN WHICH WAY DOES MAN EMULATE THE DIVINE?

Just as the Almighty is completely unlimited and may choose to do as He wishes, with no internal or external factor affecting His Will—as the prayer liturgy proclaims, "Who will tell You what to do and what shall transpire"—so too man may choose to do or be anything he favors. In the final analysis, man's choice is not affected by any outside interference or innate mental or genetic predisposition. Judaism rejects the assertion of determinists and behaviorists that we are not fully responsible for our actions or are lacking the power to determine whether we will be good or evil.

Thus in man there exist two integral faculties: (1) the intrinsic nature and genetic tendencies special to man and (2) the ability to transcend those human limitations and predispositions and to live by personal self-determination and will. Beneath the defined components of man there exists the undefined simplicity that can enable man to transcend the shell of his own nature into which he was born.

This is the true innate essence of the Jewish soul. In that the soul is an actual part of God and God is infinite, then the soul too is essentially infinite. So the Jew is able to springboard above his material composition because of his soul. Thus, the Jew in essence is a rational, yet suprarational being: rational and fixed in his temperament and suprarational in being unlimited by anything human. The latter faculty is removed from and far superior to the former.

It is in this second faculty, the inner recesses of the human soul, that his power of choice is lodged. Because there is an underlying level of undefined simplicity in man, he may do as he pleases. For no matter what influences may be affecting him, underneath he harbors a form of simplicity and lack of material definition, which remains unmolded and unshaped by those forces.

CHOICE WITH A CAUSE IS LIMITED BY THAT CAUSE

Taking this principle a step further, the fact that all of creation with the exception of man is inherently limited applies not only to the physical elements but to the spiritual ones as well. Just as all physical materials possess their own special properties and limitations—for example, rubber can bounce whereas metal cannot—so too the various gradations of divinity that animate living creatures possess intrinsic properties. These spiritual properties dictate the abilities, indeed the very thought patterns of the animal. The raven, a bird of prey, who has a defined nature toward belligerency and hostility, will always act accordingly, since the source of its animating force stems from the Divine attributes of *gevurah*, severity and stringency, discussed earlier. Conversely, the eagle, whose spiritual life force arises from the Divine attributes of *chesed*, mercy and compassion, will always act in a characteristic fashion and practice magnanimity with and offer protection to its offspring.

Although no two people are alike, man also possesses inborn character tendencies that seem to be a governing force, enabling us to make predictions of future behavior based upon past actions. Yet, in addition, there exists in man a dimension well above any definition: the Godly soul, a measure of the Infinite. This enabling power transcends any constraints inherent in the human. Thus, man may choose anything his heart desires, notwithstanding any predispositions with which he is born.

From this concept one may appreciate how the love of a father for his son is rooted extremely deeply, unlike a love that stems from mere choice. For a father is as if forced into loving his son from the moment of the child's birth. He has no choice. This love retains elements of physical coercion, and he cannot help himself. It is in his nature, and essentially, not loving his son would be an unnatural act. His very genes cause him to harbor an undying and unbreakable affection for his son, which causes the parent to treat the child with compassion. Society harbors a moral indignation for a parent who does not display a caring attitude toward his child. It is as if we all automatically regard such a parent as a curiosity, and we become immediately indignant.

Thus, even at this sublime level of love, there exists a reason, albeit superrational and internal, for the love. Since it possesses a reason, it is intrinsically limited by that reason. It follows then that this love sprouts from the lower faculty of man, that which is limited and finite. For this love does not transcend the definition of man. The love of a father to his son is a defined love; it can be categorized and classified. It is a rational love. Logic dictates that the nature of man is to love his own son. It is not a love that arises from the highest faculty of man, namely, the underlying, undefined infinite soul, which has the ability to transcend nature.

TRUE CHOICE IS INFINITE

But when one chooses something by way of his free will, without any predisposition or partiality, without influence or coercion, his deepest will is aroused for what he has chosen. The choice stems from the nethermost reaches of the soul, a place that is infinite. For this reason, this will is stronger than all others. Since it is not governed by any external factor, what can stop it or dictate the degree of its passion? Thus, the will aroused by free choice and the subsequent love arising from that choice are the deepest, most intrinsic, and most formidable of any love within the powers of a human being.

Just as man possesses these two faculties of limitation and transcendence, along with the ramifications of each that extend to the will and attraction that arise from each, the same is true concerning the Almighty.

A contradiction arises concerning the spiritual likeness of God. The prophet Ezekiel says, "And behold, upon the throne there sat the likeness of a man." Yet elsewhere in the Prophets it is written, "But He is not [and possesses not the likeness of] a man." Which is the correct description? Furthermore, how is is possible to ascribe any anthropomorphic features to the Creator?

THE EFFECTS OF *TZIMTZUM* ON GODLY DESCRIPTION

Hasidus resolves the contradiction concerning the spiritual likeness of God by explaining that the Almighty is certainly immune to any anthropomorphic description, but that in the course of the creative process God must undergo a series of contractions, or better, condensations, in order to arrive at a more finite level and thus create a physically limited world. Since this process of contraction, or *tzimtzum* as it is called in the Kabbalah, is the origin of physical existence, it is after this process has been effected that the Almighty may be referred to as possessing the likeness of man.

The reason why God may be described in anthropomorphic terms after the *tzimtzum* that enables creation is that now God must sustain and therefore interact with the world He has created. For this reason, he suddenly becomes manifest. These manifestations of Divinity are referred to as *sefirot*, and are in effect ten distinct channels of Godly revelation. Each *sefirah* denotes a different Divine emotion or attribute, which in turn corresponds, in kabbalistic analogy, to a different human emotion. When these *sefirot* are systematized and ordered into a hierarchical structure, they begin to represent, in metaphor only, a human image. Thus, the Kabbalah says that God's attribute of *hesed* corresponds to the human right arm, whereas the attribute of *gevurah* corresponds to the left arm, and so on.

The prophetic verse quoted above concerns itself with a time before the contraction. Hence, "God is not like a man." This rule similarly applies when God is referred to as Father (of the Jewish people). Before the contraction of His Limitless Self, God cannot be referred to in such anthropomorphic terms. Only after the contraction may we say that He is our Father. It is written in *Koheles* regarding God's existence before the series of contractions, "He possesses not a son, even a brother." At this highest of levels there are no relationships to which God is subject. He is completely removed from the world and does not even serve as its point of origin. Thus, when it is said that the Jewish people are children to the Almighty, this expression refers to a relationship that exists only after God has contracted and reduced Himself to a lower spiritual level.

"'YOU' HAVE CHOSEN US"

How do these concepts relate to God's choice of the Jewish people at Sinai? The love that God displayed to the Jewish people when He chose them at Sinai was far greater and deeper than anything preceding it. Before the giving of the Torah the Divine relationship that the Jews enjoyed was that of a parent to his child, which, as we have seen, is inherently limited. It was as if the Almighty had no choice but to love the Jewish people.

Yet at Sinai the Almighty had no rational basis by which to choose the Jewish people. After dwelling in Egypt for over 200 years, they had adopted and had been assimilated into the prevailing Egyptian culture, so much so that at the parting of the Red Sea when God saved the Jews and drowned the Egyptians, the angels of heaven proclaimed: "Why do you save this people and consume the other? Both are worshipers of idols and foreign gods" (*Shemos Rabbah*). Thus, with no apparent partiality, coercion, or predisposition, God chose the Jews as His people, thereby forming an infinite, quintessential love.

Therefore, the giving of the Torah represented more than the physical body of the Jew becoming attached to God. Rather, the bond itself was infinitely higher than that which existed previously. It is for this reason that at the giving of the Torah the body of the Jew was chosen. Before the giving of the Torah, when the Jews were connected to God by means of the soul, the relationship the Jews shared with God was similar to that of a parent and child. Just as the son is an integral part of the father, so is the soul a part of God, and so it was only natural that God love the Jew, a part of God Himself. But at the giving of the Torah, God was not compelled to choose the Jewish body, which was, after all, similar to that of all other nations. Thus, God's choice formed an unlimited, infinite link between the Jewish people and their Creator. The Almighty chose the Jews of His own free and infinite Will.

This was the accomplishment of *Mattan Torah*, that God should totally upgrade His relationship with the Jewish people to an infinite level, thus forever forging the Jewish people with their Creator as one. God's choice originates in the loftiest reaches, a level at which all limitation is nonexistent. At this level of God's infinite Essence, there is no contraction, hence external dimension, in the relationship between God and the Jews.

It may seem that at this infinite level it is impossible for God to share a relationship with anything at all, and this is why God must contract Himself in order to create the world and descend to a more finite level. The very concept of relationship applies only with something tangible, and at this level God is utterly transcendent. Nevertheless, when God chose the Jewish people, He established a connection with them even at this pinnacle.

This is what we refer to when we say, "*Attah behartanu*"—You, the Infinite Divine Essence, have chosen us, the Jews. At the level in which You are totally incomprehensible and transcendent, You have chosen the Jewish people, with your unlimited and uninfluenced power of choice, with no external reason whatsoever, to be Your nation, establishing an unbreakable bond with them, and showing them eternal love.

12

THE LAYERS
OF GOD AND MAN

THE ALMIGHTY OFFERS
THE GENTILE NATIONS A DEAL

The Talmud tells how, before the giving of the Torah at Mount Sinai, the Almighty approached every nation on the earth and suggested to each that it accept the Torah. The nations in turn asked what was written in the Torah, and, after receiving God's reply about the various prohibitions contained therein, such as adultery, theft, and murder, and its demands for ethics and a monotheistic faith, they refused to accept it. It was only the Jewish people who answered, "*Naaseh Venishma*"—"we will do and we will listen." Thus, the Jewish people were the only nation to receive the Torah.

The obvious question that this narrative raises is that since surely God knew initially that the Gentile nations would not accept the Torah, why did he offer it to them in the first place? Was he not aware, by way of His omniscience, that they would decline His offer?

A far more difficult question arising from this narrative is what would have happened if the nations of the world had indeed accepted the Torah. Suppose God had not mentioned the moral codes inherent in accepting the Torah and the nations had agreed to accept it? Would the Almighty have granted them the Torah? May we even mention that possibility? The Torah abounds with references to how the two things in existence before the creation of the world alongside God were the Torah and the Jewish people! Furthermore, according to Jewish theology the very reason for the creation of the world was to serve as an arena for the Jewish people to follow the Torah and observe its precepts. In fact, the Almighty made a condition with the world that if the Jewish people accepted the Torah and lived by it, then he would keep the world in existence, but if not, he would return the world to nothingness.

From all of the above it is clear that the Torah was destined for the Jewish people even before the creation of the world and that its acceptance by the Jewish people was a fundamental tenet in the plan for creation. Yet, the Talmud relates that the Almighty offered the Torah to the nations of the world and, only after they rejected it, did he give it to the Jewish people.

Hasidus explains that in truth the Torah belongs to the Jewish people; the Gentile nations have no affinity with it but rather with the seven Noachide laws and that is why they rejected it. Yet, surely then, the Almighty also knew that they would refuse it. The very purpose for the seemingly futile attempt at offering the Gentiles the Torah was to amplify the greatness and the sublime dimension of the occasion of the Jewish people's accepting the Torah, to transform the already existing connection, and to inaugurate a new form of connection between the Almighty and the Jewish people. We can understand the significance of this bond by placing it in perspective among the other forms of relationships attained before this point. Let us briefly review the differing types of human relationships that we discussed at length in the preceding chapters.

THREE KINDS OF LOVE

There are three levels at which humans relate to each other, as well as to everything else around them. First is the external attraction, the main cause of which is intellectual apprehension and which relates only to the external faculties of the beloved. The prime example is the affection between two friends, which is based on an appreciation of each other's qualities and character.

A step higher on the relationship ladder is the intrinsic bond, a prime example of which is the love between parent and child. This love is not based on external abilities, as even a child with negative characteristics is loved. The parent loves his child, because it is his child, a part of himself. As the Talmud teaches, "A son is a limb of his father." There is no logical reason for this love, just as there are no rational causes for self-love. It is a fact of nature that man loves himself, as well as anything that is a part of himself. Without this self-love, he could not live and could not prosper. This love is an intrinsic one that emanates from the quintessential nature of man.

The difference between this intrinsic bond and the love between friends is obvious. In love between friends the individuals have no real ties to each other and were originally strangers. A child, however, is no stranger to his parent. A child is not loved because he arouses affection by his parent. Rather, a parent loves his child because his very nature forces him to do so. Stated in other words, he cannot help but love his child. Whereas the love directed from one friend to another resembles a suctioning action in which the beloved plays an active role in soliciting the affection of the lover, the love between parent and child is an outpouring of affection from the parent to the child, who plays a passive role in the relationship. And although the child may love the parent in return, the child does not *actively solicit* the love from his parent. It occurs naturally. This latter love is therefore far more innate and rooted in the bedrock of man's being, in the very definition of who he is and who his child is.

Yet, notwithstanding the supremacy of the intrinsic bond over the love between friends, they have a common denominator: in both, the one who is loved is deserving of the love. There is a stark reason that justifies the love. The attributes of the beloved and the fact that the child is part of the parent, although quantitatively the space between these two pretexts is indeed vast, both constitute valid and rational reasons for the development of an affectionate bond. The fact that a parent loves a child because it is his also constitutes a reason, when "reason" is understood in the sense of being not an integral part of man, his essence, but rather an external cause that brings about an external outcome.

Although the love a parent harbors for a child is far deeper than an intellectually motivated love, nevertheless it is not a love without a cause. There is no *intellectual* reason, but there is a natural reason, a rationale. The parent's nature induces him to love the child, who is a part of himself. Man's natural instinct also serves as a reason in contrast to the intrinsic essence of man, which transcends intellect, impulse, or definition. This is not the essential "I" that represents the individual in his totality without employing any external expression.

The third level of relationship so completely transcends any rational causes that it cannot be induced by external catalysts, such as a person's attributes or the instinctual love toward one's child. This love stems from a level in man in which external motives of virtue and even blood relationships have no significance. This love issues from the very essence of the soul, the "I" that is blind to anything external. This quintessential point in the soul of man is the source of free choice. Free choice is exercised when one chooses a given item uninfluenced by any prior cause or natural predisposition. One has no tangible rationale, either intellectual or instinctual, for choosing one thing over another. Why then does he make his choice? There is no logical explanation. From the innermost reaches of the human soul, a point at which man is not consciously aware of his existence, stems the ability for him to choose. At this subterranean level man can no longer be defined. Here man is infinite and the possibilities limitless. A relationship established by man through an exercise of his free power for choice is thus the deepest of all human relationships, because there is no external element that can dilute the love, just as there was no external factor that influenced the choice. He chose to love with his own free will, not because of a friend's attributes nor out of the instinctual impulses of a blood relation. Rather, it was willed in the depths of his soul, the most private, innermost recess in man. This is the highest level of association that can be attained in the human's attachment with something outside himself, an attachment that is truly infinite.

In order to appreciate the pivotal differences between these three bonds and how man relates to them, let us briefly explore man's reaction when any of the relationships is endangered.

If a grave mishap befalls a very close friend, one whom a person loves with all one's heart, the person feels the pain of his friend, sinks into depression, and is willing to offer any assistance to alleviate his friend's anguish. Nevertheless, it cannot be inferred that he feels the same pain that his friend feels. The calamity has jolted him, but not devastated him. He can still continue with his life. After a brief recovery period, he can return to his everyday routine. He is disturbed and most willing to aid his friend, but he is not completely devastated and is seldom willing to sacrifice everything on behalf of his friend.

When misfortune meets a child, however, the parent's entire being is ravaged. The traumatic effect begins to consume his everyday activities to the point where he cannot eat, sleep or engage in normal conversation; he is truly devastated. His every thought is of the child's trauma, and he will move the foundations of the earth, sacrifice anything, in order to save his child. No obstacle is too high, and no price is too exorbitant to bring redemption to his child. The plight of a child reaches the very depths of the parent's being.

One of my childhood friends was a boy named Michael who lost his father at the tender age of six. The family had been vacationing in Hawaii, enjoying the warm waters and sunny surf. One day when he and his father were at the beach, a mighty wave came along, completely engulfing and submerging the young boy under the water. Without a moment of hesitation, his father plunged into the full force of the wave, grabbed his son by the arm and, while still underwater, forced his son to the surface so that he might breathe. The father unfortunately was not so lucky. As he propelled his son to safety, he was carried out by the tide and drowned. However courageous, a story like this does not necessarily surprise us. Does there remain anything that a parent will not do for a child?

Yet, even this degree of sacrifice falls short of what a person is willing to do if the bond he established through free choice becomes endangered. In such an event, there are absolutely no limitations to what the person is willing to do to salvage what he has chosen. Not only will he overturn the world, but he will even sacrifice his own life *as well as that of his children.* Even those things that a parent is not willing to do for his own child, he does without hesitation for that thing with which he chose to align himself. For the bond established by means of choice emanates from the very bedrock of man's existence, and all else sinks into insignificance in the face of it. It was for this reason, then, that Abraham was willing to sacrifice the life of his beloved son Isaac, for the sake of the God that he had chosen, when he was commanded to do so by the Almighty. His affinity with God struck deeper even than his love for his long-awaited son.

PIERCING THE INNER LAYERS

In another analogy let us picture man as constructed from many different layers, as if man were like an onion, or as if he were wearing hundreds of layers of clothing that constituted his being. Certain things he encounters affect only the very outer layers. Other considerations, being more internally oriented, penetrate the outer layers and reach the deeply seated inner layers. Finally are those things that infiltrate all the outer layers and reach the essence of man, which lies deeply below them.

Intellectual and emotional stimulation are exemplified by the outer layers of clothing. The love that arises from them is externally oriented, and so when someone who is loved by an intellectual love is endangered, the trauma reaches only the external shell of man.

Natural instinct, such as the congenital love of a parent for a child, represents the inner layers, those existing beneath the outer surface. Thus, the love from parent to child is equal to the love one harbors for oneself, since it reaches the fundamental components that define man. When a child is endangered, the parent is affected internally and is shaken to the depths of his soul.

Beneath all these outer layers, however, is the quintessence of man, the element that below all the external garb and expression formulates the "I," the "Me" of the soul. This deeply seated "I" is not affected by any of the occurrences taking place in the outer coverings of the soul. It is affected only by those things that emanate from this sublime plateau, that is, those things chosen by man with his own free will. Thus, when the chosen entity is endangered in any way, the effect permeates all the outer shells and reaches man's essence, and he is willing to sacrifice anything and everything in order to recover it.

With the above in mind, we may better appreciate what occurred at Sinai when the Jewish people were given the Torah.

THE MANY LAYERS OF THE GODHEAD

A recurring theological enigma concerns the frequent expressions of the Almighty's pleasure and displeasure over the actions of man. The Torah bears witness many times to the display of Divine wrath after unsatisfactory activities on the part of the Jewish people. In *sidras Haazinu* of the Bible we read, "They [the Jewish people] have angered Me with their follies." Conversely, the Torah at times bears witness to the fact that the good deeds of the people elicit Divine pleasure. Observe the verses "The Lord rejoiced with you and was good to you." How is it that inconsequential man, who in the presence of the Infinite perfect Creator is utterly insignificant, has the ability to arouse Divine happiness, anger, and displeasure by way of his actions? (Of course, the Torah uses anthropomorphic expressions to convey its message to man, and the implication made here is not that God actually becomes angered or calmed. These are mere expressions. Yet, even by way of analogy, how can mortal, finite man cause Divine satisfaction and dissatisfaction and incur Divine wrath?)

In answer to this question, it is explained that there are various degrees of the manifestation of Godliness, as was described in the previous chapter, based on the verse, "And on the throne sat the likeness of a man." It is necessary to recognize two fundamental levels of existence in the Godhead. First is God the way He exists in Himself, on a totally self-relating plane, before any form of self-contraction or revelation that could give rise to anything existing outside His unity. At this level, God is completely removed from any kind of tangible description or revelation. Then there is God the way we perceive Him. After undergoing an immense series of contractions of the intensity of His light, thus giving room for external existence, for creation, the

Almighty descends to a plane at which He relates to the created world. Since at this level there is Divine interaction with created existence, one can ascribe to the Almighty corporeal and anthropomorphic features, but only as a device for analogy. In this way, we can appreciate that, at this level only, the deeds of man may elicit an "emotional" reaction from the Creator.

In understanding this deep theological principle, we can employ an analogy from a mortal king who also constantly moves between two levels of existence. There is the king as an individual, conducting a private life with his family, and there is the king who sits on his throne, governs his empire, and judges his subjects. When the king is alone in his private chambers, none of the problems of state affect him. He is completely removed from his everyday obligations and is submerged in personal thought. He is more concerned with the welfare of his children than with affairs of state. The king later makes his way to the throne room, dons his royal garb, and concentrates on the everyday responsibilities of a ruler. Now, the economic, social, and welfare concerns of people of lower standing than him occupy his time and energy. Concerns that in his room while he was alone were totally abstract are now significant and urgent. And if we were to ask if the king is truly concerned with all the petty details of government, the answer would depend on which moment we were referring to. In his withdrawn, solitary state, the king is indifferent to these trivial concerns. Yet, when he is in his active role as ruler of the land, these details assume tremendous significance. Even the slightest infraction on the part of a royal gardener in fulfilling the king's command of how to cut the grass could incur the king's wrath. The same reclusive individual who ponders the meaning of life and existence in his private quarters assumes the mantle of sovereignty upon entering the throne room. He is now in a different state of existence.

ONLY ONE ENTITY RELATES TO THE ESSENCE OF GOD

So it is with the Almighty who condenses Himself from the loftiest reaches of infinite Divine light to the limited confines of created existence. When He assumes the mantle of Ruler of the

World and King of Kings, the deeds and misdeeds of man elicit His response. It is only concerning the higher levels of existence that it is written, "If you are righteous, you have done nothing for Him," meaning the righteous and sinful are equal before him. He is too far removed at this level for either to be of any consequence.

There is only one entity whose existence affects the Almighty even before the condensation. That is His people Israel. Since the Jewish people are "His children," they relate directly to the essence of God. For this reason, the verse that proclaims the Jewish people as God's children, "A part of the Almighty is His people," uses the tetragrammaton, the name representing God's essence, rather than *Elokim*, which connotes Divine contraction and revelation, in short, the God of nature.

Nevertheless, the Jewish people in the role of God's children still do not reach the absolute essence of God. Although a son is a part of his father, he is still an external entity and therefore relates to the element within man that is defined as a father and is therefore governed by fatherly instincts. Likewise, the Jew as a child does not relate to the quintessence of the Almighty. Again we can look to the lofty tetragrammaton. Although this name represents God's essence, it is still a name. The very necessity for a name implies the existence of an outside entity and boundaries: an entity that must be defined. Furthermore, a name is itself a limiting force. When an object is labeled, it can no longer be something else. It has been defined as that specific object. Similarly, a son can relate to his father within the confines of the father–son relationship. He will never be just a friend or just another acquaintance. Thus, the relationship is deep, yet inherently limiting. Furthermore, a name represents definition, making it possible for one entity to relate to an outside entity. Certainly, if one were marooned on a desert island, one's name would be totally useless. The individual makes use of his name only so that those around him might refer and relate to him.

Beyond this level is another one at which God has no form or definition whatsoever and cannot be apprehended. At this level God does not relate to any external existence. This absolute state of self-existence and absorption is the source for free choice. Since God does not even acknowledge the existence of an external entity, at this level all things are equal. Even congenital relationships, such as that of a son, are not discernible. Thus is it written, "He has not a son, nor a brother." Since there is not the slightest preference for one thing over another at this level, there remains room for a choice—God's uninfluenced, unadulterated choice.

Therefore, when the Almighty chose the Jewish people at Sinai, the relationship between God and the Jews was elevated to the highest of all possible levels: veritably the quintessence of God from God's perspective. At this level of essence there was no distinguishing characteristic between the Jews and Gentiles. And yet God chose the Jews.

SOLICITATION OF OTHER NATIONS ENHANCED THE CHOSENNESS OF THE JEWS

The reason why God solicited every nation to accept the Torah was to emphasize that He was now choosing the Jewish nation above all others. Before Sinai, God loved the Jewish people as children. They were a special holy nation with a Divine soul. Now, however, God was establishing His connection with the Jewish people from His infinite inner essence. At that level all nations are equal, so the Torah was offered to everyone. There was no rational reason for the Jewish people to take preference and receive it over any other nation. They had not as yet distinguished themselves through moral or ethical excellence. Indeed, they had absorbed the pagan and idolatrous practices of their Egyptian overlords in whose culture they were immersed and thus could not have been more worthy than other nations. Yet, God chose the Jews. The deepest of relationships was enacted at the foot of Sinai. The prophet proclaims, "Is Esau not a brother to Jacob?" So why should Jacob take preference over Esau? But, the prophet continues, "Yet I love Jacob and have rejected Esau." Thus, irrespective of the qualities of the Jewish people over the other nations, God chose them and gave them His Torah. And they have remained God's beloved nation ever since.

13

What the Angels
Study in the
Heavenly Academy

"*Bereishis*"—"In the beginning the Lord created the heavens and the earth." Thus the Torah begins with the letter *beis*. This immediately leads to an unavoidable question. Why not begin the Torah with the letter *aleph*, the first letter in the Jewish alphabet? *aleph-beis*? It seems inappropriate to begin the Torah with the second, seemingly less significant, letter of *beis*.

An interesting story is related in the Talmud. The Egyptian king Talmai ordered seventy of Israel's greatest sages to translate the Torah into Greek, making it accessible to non-Jews. He placed them in seventy separate chambers, so each sage translated the Torah independently of all the others. When they had all finished, all the translations were miraculously identical. Moreover, even those areas that the sages chose not to translate literally or that they slightly modified in order that the content not be misconstrued were also identical in all of the translations. One of the changes the sages uniformly made was that instead of writing, "*Bereishis bara Elokim*"—"In the beginning God created," they wrote "*Elokim bara bereishis*"—"God created in the beginning." Their reason was that they feared that if they had left the text intact, the king would think that some deity named *Bereishis* created God. Their alteration thus ensured that the pagan king would fully comprehend that it was the one God who gave a beginning to the world and not some outside power. The relevant inference from this story, however, is that in the translation, the Torah began with an *aleph*, the first letter of the alphabet, instead of a *beis* (*bereishis*), the second letter.

An important conclusion we can draw thus far is that for the Jews the Torah in its original state begins with a *beis*, whereas for the non-Jews it begins with an *aleph*.

"THE PROVERB OF THE ANCIENT ONE"

We may gain valuable insight into exactly what the Torah is by examining a special name attributed to the Torah in the books of the prophets. The young King David rebukes his predecessor Saul with the words "As the proverb of the ancient one says, 'Out of the wicked comes forth wickedness,' but my hand shall not harm you." According to *Rashi*, the proverb of the ancient one is a reference to the Torah. He writes explicitly in commenting on a verse in Exodus, "This is what David said, 'As the proverb of the ancients says, "Out of the wicked comes forth wickedness."' And the proverb of the ancients is the Torah for it is the proverb of the Holy One Blessed Be He who is the ancient of the world."

This description of the Torah as serving as God's proverb informs us that the Torah we learn is not an end unto itself. Rather, it is a parable for higher concepts. The Torah is an allegory for metaphysical concepts that we, as mere mortals, cannot comprehend with our limited intellectual capacity. Thus the Torah serves as a medium to convey to us the infinite wisdom of the immortal Creator, which transcends the constraints of human intellectual grasp.

Virtually any law mentioned in the Talmud can serve as an example; let us consider the law found in the Talmud discussing "he who exchanges his cow for someone else's mule." Superficially, this law seems to concern itself only with a simple business transaction between two individuals, as well as the necessary laws governing such an agreement. If this were so, then the Torah would obviously be incompatible with the loftier spiritual realms where there are no cows or mules, or anything else of a physical nature. In truth, however, the Torah is, at the same time alluding also to a more profound concept in the spiritual realm.

The animal soul found in man is subdivided primarily into two archetypes. One animal soul is classified as a "cow," and the other as a "mule." The soul symbolized by a cow represents someone who, like a cow, is satisfied with the basics of life. He is not a glutton for material wealth or lust. Nevertheless, like a cow, he is unmotivated and likes to take the easiest way out in life. He is happy to chew grass all day long and aspires to nothing higher. The human being possessing this kind of animal soul is unwilling to excel in spiritual matters. In short, he is unmotivated and lazy and, although he does not indulge himself in gross material pursuits, he does not pursue spiritual enlightenment either.

The animal soul symbolized by a mule represents someone whose faults lie in a completely different realm. This person is a glutton for material pleasure, and his inability to excel in holiness has nothing to do with laziness, but rather involves his insatiable desire for materialism and for aesthetic pleasure.

When man is endowed at birth with either of these two souls, his purpose is to refine it and redirect it to good, thus salvaging the immense potential for holiness contained within evil. Yet, at times, certain individuals whose animal soul resembles a cow exchange their designated service of refining that soul and concentrate on refining a mule-type soul. The law in the Talmud addressed the details of the law meant for one who has effected this spiritual exchange.

This is but one example of how the Torah alludes to lofty concepts of a supernal nature by using the confines of the empirical world as a medium for expression.

To be sure, even the above explanation of this particular law does not exhaust the literal meaning nor the literal pertinence of the law. The animal soul, although a spiritual entity, is spiritual only by comparison with our physical world. In the higher world there are countless entities whose spirituality far transcends that of the animal soul. And each of these worlds possesses its corresponding "cow" and "mule" as they apply in their respective realms, and in them too there exists the same pertinent halakhic details.

"BLEMISHES" AND THEIR SPIRITUAL COUNTERPART

On the basis of this premise, the Alter Rebbe explains the talmudic description of a heavenly debate in the supernal study house. The angels were engaged in a halakhic discussion of leprous skin blemishes: which are ritually clean and which not. How could such a debate have taken place in the spiritual realm, a world not only void of all things physical, but also where even the very grasp of physical existence is naught? The most fundamental work of Jewish mysticism, the *Zohar* itself states that, before a soul may enter the Garden of Eden, it must first be purged of "any vestige of this [physical] world," because any remembrance to the corporeal world serves as an obstruction to fully grasping the sublime concepts to be found there. How then could spiritual beings in a disembodied spiritual dimension debate the physical properties of tangible creation, when to them it is intangible?

The answer lies in the aforementioned premise. The angels' discussion was not of physical properties, but of the spiritual equivalent of leprous blemishes, the form in which it exists in their world. As they undergo the contraction necessary to bring about the physical world, they materialize in our world in the form of leprous blemishes. Our understanding of these concepts is a mere trace of the similar ideas in the celestial realm. Thus, the Torah and talmudic laws governing these blemishes serve as an analogy to help us understand the hidden, transcendental ideals that are their origin.

Therefore, the same laws and ideals exist throughout the spiritual ladder of worlds and achieve expression in a variety of ways. This explains why the Torah is referred to as "the Proverb of the Ancient One." As the word *proverb* or *parable* implies, the laws of the Torah are no different in the physical world than they are in the spiritual world, although the celestial Torah differs considerably from the terrestrial one. Their essence, of course, is the same, but the manner in which they manifest themselves and the matters with which they are concerned are very different. They are merely expressed in a different manner. The Torah then serves as the proverb, the medium by which to understand the higher worlds, even God.

It is for this reason that the Torah is said to be infinite. Every level of the Torah has a higher level that precedes it and to which it acts as an antecedent, expressing the ideals of the world while at the same time proposing laws that govern that concept within each respective realm.

We must now clarify whether the multiple allusions of a single law or concept are indeed directed at many unrelated concepts. That is, does the law of the exchange of a cow and mule on the one hand discuss the actual physical exchange and in addition allude to the different types of animal souls in man, as well as many other nonrelated meanings?

Hasidus emphasizes emphatically that this is not the case. Rather, every law of the Torah has only one meaning, albeit with many different forms of conceptual manifestation. These forms of expression are all tailored in accordance with the spiritual world in which the idea is being expressed. Thus, there are not countless unrelated meanings to a single law, but rather a single meaning that may be clothed in different images in which each is pertinent to the world in which it is manifest.

CONCEPTS EXPRESSED IN DIFFERENT LEVELS OF MEANING

To illustrate this concept, let us use a simple concept in the empirical world: sweetness. Actually, sweetness exists in a hierarchical state. First, there is sweetness in its literal connotation: something that causes a pleasing taste to the palate, typical of sugar. This is sweetness in its simplest, most basic form. Then there is sweetness of a higher form, such as a sweet melody. A person who listens to a sweet melodious tune is captivated more than he would be if he ate a sweet apple. He is not satiated until he hears the tune over and over again. Still higher is sweetness as it exists in the form of a brilliant intellectual insight. When an individual fond of learning hears a penetrating, philosophical insight, the sweetness of explanation overcomes him. Thus, sweetness is expressed in a hierarchical spectrum from the lowest human indulgence to the most sublime of human pursuits.

Now, are these three examples of sweetness really three completely different themes whose only common denominator is a similarity in name only? Can we really say that the sweetness found in an apple and the sweetness of a beautiful melody are qualitatively different entities? Obviously not. They are really all the same type of experience, each evoking the same kind of feeling—a certain sense of enticing pleasure. The differences are due only to the different arenas of expression. Within the elevated world of intellectual experience, sweetness is expressed in the form of pleasurable scholarly stimulation. Descending to a lower plane, but not as low as the corporeality of our physical world, the sensation of sweetness finds expression in the form of pleasure brought to a connoisseur of music. And finally, as we enter the realm of tangible human experience, sweetness finds expression even in the form of lowly physical substances that can produce aesthetic, sensual pleasure that is so tangible it can be touched and felt, in this case by the tongue and palate. Therefore, the very same concept, a certain experience of delight and pleasure, is expressed in differing hierarchal form in accordance with the experience that evokes the sensation in the first instance, be it music, an apple, and so on.

Another example illustrating this point is the concept of light and darkness. Light and darkness exist in the physical world as well as the theoretical plane, where they assume a more homiletic meaning. The fool is said to be "wandering in darkness," whereas the sages and leaders of Israel are referred to in the Torah as "the eyes of the congregation." Every student has had the experience of struggling to comprehend a difficult passage, and when he finds the meaning he suddenly feels illuminated and enlightened. Whereas previously he was "in the dark" as to its meaning, "light" finally sets in and he now comprehends. We all have seen the pictorial display of a light bulb over a person's head, representing the flash of an idea in the mind. The Dark Ages are so called because they represented a period of human stagnation in scholarship and the arts. Similarly, the

Zohar, commenting on the biblical verse "And there was light" explains, "this [refers to] wisdom."

It is evident that here too the empirical and spiritual connotations of light are really one and the same, the only difference being the arena in which light and darkness are used: one being the spiritual realm, the other the physical realm. The implication of light is illumination, which makes perception possible. Where light shines, everything becomes revealed. And although light itself might leave shadows, a small crevice for doubt and subterfuge, the objects themselves are disclosed.

This connotation applies in both a physical and in an intellectual realm. In the latter realm, light conveys intellectual illumination and clarification of a scholarly subject along with its wealth of details and depth. In the physical world, it simply means white light that brightens the surroundings, enabling one to perceive the world. Whatever the connotation, however, the essence of light remains the same.

These examples are but small parts of a much greater whole. In truth, even concepts as basic as light and sweetness manifest themselves at an infinite number of spiritual levels, continuing all the way up the hierarchal ladder of spiritual worlds and finally reaching the pure essence of these concepts, which is the source for their manifestation in their disparate worlds. But it is only in the physical world where they clothe themselves within time and three-dimensional space and become something that we can see, touch, taste, hear, or smell.

In the same fashion we can elucidate how the Torah serves as "the Proverb of the Ancient One." A parable and its moral lesson are qualitatively related, since the parable illustrates the moral. A truly accurate parable is one that is derived from the moral, with the moral serving as the very source that brings it forth into existence. If the parable were merely an outside story brought in to illustrate the moral, it could never accurately convey all the intricate details of the moral.

Returning to our previous example, if a theoretical physicist wishes to convey to his young child the sweetness he felt upon comprehending the brilliance of the theory of relativity, he might compare it to eating candy. And although there is an immense difference between the two, the analogy is still accurate for in essence the sweetness in each experience is the same. Both convey a pleasant reaction to an empirical experience. The difference is merely their realm of expression—one being the intellectual domain and the other the physical domain. As they both emanate from the same source, one may serve as a symbol for the other.

THE LEVELS OF TORAH INTERPRETATION

Likewise, the law of "exchanging a cow and donkey" is really a single principle: the exchange of a cow with a donkey. In the physical world this principle stays within the confines of the material world and thus concerns itself with a donkey and a cow as they exist in this world. In a higher spiritual world the same principle relates to the concepts of donkey and cow as they appear there, namely, as different types of animal souls. And as we ascend the spiritual hierarchy of worlds, the corresponding concepts of cow, donkey, and their exchange become ever more refined, yet all born of, and relating to, the same principle.

We may now appreciate how it is possible that the "*Yeshivah* of Heaven*," as the Talmud refers to the celestial academy of learning, should study such subjects as leprous blemishes. They are studying the blemishes as they appear in the spiritual realm. They are not studying another Torah, since there is only the one. Yet, the principles and laws of this Torah achieve different forms of expression in each world in accordance with the makeup of that particular world.

In other words, in essence there is only one Torah. And when it discusses the "exchange of a donkey and cow" it is referring to a single but flexible concept, the expression of which would vary in each world. Thus, the lower forms of expression in the lower worlds automatically constitute a "parable" or "proverb" for the Torah of the higher worlds.

We can now appreciate why we find throughout Jewish scholarly works what have come to be known as *pshetlack* or homiletically inspired interpretations of straightforward passages of halakhic homilies. These *pshetlack* abound specifically in the hasidic schools of thought. We might have been led to believe that after all they are merely homilies; for example, the true meaning behind the *halakhah* of the "exchange of a cow with a donkey" is exactly what it professes to be. The other explanation, that of the different brands of animal souls would be considered a mere *pshet'l*, or homily. This is a gross misunderstanding. Rather, the spiritually inspired interpretation is a reality in a higher spiritual realm, whereas here in the physical word it has actual physical applications and connotations.

The more we can comprehend the Torah on a loftier spiritual plane, the closer we draw to its original unadulterated principles as they exist before they descend and are made to fit into the human realm of experience. For the lower the world at which the Torah appears, the more vestments—hence concealment—it had to undergo to reach that world. And when the process is reversed—that is, when the Torah is divested of its camouflage—we arrive at a truer projection of Torah.

Returning to our previous illustration, just as no one could say that the use of the terms "light" and "darkness" to represent intellectual illumination is any less valid than their empirical uses, the same applies to different levels of Torah. On the contrary, everyone can appreciate that intellectual darkness is far more severe than a lack of physical visibility. If one were forced to choose between losing one's intellectual capacities for light and one's physical capacity for sight, one might feel that the intellectual loss is worse. Just as this form of light is as real as the physical form, so different mystical interpretations of Torah are as real as the physical laws, the former in fact serving as the source of the latter.

The Torah teaches that the wisdom of King Solomon was so great that "he spoke three thousand parables" on every point of Torah law. The Alter Rebbe explains that this statement does not mean that he gave three thousand independent parables all of which were used to teach the same point of law. Rather, the wisdom of Solomon was so great that he explained a single principle *on three thousand different levels*, each parable corresponding to a separate level of expression and metaphysical existence. Solomon would begin by stating a simple halakhic ruling involving a physical act. He would then proceed to explain how the literal interpretation was a mere parable for a higher, spiritual meaning, and he defined exactly how the same concept existed at that spiritual level. On and on he would go, climbing the ladder of Torah dissertation until he had expounded upon the correlation of the law in three thousand different worlds!

We often employ the same method, but in reverse order. In the course of instructing a young child about a complicated theological passage, the teacher makes use of a parable that illustrates the point at a lower, simpler level. At times even this anecdote is insufficient, and a still simpler example must be given and so on until the information is finally apprehended by the child.

Concerning Solomon, it is taught that he understood the Torah the way it exists in the highest of the four general spiritual worlds, the world of *Atzilus*, emanation. To convey this lofty perception, he was forced to construct for his listeners an ascending ladder of three thousand parables: one thousand from the lowest world, *Asiyah*, action; one thousand from the next highest world, *Yetzirah*, formation; and a thousand from the world of *Beriah*, creation (in every world there are generally one thousand levels according to the Kabbalah). The scarlet thread running though this entire spectrum is one and the same law, but that is manifested at three thousand different levels, and Solomon expounded all of them. This is the Torah as "the Proverb of the Ancient One."

"BEIS" SIGNIFIES A SUBSTRUCTURE

It is for this reason that the Torah begins with the letter *beis*, signifying that the manner in which we possess it is not the *aleph*, the true source—Torah in its unadulterated form—but the *beis*, which has a numerical value and place in the *aleph-beis* as two. Our Torah is a parable and a product of the supreme spiritual Torah, of which we have no true comprehension. What we have is the by-product, a secondary-level manifestation of Torah. For the great kabbalist Rabbi Isaac Luria, known as the Lion, the phrase "And for Your Torah which You have taught us" symbolizes the Torah as it has descended into the world of

Beriah, the world in which created reality begins to take shape, and lower.

The Torah then exists at two fundamental levels: (1) with the Creator before it has descended or contracted into the confines of created existence and hence is completely unaffected by it and (2) after it has descended, at which time it has to some extent assumed the properties and matrix of created existence so that we can comprehend it. Rabbi Luria went on to explain that his idea is further alluded to in the fact that the world of *Atzilus* also begins with an *aleph* whereas *Beriah* begins with a *beis*.

Thus, the letter beginning the Torah reminds us that the Torah as it exists before us is not its final form, so that we not think that what we study and comprehend is the whole Torah. There is another aspect of the Torah—Torah that transcends all boundaries and leaps beyond all heights, Torah as it exists with the Almighty. This is the *aleph* of Torah, something of which we mortals have no comprehension, as it utterly transcends the realm of human experience.

However, when the Torah is translated for the benefit of the Gentiles, it begins with an *aleph*. For the Gentile, this is the entire extent of the Torah. The Jew, notwithstanding his lack of comprehension, has an intrinsic connection to the Torah as it exists with the Creator, because the Jew contains a spark of the Divine and as such is one and the same with God. For the Gentile, however, his comprehension of the Torah is his entire reality. As the highest life form within creation, he relates to the Torah the way the Torah is clothed within the creation, but not higher. This difficult concept is further elucidated in the next chapter.

14

THE PROVERB
OF THE ANCIENT ONE

In the previous chapter we explained that beginning the Torah with a *beis* is not merely a coincidence, but a matter of profound significance. It teaches us that the Torah that we study is only at a secondary level. Our Torah serves as a "proverb" for the mystical Torah that exists in a revealed state in the spiritual worlds. Those laws we study that pertain to earthly matters are actually a reflection of loftier concepts that materialize in a different manner in each world. Thus, the Torah resembles a parable that is used to explain a single concept at various intellectual and spiritual levels.

Using the example of sweetness, we saw how the sweetness experienced in tasting an apple, listening to a beautiful tune, and fathoming a deep intellectual insight are indeed different but qualitatively they express the same principle: the experience of something pleasurable and pleasing. The Torah similarly comprises singular principles whose only differentiation is their manner of expression and manifestation in the different stages of the hierarchy of spiritual and physical spheres.

If this be so, we will encounter difficulty in explaining why only the Torah, and not all other physical objects, is referred to as "the Proverb of the Ancient One." In Jewish mysticism it is repeatedly stated that the same principle applies to all created matter. Every material object possesses a spiritual source and a counterpart, as is apparent from the example about sweetness.

Thus, not only the Torah, but indeed every physical object serves as a parable in grasping and appreciating their intangible spiritual counterparts.

TORAH IS UNAFFECTED BY *TZIMTZUM*

Yet there is a basic difference in the appearance of the spiritual source of Torah and all created objects once they descend into the physical world. *Hasidus* explains that, even after the Torah has contracted and descended into the physical world, it still retains all of its spiritual properties. In essence, it is unaffected by the contraction. This means that the contraction of the source of Torah is a condensation of the source's intensity, and the whole of the source is fully contained within the physical product. Within physical objects, in contrast, there remains only a faint vestige of its spiritual source. Although it is true that the sweetness that exists in a grasping of intellectual concepts is the same idea of sweetness that is found in a candy, nevertheless in the candy it has lost its abstract nature and is no longer as refined as it once had been. The purity of the spiritual ideal was lost once it clothed itself within the material world, although the ideal itself remained whole.

Because this purity is lost, it is difficult to say with accuracy that physical objects serve as parables to their corresponding ideals in higher realms, for the corporeality and material construct of the object indeed masks and conceals the inner spiritual correlate to the point where the object appears to be purely physical with no spiritual counterpart. Therefore, although we may say that the physical has descended from the spiritual, to say that it is a true reflection of identical ideals in the higher realms would be true only in a very general sense. They are similar and are expressions of the same concept, but they are far from identical.

The Torah, however, loses none of its intensity or purity as it descends into the material world. The physical law of exchanging a cow for a donkey incorporates within itself all the metaphysical meaning of the same law as it exists in the spiritual world, up to its ultimate source. Nothing of its intrinsically spiritual nature is compromised at even the lowest possible levels. Even as we study a passage of Torah within this world, it is identical to the passage of Torah being studied in the world of *Atzilus*, the only difference being that the higher implications of the passage are hidden from us and the lower ones are manifest.

CONTRACTION VERSUS CONDENSATION

From this distinction we understand that there are two types of *tzimtzum*, that is, two means by which a spiritual entity may contract itself in order to arrive at a lower, more mundane plane. One is the dismembering of parts. For example, if an instructor wishes to teach a complicated theory, such as general relativity, he might disregard the difficult details such as the complex mathematical equations and instead concentrate on the general idea, that matter and energy are equal and therefore time and space are not absolute. To be sure, the theory is far more involved, and this fragmented explanation is but a generalization that ignores the important particulars. In this form of *tzimtzum*, therefore, the theory is splintered and loses its integral parts. It emerges as a somewhat different theory than it was before the contraction.

The second type of *tzimtzum* does not alter the content; it acts more as a condensational process. The subject is not stripped of its details. Rather, they are compressed into an all-encompassing generalization in which some details are revealed and others become hidden, although they are still present. For example, concerning the Divine Presence in the holy Temple, it is said that "the Almighty concentrated His Presence between the two staffs of the Holy *Aron* (Ark)." Although the Divine Presence may have been concentrated, nothing of its essence was lost. On the contrary, its sublimity was manifested in this ability to compress its full intensity within defined borders.

The former *tzimtzum* is that which acts upon the material aspects of this world as they descend from their spiritual origin. As every material object passes from its spiritual source, only a faint glimmer of the original finally reaches earth, with the quintessence of the object remaining aloft. The materialization of the Torah, on the other hand, is accomplished by the second type of *tzimtzum*. Nothing is lost in the descent. Rather, the infinite implications of the law are compressed within it as it arrives within our world. The only change the *tzimtzum* makes is to render all the spiritual explanations invisible until they must be rediscovered by the probing mystical mind.

It is for this reason that the blessing the Jew makes on the Torah before he studies is worded, "He who has given us His Torah," for indeed the Torah that we study remains His exact Torah, with no change. The way in which it was given is the same way it exists today.

This is the meaning of the statement of the Talmud concerning life in the hereafter: "Fortunate is he who comes with his learning 'in his palm.'" If we understand this statement superficially, of what use does the Torah learned in this world have in the World to Come, whose reference points are completely different? To what use can the Torah studied in a physical body be put in a completely metaphysical world when the soul is a disembodied existence? The explanation, of course, is that the Torah of the World to Come is submerged within the Torah of our world; its mystical aspects merely remain hidden until one's arrival at the higher worlds.

"*BEIS*" SIGNIFIES THE RETENTION OF ALL PREVIOUS LEVELS

With this in mind, we arrive at a deeper appreciation of our explanation as to why the Torah begins with the letter *beis*. We perceive only a secondary aspect of Torah, the part that descended and assumed spatial–temporal coordinates. This Torah is a derivative of the Torah of the higher spiritual realm. Nevertheless, there cannot be a *beis*, a latter, without an *aleph*, the former. In fact, within the number two the number one is already included; it is this inclusion that makes it a number two! If a later item becomes completely independent of something that preceded it, then it becomes a first unto itself. Thus, by proclaiming our Torah as the *beis* of a higher Torah, we are simultaneously implying that included within this Torah is the *aleph*. They are not only inseparable but are one and the same thing whose only differences are in their respective spiritual and material realms.

This principle applies specifically to the Jew. When the Jew studies a passage of the revealed Torah, he simultaneously amasses all the hidden implications of that passage. Yet, when the non-Jew studies the Torah, even those parts that were specifically designed for him to study—Torah's universal code of ethics and morality known as the seven Noachide laws—he amasses only what he comprehends. The principle of "He who has given us His Torah" applies specifically to the Jewish people to whom the Torah was given at Sinai.

Thus, what the Torah means to the Jew and what it means to the Gentile are very different. For the Gentile, it is a lofty moral code of ethics that instructs him how to act, but it does not contain the infinite spiritual levels beyond the perceivable aspects. Therefore, when the Torah was translated for the Egyptian king Talmai, it automatically emerged beginning with an *aleph*: "*Elokim bara bereishis.*" For the Gentile Talmai, this was the entire Torah, the first and last levels.

Notwithstanding all of the above, a major inconsistency still remains. We mentioned that the Almighty gave us "His Torah"; that is, the Torah that exists in the highest of worlds, *Atzilus,* is the same Torah that we have. There is only one Torah. There cannot be any discrepancies or changes. The way our Torah is written must therefore be identical with the Torah in the world of *Atzilus.* Thus, the Torah of *Atzilus* must also begin with a *beis*.

Further proof of this observation is the biblical commentary of the great Rabbi Moshe ben Nachman in which Moses' writing of the Torah is analogous to a scribe's copying from one text to another; that is, it was dictated to him word for word, letter for letter. In other words, God dictated to Moses, and he faithfully recorded the Torah in the manner in which it appears to God. And even there it begins with a *beis*. Yet how can this be? What is the significance of the Torah of *Atzilus* beginning with a *beis* even in the heavens?

THE KEY TO UNDERSTANDING THE DIVINE ONE

Here we arrive at a far deeper understanding of the metaphor labeling the Torah "the Proverb of the Ancient One." Thus far, we have shown *proverb* to indicate that, because the Torah has an infinite number of levels, each lower level serves as a parable and a key to understanding the level above it. In this context, the word *proverb* applies to each individual level. Yet, in a deeper context, the Torah as a whole serves as one big parable explaining the Ancient One, God Almighty!

What is the Torah? In its highest and purest form, the Torah is the very wisdom and knowledge of the Almighty Himself. It is His very thought process which has descended to us. Thus, it serves as a link between all the lower worlds into which it has descended and the Creator of those worlds. But once the descent is initiated even in the highest of worlds, this Torah loses its original form as the intellect of the Almighty. God's wisdom cannot descend into any world without first assuming another form. Otherwise, it would completely overwhelm and destroy any world it entered. It is simply too lofty. Thus all the Torah, even of *Atzilus*, is a derivative of that original Divine seminal thought and serves as a "parable" in understanding the ways of the Creator. Of necessity, it has undergone some form of contraction.

Therefore, even the Torah of *Atzilus* begins with a *beis*, teaching us that the Torah of every world, even of the highest, is secondary in comparison with how the Torah exists on the plane of the Creator. Yet, all of the Torah, from the highest to the lowest realm, serves as a means by which to understand the thoughts of the Creator, thus unifying one's thought, speech, and action with the Master of the Universe.

15

WHY THE TORAH CANNOT CHANGE

ATTEMPTS AT TORAH MODIFICATION

Over the past two centuries, and especially over the last few decades, movements somewhat outside traditional, mainstream Jewish Orthodoxy have arisen within the Jewish nation. These movements have had different names, such as Enlightenment, Liberal, Reform, and Reconstructionist. Although they differ with regard to outlook, they share a common underlying premise —encouraging the alteration and modification of the Torah so that it better conforms to modern times and ideals. I do not doubt the sincerity, dedication and devotion of Reform, Conservative, and Liberal Jews, and I am sure that in their opinion and in the opinion of their leaders they are practicing a Judaism that is in the best interests of the Jewish people. Indeed, many are profoundly dedicated Jews. Nevertheless, it cannot be denied that within these movements many have adopted new methods of practicing Judaism that in many cases are profoundly different distillations of the traditional Jewish observance that has been in existence since the giving of the Torah at Mount Sinai more than 3,300 years ago. In justifying their actions, they contend that the "modernization" of Judaism to suit contemporary times is imperative if Judaism is to survive and prosper in the modern era. An "outdated" religion has no hope of surviving and competing with the forces of modern-day society.

So if Judaism is unwilling to change, it runs the risk of becoming completely irrelevant to the lifestyles and daily challenges of most modern Jews.

Rationally, however, the idea of adapting Jewish practices to suit modernity seems illogical. Judaism is a religion predicated on the belief in Divine revelation, which entails a God-given Torah and God-given commandments. How then may man alter what God has given and decreed? Once this is done, the new product, irrespective of its virtue or greater suitability, is no longer Judaism. A religion modified by man has no resemblance to a religion born of Godly revelation. Man cannot change what God has instituted, even if he seemingly has good reason for doing so. Moreover, rationalizations for the alteration of Torah seem completely unjustified, since Judaism and those who adhere to it are the only ones who have survived from all the nations of the world throughout the generations. It is, in fact, the Torah itself that has enabled them to survive.

This point is expressed aptly by the non-Jewish author of *History of the Jews*, the celebrated contemporary British historian Paul Johnson. He writes: "Countless Jews, in all ages, have groaned under the burden of Judaism. But they have continued to carry it because they have known, in their hearts, that it carried them. The Jews were survivors because they possessed the law of survival. Judaism created the Jews, not the other way around. As the philosopher Leon Roth put it: "Judaism comes first. It is not a product but a program, and the Jews are the instruments of its fulfillment."

To demonstrate this point, we can examine a game of chess. One who wishes to modify only the position of the pieces on the board—for example, moving the rook to the knight's position, the queen to the pawn's, the bishop to the king's, and so on—can continue to play the game and may even enjoy it more than the original. But the game he is playing is not chess. It is a new game that he has invented and that happens to incorporate some of the rules and pieces of chess. But it is not chess. So, too, individuals may continue to modify Judaism and justify the necessity for their actions in a logical and rational manner. Nevertheless, they are not following Judaism, but rather some human system of belief that is based on Judaism and may somewhat vaguely resemble it but has changed considerably. The basic premise of Judism is that the Torah was given by God and therefore cannot be altered by man.

Yet notwithstanding these rational arguments, the mistake made by the proponents of these changes is not one of irrationality but is born more of ignorance. Their mistake in modifying the Torah is that this action betrays a lack of a truly deep and penetrating understanding of what the Torah is and what it is designed to achieve.

In this chapter, we describe the reality of Torah and show why, by its very definition, it is not subject to modification. Any attempt to do so betrays a superficial understanding of the Torah, God, and Judaism.

SHOULD NOT THE TORAH ACCOMMODATE CHANGES IN SOCIETY?

As part of his thirteen cardinal articles of Jewish faith, Maimonides includes the premise that the Torah shall never be changed, even to the slightest degree. No *mitzvah* shall be added to the Torah and none subtracted. This means that not only will man never change the Torah—this, of course, should go without saying for it is not his Torah to change—but even *the Almighty* will never change any aspect of the Torah. The Torah that was given on Mount Sinai will endure, without the slightest modification, forever. This, in essence, captures the ninth principle of Maimonides' thirteen cardinal articles of Jewish faith.

The commentators ask why this is so. Why is it that even God will never change the Torah? Why cannot God add or remove a *mitzvah*? Furthermore, why is one of the cardinal principles of Jewish faith to believe in the immutability of the Torah? Why must we say that the premise of the Torah remaining eternal is so significant that anyone who does not accept it has compromised his faith in God and the Jewish religion?

The commentators who ask the question strengthen their query with an analogy of a doctor and patient relationship. A doctor tells the person who is ill what he should do in order to be healed from his illness. The doctor's instructions must coincide with the current medical situation of his patient, and as that situation varies, the doctor's instructions must vary accordingly, for the function of the doctor is to heal his patient. If the status of the patient has changed, then it is as if this is a new patient, so the doctor must correlate his instructions to coincide with the new circumstances.

A similar analogy may be taken from the education that a parent gives his child. A parent brings a child into the world and subsequently guides the development of that child so that he may grow to be a responsible and mature adult. This process continues throughout the younger, adolescent, and even older years of the child. The tutelage the parent gives must correspond to the child's every stage of life and development.

With an infant, the parent teaches the child what to eat and when to sleep. Then the parent toilet trains the child. Later, when the child is being taught to read and write, his young character is carefully molded by his concerned parents. At all the stages of this process, the parent's education must grow with the child. Whether the child is maturing slowly or quickly, the guidance of the parent must correspondingly coincide with and accommodate the child's progress.

In light of these two examples, why is it improper and sacrilegious to maintain that there will come a time when the world will alter, and the Torah, which was given for the benefit of the world, will similarly require modification? If the Torah is to be fulfilled in this world and the Torah is meant for the benefit of this world, then should it not follow that the Torah should change in accordance with the changes in society?

For example, *tefillin*, our sages explain, is a *mitzvah* done to facilitate the sovereignty of the mind over the heart, that is, the intellect over the emotions. To this effect, the *tefillin* are placed both on the head, which is the seat of the intellect, and then adjacent to the heart, the seat of the emotions. There may, in fact, come a time when the mind and the heart may change, not biologically but by becoming more refined or more coarse. The moral stability of man may change for the better, or even for the worse. So, in accordance with that change, should not the *tefillin*, which are given to facilitate the subservience of the heart to the soul, change as well?

Why is it such a great contradiction of faith to assume that the Torah will one day change?

COMMANDMENTS HAVE IN FACT BEEN ADDED

Thus far, we have used an argument based strictly on logic. Yet, if we briefly consider actual occurrences, we will see that in truth, with respect to certain individuals in history, *mitzvos* were added and removed. For example, *Adam Harishon* (the first man) was given six commandments by God, yet later, with the advent of Noah, a seventh commandment was added in the form of *eiver min hahai*—the prohibition of extracting a limb from a living animal and otherwise treating animals sadistically.

Certain Divine commandments were subtracted as well. *Adam Harishon* was permitted to eat only vegetation. Later God removed the prohibition of eating flesh and permitted Noah to do so, making him an omnivore. These instances are not only logical but also practical, examples before the actual giving of the Torah of *mitzvos* being added and subtracted. So why is it such a denial of faith to assume that the Torah will itself be modified?

A seemingly logical conclusion might be that the Torah, as God's Will, can never be modified, for doing so would imply that God's Will is not constant but changes, an assumption bordering on heresy because it presupposes that God Himself changes and is therefore not eternal. Then how can we reconcile this fact with those presented above, that before the giving of the Torah *mitzvos* were, in fact, added and removed? Do these examples represent a variation in God's Will?

The only possible solution to this dilemma is to state that there was no variation in God's Will, because it was not the Will or the *mitzvos* that changed, but rather the status of the world that changed and the Torah had to be modified accordingly. The change is therefore not an inherent fault in God's Will. On the contrary, the *mitzvos*, which were given for the world, were modified in accordance with the modification in the world itself, just as in the analogy of the doctor and his patient.

Now if this principle applies to the commandments given before the giving of the Torah, why does it not apply to the commandments given after as well? Why does Maimonides write that one of the fundamental tenets of Jewish belief is the premise that the Torah is immutable and will forever remain in the identical form in which it was given and received at Sinai?

One may answer quite simply that Maimonides had proof, either from a talmudic or some other Jewish source, that the Torah would remain in its present form forever. Yet, this still does not answer the most pressing question as to why Maimonides incorporated this premise as one of the cornerstones of Jewish belief, alongside such colossal principles as the very belief in the existence of the Creator?

GOD AND HIS TORAH ARE NOT MEDIA THAT FACILITATE AN END

The entire question of why the Torah does not change to suit changing circumstances in society is based on a terribly flawed premise: that the Torah and organized religion were created for society and that therefore the Torah must seek to accommodate societal changes. Without this underlying premise, no one would even raise the question of why the Torah does not change alongside society. And here we have to ask why most people take it as a given that indeed the Torah, and all organized religion, is a medium to suit the world's needs and to cure society's ills? Why do we ask the question so easily of why the Torah does not change?

I suggest that this readiness to ask has to do with the influences of Christian culture on our theological attitudes. As we are immersed in a Christian culture, we sometimes inadvertently adopt preconceptions that are foreign to Judaism. In Christianity, Jesus is a means to salvation. Jesus died on the cross so that man might be saved. Thus, Jesus came to assist man. He serves the purposes of man, and if people have enough faith in Jesus, then they will be rewarded with salvation and eternal bliss. Thus, the Christian deity is not a goal in himself, but rather a means to an end. He is the path to the redemption and salvation of humankind.

Although Christianity has the right to postulate any beliefs it wishes and people have the right to embrace such beliefs, Judaism utterly rejects such a notion. Neither God nor his Torah is a means to any alternative or higher end. Both are goals in and of themselves. Thus, the Jew is encouraged not to be like a servant who obeys his master in order to receive a reward (*Ethics of Our Fathers*). God is not here to meet our needs. Quite the *opposite* is true. We were created to meet His needs and to execute the Divine Will (see chapter 1). Obeying God in hopes of a reward would be treating God as if He were an end to human needs. This concept is found in the statement of the *Zohar*, the foremost work on Jewish mysticism: "The Almighty, the Jewish people, and the Torah are all one." The Torah is one with God and vice versa.

This means that the Almighty is not a means to an end. He is rather the foremost and primary existence, independent of all other existence, and the source of all subsequent existence. In that all of creation and everything contained therein rely upon God for their existence, God is the very goal of everything in existence and in no way is a medium for something else. And in truth, this concept requires no elaboration. Any thinking individual will arrive at the same conclusion. It is illogical to believe that the Creator of the universe is a means to an end that serves the purposes of the universe He created. Since the Torah and *mitzvos* are part of the one God, they too are goals by themselves. They serve as no medium for anything external to them. Torah is not a means, but an end. And *mitzvos* are not a means by which man may achieve a higher degree of human perfection. On the contrary, *mitzvos* are an end in themselves. This does not mean that the fulfillment of *mitzvos* will not elevate a person, refine him, and help him achieve a certain degree of perfection. It does mean that this function is definitely not the most fundamental aspect of the *mitzvah*. Although a *mitzvah* does perfect man and add meaning to his life, this is not the essence of the *mitzvah* but rather an offshoot of the *mitzvah* and is an ancillary consideration in the fulfillment of the Torah's divine precepts.

So when people say that they love to observe the Friday night *Shabbos* meal because it brings the family together or they love to go to synagogue because everyone sings together and the experience is very moving, all this may indeed be true. The beauty of a *mitzvah* is appreciated by all, and that beauty should continue to inspire us to bring more and more *mitzvos* into our lives.

Yet, at the same time we must be aware that this beauty is not the essence of the *mitzvah*. A *mitzvah* is not a means by which we bring beauty into our lives. A *mitzvah* is a goal unto itself. And an ancillary and extraneous, yet important, facet of a *mitzvah* is that it has the capacity to enrich our lives. But this should never be the basis for its fulfillment.

Therefore, the understanding should not be that, given that there is a world and in that world are people who presently lack meaning and Godliness in their lives, therefore the Torah was given for them as a means to bring spirituality and something valuable into their lives. Quite the contrary, the world was created for the Torah! God created the world as an instrument and an arena for the fulfillment of the Torah.

Because the Torah is God's intrinsic Will, God therefore established a place in which the Torah could be translated from the potential into the actual. Everything in creation has a desire to reach its highest state of perception. In order to do so it must translate its potential into the actual. The goal of everything created is to exist in its highest possible form.

In the same vein, God's intrinsic desire is for the Torah to be realized in an actual form. In order for that to happen, a place that would facilitate that manifestation had to be established. God therefore created the world as an arena in which the Torah could achieve fulfillment. Thus, the world was created for the Torah, not vice versa.

As quoted earlier, this point is stated by the classical biblical commentator Rashi, who, quoting from the Talmud and the *Midrash*, states that the word *bereishis*, "in the beginning," implies that the world was created for two beginnings (the word *bereishis* when dissected becomes *beis reishis* or "two beginnings"). Those two beginnings are the Torah and the Jewish people. Once again, the world was created for the Torah; the Torah, as an end in itself, was not created for the world.

Any capacity in which the Torah serves only as a medium for the achievement of something else is only a single or ancillary aspect of the Torah. To be sure, it is written in the *Midrash* that "*mitzvos* were given to perfect the creation," but this capacity of the Torah is an external aspect, and not its central purpose.

INTERNAL AND EXTERNAL WILL

It follows, then, that the Torah, being God's intrinsic Will, can never be altered in any way, for just as God is everlasting and unchanging, so too the Torah, an intrinsic part of the Creator, can never be changed. It is similarly inaccurate to maintain that, as the world changes, the Torah must adapt accordingly, for the world is dependent on Torah and was created to serve its purposes, and not the reverse.

Had the Torah been created to suit the needs of the world, then we could say that the Torah must conform to the changing needs of society. Otherwise, it would become outdated, defeating its own purpose. But since Torah and *mitzvos* are God's intrinsic Will and ends in and of themselves, their stability is not dependent on any outside factor. Just as God does not change, the Torah does not change.

Now, if we are to engage in a deeper study of will, we will discover that there are essentially two aspects of will, internal and external, and these two aspects exist on every plane at which will exists, including human will.

External will means that one wills or desires a certain thing only because it will lead to something else. Under these circumstances, if the long-term desire changes, then the will changes accordingly.

For example a person who works in a law firm may spend a considerable amount of time trying to impress his superiors so that he will get promoted. He buys his boss tickets to the opera and invites him home for dinner, not because he cares about him as a person or friend, but because he wants the boss to help him get ahead. But if the boss is fired, the employee would immediately stop doing anything for him, because his desire to treat the boss nicely was an external will. There was something internal, an ulterior motive concealed within. The moment that ulterior motive can no longer be satisfied, however, the external will that is its product disappears.

Internal will, conversely, refers to something that is desired as an end unto itself. A classic example is man's desire to live. Man desires to work, but not as an end unto itself. Rather, he works in order to receive a paycheck. The money he acquires is not an end unto itself either, but rather a means for acquiring food, clothing, and shelter. And why does he desire these things? In order that he may live. In short, physical labor provides for human sustenance. But it stops here. There is no further cause, or more of a will to which man strives. We cannot ask why man desires to live. There is no answer to such a question. The will to live is an involuntary, suprarational desire and as such is an intrinsic part of man, without any ulterior motive. This will reaches the very essence of man, which is not subject to any fluctuation or change.

Likewise, Torah and *mitzvos* are God's intrinsic Will and are not subject to change. They are, as it were, the equivalent of God's life, or will to live. Torah is an essential, internal Will of God that is the very culmination of all other wills. Therefore, although God willed the establishment of the world and willed that in that world there should be society, morals, and civilization, all these served only as a medium for the Torah in order that there be a place in which the Torah might be kept and translated from the potential into the actual. God created a world and furnished it with people so that there would be someone to observe the Torah.

We saw earlier that the *mitzvos* that were given before the giving of the Torah on Mount Sinai were indeed modified. Noah was forbidden from engaging in the sadistic treatment of animals (eating the flesh of a living animal) and was given permission to consume animal flesh, and neither commandment was among the original ones given to Adam. It would seem from this example that Torah and *mitzvos* may indeed be modified. Yet as we gain a keen insight into the difference between the *mitzvos* before and after *Mattan Torah*, we see there is no contradiction and are introduced to two types of commandments.

TORAH AND NOACHIDE LAW
SERVE DIFFERENT PURPOSES

The seven Noachide laws, which form the Jewish universal code of ethics and morality, by their very nature ensure the establishment as well as the preservation of the society. They are laws that regulate the activities of man and ensure that he behave within the norms of a moral, humane society. As such, they serve as the governing arm over mankind, making the world a habitable and peaceful place of dwelling. The Seven Laws are the minimal standards of decent moral conduct and behavior by which a civilization prospers and ensures its own continuity and advance.

If one should study the seven Noachide laws in detail, one would discover that they all fall within these guidelines of establishing a decent and just society. For example, one law is that the inhabitants of the world must establish a proper judicial system so that all people will be tried and judged fairly. Without a command of this nature, a fair and just society would be impossible. The prohibitions of theft and adultery similarly demonstrate the attainment of the objective that the world be suited for the dwelling of man, for if everyone steals or defiles what belongs to his fellow, the world would be insufferable.

Therefore, we arrive at the conclusion that indeed these *mitzvos* of the Sons of Noah are not similar to the commandments issued at the giving of the Torah. Whereas the *mitzvos* after *Mattan Torah* are an end unto themselves, the seven Noachide laws are a means for preparing the world as a settlement of mankind, subsequently enabling the receiving and fulfillment of the Torah.

The Torah and *mitzvos* that were given after the stand at Mount Sinai, on the other hand, are not in any way a means to some other end. This is best illustrated by the fact that at the giving of the Torah God revealed Himself and gave the Torah with the words *Anohi Hashem Elokeha*—"I am the Lord your God." It is interesting to note that God, although using three different Divine descriptions (I, Lord, God), nevertheless begins the statement with the description of "I." What is the significance of this word?

WHAT IS IN A NAME?

A name is something that permits the identification of a person, place, or thing. This identification is useful not to the person being identified, but rather to others who wish to distinguish this individual from all their other acquaintances. What this really means is that a name is not something intrinsic to the bearer of the name. On the contrary, he will always remain who and what he is, regardless of whether he possesses this name or not.

Imagine someone deserted on a desolate island. Being the only inhabitant, they would have no use for a name, for the purpose of the name is merely for others to make use of it. Without other individuals around, the very idea of a name becomes obsolete.

Bearing this in mind, we can appreciate that, although God possesses many different names, each representing a different attribute in the hierarchy of Divine levels, all of these names, even the greatest of them—the tetragrammaton (Y-H-V-H)—are not intrinsic to the Divinity per se. They rather constitute a channel for Godly revelation, just as a human's name is a "handle" by which others may refer to him. These names connote the manner in which the Creator interacts with His creation, not with Himself.

On the other hand, going back to the individual stranded on a deserted island, we can appreciate that, although he needs no specific name, he must still relate to himself. He must still think to and of himself and interact with himself. The term "me," therefore, even to this individual, is invaluable. Whenever he thinks of himself in his own mind he sees and describes himself as me, the self whom he is addressing.

In relation to oneself, then, the terms "I" and "me" are expressions of essence. They connote man in the manner in which he relates to himself, the way he is, without outside considerations.

THE NAME "I" DENOTES ESSENCE

So, too, in relation to God, the term "I," as it was used at the giving of the Torah, connotes God's essence. All other Divine names and attributes denote God at the stage in which He communicates with His creation. A Divine name is used to demonstrate only a certain aspect of Divinity with which God expresses Himself to His creation. Therefore, it is merely a manifestation of God. It does not involve God's intrinsic essence, the revelation of which would completely overwhelm and nullify the Creation. The term "I," however, denotes that aspect of Divinity that is completely removed from creation. It is the level at which God exists completely by Himself.

As our Rabbis have pointed out in the Talmud this concept is also manifested in the fact that the word *Anokhi*, "I," forms the acrostic *"Ana nafshi kesovis yehovis"*—"I God have put Myself into the Torah." That is, in the Torah is found God's intrinsic essence that He instilled into it. This is comparable to someone who, upon completing a given project, states, "I have done it." The person is saying that he has put his entire self into that project; it is *his* project. So too God states that He has inserted Himself into the Torah. God and the Torah are indivisible, and therefore, just as God is not a medium for another end, likewise the Torah is not a medium but an end.

We can now understand why Maimonides included the principle of the immutability of Torah in the Thirteen Articles of Jewish Faith. By making this point, he is essentially teaching us what the Torah is. In other words, this principle is not teaching what the Torah *will be like* in the future—that is, that it will never change and will forever remain the same—but rather *what Torah is today.* By knowing that the Torah will never change, we understand that it is an intrinsic part of God and that the world and all its inhabitants, from the beginning to the end of time, were all created to serve the purposes of the Torah, and not vice versa.

A Jew, upon studying Torah or performing a *mitzvah*, must know that this is something that will never change, for it is one with God. It is through an apprehension of this unique relationship that the significance of the Torah can be put into proper perspective. The fact that the Torah and all its laws are completely immutable teaches us that the Torah is always attached to God as His wisdom and knowledge. Just as He will never change, so too the Torah will never change.

16

So That the World Not Be a Jungle

The *mitzvos* that are actually commanded by God can be categorized chronologically: those commanded by God at or after the giving of the Torah and those given before the stand at Mount Sinai. According to *Hasidus*, the difference between the two categories is so great that there is no comparison between them. The concept of a *mitzvah* as a Divine revelation on the part of God guiding man to certain acts is applicable only to those *mitzvos* given after the Torah. The earlier *mitzvos* should be viewed as something totally different, a means for preparing the world for the *mitzvos* that were to follow.

The most intelligible reason we have for the creation of the universe and its inhabitants was to "establish a dwelling place for the Almighty here on earth." Thus, our Rabbis commented many times that the world was created for "Israel and the Torah," that is, the Jewish people make the world suitable for the Divine by fulfilling the Torah's commandments. Just as a king must dwell only in a house fit for a king, such as a magnificent palace, the same applies to the Almighty. Thus, man must work to ensure that this world is made beautiful spiritually by fulfilling the Torah and thus creating a suitable dwelling for the King of Kings. It would follow, then, that this process began at the giving of the Torah at Sinai. The purpose of the *mitzvos* given before Torah was to elevate the world to the point where it could be worked with and elevated for the purpose of achieving a Divine goal.

To better understand this fundamental concept, we must examine the *mitzvos* given by God to the first man, Adam. These *mitzvos*, which have come to be known as the seven Noachide laws, are universal laws intended to be kept by all people, Jew and non-Jew alike.

THE SEVEN NOACHIDE COMMANDMENTS: CONSTRUCTING A MORAL SOCIETY

The world cannot function as a jungle. Before any spiritual considerations are addressed, the orderly day-to-day running of the world must be established. The Jewish people, as well as the Torah, are part of and must live in the physical world. The majority of *mitzvos* can be fulfilled only with physical objects: wool for *tzitzis*, parchment for *tefillin*, and meat and wine to celebrate *Shabbos* and festivals. Therefore, the first premise that needs to be established for the proper performance of Torah is that the physical world not be in shambles or bereft of goodness and virtue. How could people study Torah, to take but one example, in the midst of revolution and war?

If the purpose of the world is for the Jewish people to infuse it with holiness by fulfilling God's commands, then the more ethical and moral the world to begin with, the easier it is to bring Godliness into the world. A pure world serves more as a receptacle to holiness than a base or decadent society. The world must have a certain refined quality before the Jewish people can begin working on it. It is this crucial premise that facilitates the later sublimation process that the world must undergo.

To achieve this goal, God gave all of humanity a universal code of morality and ethics in the form of seven laws governing both interhuman and God–man relationships. The laws governing interhuman relationships, such as the prohibition against theft, ensure stability and social justice so that mankind could prosper in peace. The *mitzvos* between man and God, such as prohibitions against idol worship and blasphemy, preserve the spirituality of the world and ensure that it not be marred by man's perversions.

Nevertheless, even a just and moral society is still only a coarse physical place. A decent world is not necessarily suitable for God to dwell in. Coarse materialism still presents an obstacle to the spiritual. It is for this reason that the performance of *mitzvos* is necessary, since a *mitzvah* is a synthesis of the two worlds: a physical object becoming consecrated through a Divinely prescribed act. Thus, the seven Noachide laws facilitate, without actually accomplishing, the introduction of holiness into the mundane world. When they are looked at from this perspective, their importance cannot be overemphasized.

God's intention at the outset of creation was for the world to assume a certain orderliness that we call nature. Natural phenomena are visible from the irrigation of the land to the instinctive habits of the animals, as well as man. Amid this order, God also wanted certain important decisions to be made by man of his own free will. So although God desired the world to be morally and ethically sound and wanted man to preserve the sanctity of life by refraining from murder, He gave man the choice of whether to act accordingly. But He still *commanded* him to choose the path of justice.

These commandments thus form an integral part of the creation itself. In some way they are not even so much spiritual as ethical in nature. And although they serve as a means to something spiritual, they also possess a tangible goal: the preservation of the moral integrity of mankind and creation. The seven Noachide laws are thus as integral a part of the creation as sunshine and rainwater. Both are necessary for the continuity of the earth, but there is one difference: God chose not to institute the laws of morality as part of a natural process. He wanted man to choose, and He instilled in man a strong conscience and propensity toward the morally correct amid the complete freedom to choose and act otherwise.

Therefore, one who has denied his adherence to the laws has denied his right of existence. He was put on earth to help make the world a more Godly place, and instead he has added to its anarchy.

THE SINAITIC COMMANDMENTS:
INFUSING THE WORLD WITH HOLINESS

Markedly different from the Noachide *mitzvos* are the ones given to the Jewish people at Sinai. Their purpose was to elevate the world to a more spiritual plane. None of the laws prescribed by Torah can be fulfilled without some sort of material input, because they were designed to uplift man and his material surroundings and inoculate all the world with Godliness. Thus, even the laws governing man's behavior toward his fellowman are constructed, not to preserve orderliness, but to infuse man's daily life and all his activities with holiness. The *mitzvos* at Sinai, therefore, were not given to serve as human moral and ethical standards, but so that the world would be a spiritual–physical domicile housing the Almighty. In turn, man was to be elevated by the *mitzvos* from the domain of the purely physical to that of Homo spiritus, a Godly being.

In light of this explanation, we can now put the commandments fulfilled by our forefathers into proper perspective. They cannot be in the same category as those *mitzvos* after Sinai, and they also cannot be mere societal-preserving laws like the Noachide code for, if so, they have no real spiritual dimension. They were not commandments whose purpose it was to police society.

In hasidic thought it is explained that the *mitzvos* fulfilled by our forefathers did possess some vestige of the unique properties of Sinaitic *mitzvos*: they were able to bring Godly light down into the world, albeit not a very lofty one. A talmudic passage states that "until Abraham the world was sunken in darkness, and with the advent of Abraham the world was illuminated." The difficulty with this passage is that it seems to ignore all the righteous men who preceded Abraham, such as Noah, Methusaleh, Shem, and Ever. The explanation is that the word "illuminated" connotes a heavenly light that transforms the world from a place of material blackness to spiritual enlightenment. To be sure, there had been *tzadikim* before Abraham's time who led morally righteous lives and may even have encouraged other men to live by these unalterable ethical truths. Still they did not bring Godly light to radiate in the world. Thus, in a somewhat similar passage the Talmud declares, "In Abraham's time two thousand years of Torah began," the allusion referring to the power of Torah to introduce spirituality into the coarse material world.

Nevertheless, even these *mitzvos* did not approach the sublimity of the Sinaitic *mitzvos*. It was there where God proclaimed, "Anochi," "I," which the Talmud interprets as an acrostic for "*Ana nafshi kesovis yehovis*"—"It was my Essence which wrote and gave the Torah." God invested His intrinsic Self into the Torah, enabling man, by virtue of his fulfilling the *mitzvos*, to bring Him into the material fiber of the earth.

THE FOREFATHERS' *MITZVOS* ARE FRAGRANCE

It is with this intention that our Rabbis in the *Midrash* comment on the verse in Song of Songs "Your oils have a goodly fragrance; Your name is an oil poured forth," as follows: "The forefathers' *mitzvos* are considered to be only the fragrance of a *mitzvah* in comparison to our more substantive *mitzvos*." Their *mitzvos* were more fragrant, whereas ours are the actual oil that produces the fragrance.

Thus, we arrive at three categories of *mitzvos*: (1) the commandments given to Adam, Noah, and his descendants, which were for the express purpose of taming and policing man in order that he form a more socially perfect world but that did not comprise a spiritual aim in their own right; (2) the *mitzvos* of the forefathers, which, although bringing into the world something of the Godly light of the later *mitzvos*, were not as wholesome as the latter and are thus referred to as being a mere "scent" of the later *mitzvos*; and finally (3) the *mitzvos* given at Sinai, which "I Myself gave and put My essence into" and through which the Jewish people actually bring God into this world, thereby consecrating it as a material structure.

17

THE POWER
TO JOIN OPPOSITES

In the last chapter we discussed the difference between the *mitzvos* before and those after the giving of the Torah. The *mitzvos* before Sinai were essential to keep chaos from the world and thus permit the performance of the later *mitzvos*, which bring spirituality into the world and make it suitable for God to dwell therein. A *midrash* commenting on a verse from the Song of Songs explains that our forefathers' *mitzvos*, before the giving of the Torah, were fragrant, but our *mitzvos* are the "oil poured forth." In this chapter we expound upon this principle, casting light on the aims and the mechanics of the *mitzvos* themselves.

MITZVOS THAT ARE POWERLESS
AGAINST THE PHYSICAL

In expounding this all-important *midrash*, *Hasidus* searches for the intrinsic property of a scent. First, a scent is not a part of but rather is an emanation from an object. Second, it follows therefore that a scent lacks the permanence and stability of the object itself. Although it may be potent today, tomorrow it will have faded.

So too, as was discussed in the last chapter, although the *mitzvos* of our forefathers brought Godly light into the world, this light was only an emanation of God's essence. Their *mitzvos* did not have the power actually to draw God into this world, and thus they had no lasting effect on the world. There was no fusion of the spirituality they generated with the material fiber of the world, and so they produced no holy objects, such as *tefillin*. The Godly light they brought into the world merely hovered from above without being injected into physical substance. The world went unchanged. The Godly light emanated in full force so long as the *mitzvah* was being fulfilled, but quickly dissipated thereafter. It was the mere scent of a *mitzvah*.

An example may be taken from the *Zohar's* statement concerning Jacob's fulfillment of the *mitzvah* of *tefillin* with sticks. The *Zohar* explains that the mystical explanation behind the vividly recounted biblical narrative of Jacob forging sticks with speckles and polka dots for the flock of his father-in-law Lavan to gaze upon was that in this manner he fulfilled what later became known as the *mitzvah* of *tefillin*, albeit in a much different manner. The same spiritual and Godly emanations that we bring about through black leather boxes, known today as *tefillin*, Jacob did with his sticks. There is one important difference, however. The black leather boxes of today not only are the *instrument* for the fulfillment of a *mitzvah* but they are also the *mitzvah* itself. They have been transformed into a holy object, and one cannot bring them into a restroom or sleep in them. Jacob's sticks, however, remained all the while mere sticks. Although they enabled him to fulfill a *mitzvah*, they assumed no sanctity of their own, and immediately after the completion of the *mitzvah*, they could be discarded. They did not change the material structure of the world.

RABBINIC AND BIBLICAL COMMANDMENTS

In truth, the phenomenon of a *mitzvah* without the ability to transform a physical object exists even in our post-Sinaitic era. In fact, only *mitzvos de'oraisa*, *mitzvos* commanded by the Torah itself, have the ability to transform physical matter. Those *mitzvos* commanded by the sages lack that ability. In a fascinating exposition of this principle, the latter-day sages point out that when the Torah prohibits a certain object, such as not eating the meat of a nonkosher animal, it is *the object itself*, in this case the animal, that is forbidden. The animal has been transformed into a *heftza shel issur*, "a prohibited article." Yet, when the Rabbis prohibit a given act, such as consuming non-Jewish bread, the prohibition falls on the individual, *issur gavra*, and not on the object. In this case it is not the bread that is prohibited, but the individual who is prohibited from partaking of it. Rabbinic injunctions, then, cannot transform physical objects into categories of holy or unholy substances. Only God, the Creator of the earth and everything contained therein, has the power to do so.

There is a very good reason for this distinction between the two types of *mitzvos*. In order to synthesize physical matter with holiness, a special force is necessary. Since God is the sole Creator of the world and all its components, it is He alone who can grant the power to make a spiritual–physical composite of a purely physical substance. Thus, it is only the Divine commandments found in the Torah that can accomplish this transformation. Likewise, the *mitzvos* observed by the forefathers had no effect on the objects they used.

Yet, our explanation thus far is still inadequate since it does not address the most pressing question: How is it that a physical object can be sanctified at all? If the spiritual and physical are indeed antithetical, how may they be orchestrated and united together? To be sure, whenever an attempt is made to synthesize two things as one, there must be some connection between them. If they are not only separate but contradictory, how then will they remain together after we have joined them? There must be some place for the adhesive to stick. And, of course, this question applies even more so when our desire is to actually fuse two things into a single, indivisible, new entity. If they are too dissimilar or contradictory, they will remain two divisible entities that are merely fastened together, and with the passing of time they will slowly separate.

What holiness, *kadosh*, implies is separateness. Godliness is above physical matter. This is what makes spirituality special.

It is a mountain that must be climbed: one must search after it. God and Divine emanation transcend the earthiness of our world. How then can a Jew, by merely utilizing a physical substance for the performance of a *mitzvah*, defy all the natural rules and draw Godliness into that object?

OBJECTIVE: TO REVEAL THE PRESENCE OF GOD IN CREATION

The explanation is as profound as it is mysterious. Although we may perceive the world as being outside of God and His unity, even as opposing God and holiness, this is a mistaken illusion. The world and everything within it are a part of God. In the process of creating the world and giving it space in which to exist, God "contracted" Himself and left an empty space, the mystical *makom panui*. Inasmuch as there cannot exist a place devoid of God's Infinite Being, this contraction did not so much constrict God's essence as it concentrated or concealed it. Thus it appeared as if God were not there, but He was and, of course, still is. The world that emerged out of that "empty space" is in actuality only a concealment of God's omnipresence, and it is man's purpose to reveal its true, underlying nature.

The undertaking to bring Godliness into the material components of this world, therefore, goes not progressively downward, but progressively upward. Man is not meant to bring God *down into* this world. He is already here. Rather, man's purpose is to raise the world and reveal the latent presence of God in all of creation. This task in itself *is* the consecration of physical matter: to veritably lift the veil of nature and expose the Divine Creator lurking within all of created matter.

Therefore, Godliness and the physical world are not antithetical, and fusing them together is not impossible. On the contrary, they are one and the same. When a Jew uses a physical object for the performance of a *mitzvah*, he is exposing and revealing the dormant spirituality lurking within every aspect of creation. Doing a *mitzvah* is really expressing a single cohesive identity between God and the world.

GOD'S COMMANDMENTS EMPOWER
THE FUSION OF OPPOSITES

The reason that the *mitzvos* of our forefathers could not manifest this latent dimension of the world was that their *mitzvos* were
not commanded by God. The deeds they did were part of and
not higher than the world. They thus could not transcend the partition God implanted in the world to conceal Himself. A famous
maxim suggests, "A bound man cannot free himself." So, too,
since their *mitzvos* lay within the confines of the world, they were
not designed to reveal the secrets that lay higher than the world.

In fact, the very opposite is true. They did succeed in bringing Godly light into the world, albeit a limited one, but because
holiness is removed from and higher than physical existence,
it could not be fused into the world. They did not reveal the
innate holiness implicit in creation. What was lacking was the
Godly revelation at Sinai that revealed that the world does not
have a separate existence outside of God. Without this revelation, the deeds of our forefathers, notwithstanding how meritorious and righteous they actually were, were channeled in the
wrong direction and proved fruitless insofar as the sublimation
of physical existence is concerned.

At the giving of the Torah, God invested Himself into His
commandments. And just as He is all-powerful and all barriers
fall before Him, so too His commandments were imbued with
the ability to transcend all limitation, even the barrier concealing God's presence from this earth. What Godly emanation cannot do, God Himself can. The "scent" *mitzvos* of the forefathers,
although spiritual, were not of a sufficiently lofty degree to
penetrate the barrier separating the spiritual from the physical.
But God knows no bounds, and He instilled within His *mitzvos*
the ability to transcend all impediments separating one reality
from the other.

ANNULLING THE RESTRICTED ZONES

It is this fundamental idea that the *Midrash* is attempting to
convey when it compares the era preceding the giving of the

Torah to a royal decree by an emperor. The emperor had instituted a law that prohibited the inhabitants of Syria from traveling to Rome and the inhabitants of Rome from traveling to Syria. One day he annulled the decree, and to demonstrate its dissolution he proclaimed, "I shall be the first to travel between the two locations." Likewise, says the *Midrash*, at the giving of Torah God dissolved the decree that separated the spiritual and physical domains and became the first to demonstrate that annulment with His historical descent down to Moses on Mount Sinai.

Hasidus develops this *midrash* by explaining that the word *gezeira*, "decree," also means "cut off." Before Sinai the spiritual and physical domains were cut off from one another, the spiritual being too aloof and the physical being too mundane. At Sinai God annulled the decree and gave the Jewish people the ability to synthesize the two, to make a holy world.

We may now put the different kinds of *mitzvos* into proper perspective. The Noachide laws, the purpose of which is to maintain control and orderliness in the world, have no spiritual effect or repercussions. The *mitzvos* of our forefathers, although bringing spirituality into the world for the duration of the *mitzvah*, have no permanent influence on the world. They are but a means to an end. And the *mitzvos* commanded by God Himself at Sinai and fulfilled today by the Jewish people bring permanent change into the world by manifesting and bringing to the fore the intrinsic holiness and Godliness found in creation.

18

MENTAL CONTEMPLATION VERSUS PHYSICAL ACTION

In the previous chapter we discussed the differences between the *mitzvos* observed by our forefathers and the *mitzvos* that were commanded at Sinai, and we highlighted the supremacy of the latter over the former, since they have the capacity to transform the physical world into a spiritual abode for the Almighty. In truth, however, there was a significant dimension to the *mitzvos* of our forefathers that was qualitatively higher than our own. To discover this dimension, we must descend to the very core of this strange phenomenon: our forefathers' observance of *mitzvos* that had not yet been commanded by God and which were formally introduced into the world later by means of direct Divine revelation.

The *Midrash* states, "The patriarchs fulfilled all the *mitzvos* of the Torah before they were actually given." What does this mean? How, for example, did they observe the *mitzvah* of *tefillin*? It is unlikely that they affixed black boxes of leather containing scriptural text written on parchment to their arm and head. The *parshios*, or Scriptures, found in *tefillin* speak of the Jewish people's exodus from Egypt, but in the time of our forefathers the Jewish people had not yet even descended into Egyptian servitude. Nor did our forefathers likely eat *matzos* on Pesach centuries before the Jewish people themselves ate *matzos*. We must conclude that, although our forefathers did indeed fulfill *mitzvos*, they were not *mitzvos* like our own.

THE FOREFATHERS' *MITZVOS*:
INTELLECTUAL AND EMOTIONAL

In the Kabbalah it is explained that the forefathers' *mitzvos* were of a spiritual nature. They did not affix *tefillin* as do we, yet the causal chain of emanation in the spiritual worlds, brought about by the *tefillin* and other *mitzvos*, was accomplished in the same way. So although the physical accessory of the two types of *mitzvos* were not the same, the spiritual effect was. This is the pivotal difference between the two types of *mitzvos*. Whereas today the very accessory for spirituality is the physical world, for our forefathers the spiritual world was beyond the reach of the physical. As was discussed earlier, the partition separating them had not yet been removed. Therefore, they used their own spiritual faculties of intellect and emotion to bring about the same spiritual result that we do today by performing *mitzvos*.

Let us consider the practical application of this principle: while putting on *tefillin*, one is meant to contemplate the sovereignty of the intellect over the emotion. The affixing of the *tefillin* to the head and the heart itself facilitates this subjugation so that in the course of the day the intellect guides the emotion, instructing it to pursue Godliness and reject defilement and unholiness. Our forefathers accomplished the same task, but without any outside agent. Their *mitzvah* was wholly a process of introspection. Yet, both processes accomplished the same task of subjugating man's emotion to his intellect and thus enabling him to act in a Godly, rather than a base and animalistic, fashion.

Thus the patriarchs fulfilled all 613 *mitzvos*, such as *tzitzis*, blowing the shofar, eating in a *sukkah*, and so on, but their manner of doing so was radically different from the manner of our fulfillment today. Today the essential aspect of the *mitzvos* is the physical act, and the individual's intention merely adds vitality into its fulfillment. A thoughtful *mitzvah* itself consists purely of the physical act. Any added concentration merely serves to enhance or upgrade the quality of the *mitzvah*. For our forefathers, however, the reverse was true. The entire *mitzvah* was intellectual contemplation supported by emotional feeling. The *mitzvah* belonged to the soul; the body played no part. However, even this explanation seems somewhat inaccurate, since earlier we related how the *Zohar* teaches that Jacob utilized wooden sticks for the fulfillment of the *mitzvah* of *tefillin*. Thus, we observe how the *mitzvos* of our forefathers as well were seemingly facilitated by the use of physical objects and were not completely of a spiritual nature.

This story of Jacob then raises two questions: (1) Why was it necessary for our forefathers to use something physical in the performance of their *mitzvos*? Their *mitzvos*, unlike ours, were not intended to bring about an alteration in the material world, and so physical objects were not essential, as we have discussed. (2) If indeed the prime goal behind our *mitzvos* is the transformation of the physical world, then why should the *mitzvos* be tied to only a single configuration for enactment? Why must all Jews put on *tefillin* in the very same manner every day? Should we not discover as many different avenues and different objects as possible so that we can consecrate all of creation? Our forefathers themselves led the way since Jacob observed *tefillin* with sticks. And since he is singled out by the *Zohar*, then presumably Isaac fulfilled it with a different physical object, as did Abraham. And if uniformity in *mitzvos* is important, then why was it not present in their *mitzvos*, which were performed at random?

These important questions figure prominently in hasidic thought and are answered with two general explanations: (1) The physical correlative acts accompanying the *mitzvos* of the patriarchs had no significance of their own, but were rather an involuntary outgrowth of the spirituality of the *mitzvah*. (2) The physical element of their *mitzvos* was necessary so that they would in turn serve as a catalyst for the *mitzvos* of their descendants. We elaborate on both these concepts in the sections.

UNITY BETWEEN BODY AND SOUL

Regarding the first question, it is an undeniable fact that man's frame of mind or, to state it better, the moods of his soul have a direct bearing on his body and are reflected therefore in physical action. When one is jubilant, the joy can be seen on one's face. It radiates with exuberance. Likewise, when one is sad, the depression is "written" all over one's face. Similarly, the *Mishnah* teaches that the face of a wise man is not the same as that of an ordinary person, because "a wise man's wisdom illuminates his countenance."

This phenomenon is a bit mysterious. Why should the moods of the soul be evident upon the body? Are not body and soul separate entities? The answer is, of course, that although they are indeed separate, nevertheless they are joined together as one and thus have a direct bearing on each other. In fact, to assume that the body would not be at all affected by the changing conditions of the soul is ludicrous. It is the soul that animates and sustains the body, and therefore the seasons of the soul find expression in the body.

Kabbalah maintains that in man there are two souls. One, the *nefesh habehamis*, or animal soul, is the more natural and is closer to the body. The other, the *nefesh elokis*, or Godly soul, is divine and serene, but is more removed from the body. It is the former that serves as the life force of the body. One may therefore appreciate that the condition of the animal soul is what is most manifest in the body, and not the Godly soul. What this means in practical terms is that when a feeling of spiritual awe overtakes an individual, this feeling is not necessarily expressed in physical action. There is no causal chain between the Godly soul and the activities of the body.

An exception to this rule occurred in our forefathers. The unity between their Godly soul and corporal body was such that their spiritual impulses immediately found translation in the physical realm. Every Godly experience, such as a *mitzvah*, was impulsively transmitted to some physical act. Just as man's face radiates happiness when he is ecstatic, so too the forefathers' bodies brought about a correlative physical response to spiritual experience. Why was this so?

THE FOREFATHERS WERE THE CHARIOT

"Our forefathers were the chariot," declares the *Midrash*. The implications of this statement are that just as a chariot is wholly subjugated to its rider and even assumes his will, so too the actions of our forefathers were dictated by the Divine Will. The level of a chariot's subjugation is greater even than that of a horse to his rider, since a horse has a will of its own but now follows its owner's command through coercive training, or even through kindness from the rider who teaches the animal to obey him.

Our forefathers had no will save that of the Almighty Himself. They acted as incomparable and unequalled representations of the Divine Will. What *Hasidus* is further introducing into this concept is that this self-nullification encompassed not only their soul but even their bodies, so that they too became an instrument of the Divine Will. Every limb and sinew in their bodies was a vehicle for the expression of Godly ambition.

It was for this reason that any spiritual engagement they undertook was automatically expressed in a physical form as well, that is, physical objects being used for the *mitzvah*'s fulfillment. It was not their intention, nor was it within their ability, to transform those physical objects to holy ones. Rather, the absence of an impulsive physical counterpart to their feelings of spirituality would have been a sign that the body was not completely subjugated to God. The body and the physical objects surrounding it were drawn by the soul into the *mitzvah*. Stated in other words, their bodies were complete and utter "chariots" to their soul. Any dictates of the rider of the chariot, their soul, immediately found expression in the chariot, the body. Hence, the patriarchs, while practicing *mitzvos* that were purely ethereal in nature, still made use of bodily and physical existence in the execution of their commandments.

Why was there no uniformity in the physical dimension of our forefathers' *mitzvos*? For example: why did they use different material objects for the fulfillment of the same commandments, such as *tefillin*? Since the involvement of the body was only a direct response to the spiritual experience of the soul, then it follows that the different ways in which our forefathers expressed their spirituality would be reflected in correspondingly different forms of physical expression. As was noted earlier, the spiritual attribute that best described Abraham was *hesed*—mercy; Isaac, *gevurah*—severity; and Jacob, *tiferes*—benevolence. Since their prime spiritual attributes differed, the corresponding physical counterpart differed as well.

When Jacob spiritually fulfilled the *mitzvah* of *tefillin*, the corresponding physical outcome found expression in sticks. This physical expression was consistent with the *mitzvah* of *tefillin* as it is channeled by means of benevolence. It was not, however, the correct form of expression for this *mitzvah* from the aspect of severity or mercy, and thus the same *mitzvah* when fulfilled by Isaac and Abraham had different forms of physical execution.

Returning to our analogy of facial expression resulting from an individual's frame of mind, it is not the facial expression that is significant, but rather the inner ambiance of the soul that produces those expressions. An individual is not sad because his face looks gloomy, but rather the reverse. Thus, one cannot find two individuals whose facial expressions are identical during happiness or depression, for the outward expression is uniquely personal and directly related to man's inner essence.

After all, many people cry when they are happy. In the same way, the fundamental element of our forefathers' *mitzvos* was its spiritual dimension; the physical act was a mere outcome, and thus it differed between the respective patriarchs.

CEMENTING GODLINESS INTO AN UNGODLY WORLD

Of course in relation to our own *mitzvos* this assessment is not applicable. The purpose of our observance of *mitzvos* is not to bring about cataclysmic changes in the higher spiritual worlds, but to bring Godliness into an otherwise ungodly world. We put on *tefillin* to impart holiness into our arms and intellect, as well as into the parchment on which God's words are written. As was pointed out earlier, the only reason why contemplative intention accompanies the *mitzvah* is to enhance its physical performance. Yet, even devoid of concentration or intent, the *mitzvah* is still whole (albeit less desirable than one with the proper meditations).

Because the essential element of our *mitzvos* is the physical act, the manner in which they are fulfilled must be in conformity with the manner in which God commanded them. Thus, all the Jewish people keep the *mitzvos* in the exact same way.

If we were to stray even one iota from the way God instructed, the *mitzvah* would be missing God's special power, the *Anokhi* ("I Myself wrote and gave the Torah") that binds the spiritual with the physical and amalgamates them as one.

This attitude about the nature of *mitzvos* is reflected in Jewish law. One who observes a *mitzvah* even without proper intention is still credited with it and therefore is required to recite the blessing acknowledging "He who commanded us" to perform it. Even if he later regrets his minimal performance of the *mitzvah* and wishes to redo it, he is forbidden to repeat the blessing. Doing so would entail a *brokhah levatalah*, a blessing in vain, since he has already fulfilled the *mitzvah*. Similarly, if one well versed in the Kabbalah meditates into the Godly effusion caused by the *mitzvah* of *tefillin* yet does not actually put them on, he has not fulfilled the *mitzvah* in the slightest. And if one affixes *possul*, or invalid *tefillin*, even accompanied by all the mystical meditations in the world, he has not fulfilled the *mitzvah*. Once the Torah was given, the physical element of the *mitzvah* became the essential ingredient. No mental gymnastics can ever replace it. This is the cardinal distinction between the *mitzvos* before Sinai and those commanded at and after Sinai.

So much for our first explanation about the necessity for physical participation in the forefathers' *mitzvos*. Now we proceed with the second explanation, namely, that incorporating the physical was necessary as a catalyst for the *mitzvos* of our patriarch's descendants and posterity.

BRIDGING THE GENERATION GAP

Hasidus emphasizes the idea that the lives of our forefathers served as a preparatory stage for the giving of the Torah. They cleared the way for the rest of humanity by being the first humans to recognize and, at incredible risk, propagate the knowledge of God and lead holy lives. They genetically transmitted this knowledge to their descendants so that they would in turn fulfill their duty after the Torah had been given. Without that rudimentary foundation the Jews would have never been prepared to receive the Torah.

It was necessary therefore that the *mitzvos* of the forefathers incorporate a physical dimension so that there would be some tangible connection between those *mitzvos* and the ones of their progenies. Had their *mitzvos* not found some sort of expression in the physical world, we would not have been able to recover the potent strength that lay within them and that is so vital to our religious devotion today. There would have been an unbridgeable gap between the two modes of divine service, one totally spiritual and the other totally physical. Thus, the forefathers synthesized their service unto the Almighty with physical action, thereby transmitting to us all the spiritual ground they had gained.

As a case in point, many of the Jewish prophets, in the course of receiving their visions, were instructed to perform seemingly unrelated, trivial activities. For example, the prophet Ezekiel was once ordered to lean on his left side, then on his right, and subsequently to make a *kli gola*—a "knapsack." What was the purpose of these strange instructions?

The great medieval Jewish thinker Nahmanides (Rabbi Moshe ben Nachman), in his commentary to *Lekh Lekha*, and the Ran (Rabbein Nissin) explain that these physical maneuvers were necessary for the prophecy to materialize. The prophecy by itself, they explain, could just as well have remained fully spiritual, not descending to the prophet, but then its content would have been lost. Therefore, the prophet was compelled to move physically, ensuring that the message would assume a spatial–temporal dimension that he could apprehend, and that would remain with him once the Divine vision had ended.

The physical expression of our forefathers' *mitzvos* should be viewed in the same way. The intention behind it was to bridge the gap between a purely metaphysical experience and the material world so that it would be channeled to posterity and not be lost.

On the basis of this rule, Nahmanides interprets many events in Abraham's life as forming a pipeline whereby his spiritual achievements could be transmitted to his descendants. A classical example is the command for Abraham to "rise and tour the Land (of Israel)," which Nahmanides sees as the means by which Abraham transformed his spiritual connection to the land into his heirs' right to acquire the land. By actually encircling the land, Abraham performed a *kinyan*, or legal commercial transaction whereby the land was transferred from others' ownership into his own and through him to his descendants.

It also follows that since the main aim behind the physical act of the forefathers' *mitzvos* was the connection it provided with the physical world and not the act itself there was no necessity for uniformity of the *mitzvos*. What was essential was that they find some form of physical outlet, and each of our forefathers used what means suited him best.

ABRAHAM'S SINGLE HOLY OBJECT

There is one exception to this entire discussion—the *mitzvah* of *milah*, circumcision. Our forefathers, as we do today, performed this *mitzvah* by the command of God. In the transmission of the spiritual virtue of the forefathers to their descendants, it was important that at least one *mitzvah* be identical, and the chosen *mitzvah* was circumcision. This was not a random choice. Circumcision is the only *mitzvah* that actually imbeds Godliness ("My Covenant") into man's flesh. Whereas all other *mitzvos* invoke the participation of the world outside of man, *milah* takes an actual part of man and makes it a *mitzvah*. Because it is the only *mitzvah* that can actually transmit the vigor of the forefathers' spirituality into the Jewish body, it was chosen to be identical.

This concept is also the reason behind Abraham's surprising request of his faithful servant Eliezer to "place your hand under my thigh" while swearing his oath to bring back a suitable wife for Isaac. Superficially, this request seems to contravene all decency. Why would Abraham have asked Eliezer to hold his male organ while swearing an oath? The explanation is simply that Abraham wished to swear his servant by a holy object. The only one in his possession was his *milah*, for it was the only one commanded by God and thus capable of inoculating spirituality into something material. Curious as it may sound, Abraham valued the place of circumcision as the one area of his body that had been synthesized with the Divine.

THE SCENT THAT REVIVES

What remains unanswered is what special virtue was inherent in our forefathers' *mitzvos* that supersedes the Sinaitic *mitzvos* to the point where all kinds of physical action are necessary just to transmit it to us. We have discussed at length how their *mitzvos* in comparison with our own are analogous to what a scent is to a flower.

The answer is that although *scent* connotes mere emanation without substance and furthermore has no permanence and is quickly dispelled, it is still capable of restoring consciousness and life. In the course of everyday life, it is food and drink that are essential for sustenance, not scent. What we eat keeps us alive, and not what we smell. Yet, when a person has fainted and is in need of resuscitation, it is only a strong scent that can reach him, and usually smelling salts are brought.

How this virtue of resuscitation figures within the framework of our forefathers' *mitzvos* is discussed in the next chapter.

19

It's the Thought
That Counts

The *Midrash*, in distinguishing between our *mitzvos* and those of our forefathers, says, "All the *mitzvos* which our patriarchs fulfilled before you were as 'scent.'" The word *all* is significant. It suggests that not only are the *mitzvos* that they performed at their own initiative as mere "scent" but also that the *mitzvos* they fulfilled at God's command, such as circumcision, are classified as such.

From this insight we deduce that the eminence of our *mitzvos* over theirs comes not only from the fact that ours are fulfilled at the command and with the power provided by the Almighty. If that were the case, then their observance of circumcision would be identical to our own since both were commanded by God. Something else must have taken place at Sinai that places our Sinaitic *mitzvos* over and above those previously observed.

That this is true is amplified by Maimonides in his commentary to the *Mishnah, Hullin,* where he writes that it is of critical importance to be aware that all the *mitzvos* today exist only as a result of God's command to Moses at Sinai, and not to Adam, Noah, or Abraham. Maimonides goes to great lengths to emphasize that the sole basis for our fulfillment of the commandments today is the fact that God commanded them at Sinai. This includes even those *mitzvos* that God commanded before Sinai or that our forefathers kept of their own accord. In illustrating how this principle operates with respect to Abraham, Maimonides chooses circumcision and declares that our observance of it today is based not on the pretext that God commanded Abraham to observe it, but rather on God's subsequent command to Moses concerning circumcision.

Although it is relatively simple to understand why the *mitzvos* observed by the forefathers of their own initiative are only the "scent" of a *mitzvah*, it is difficult to comprehend why their observance of *milah* is viewed similarly. Before we elucidate the distinction between *milah* before and after Sinai, we must first delve deeper into the *mitzvos* the forefathers kept of their own initiative.

ILLUMINATING THE WORLD WITH GODLY LIGHT

The essential innovation resulting from the giving of the Torah was the annulment of the heavenly decree barring interaction between the physical and spiritual domains, thus enabling Godly light to permeate and consecrate the material world. This transformation is inclusive of man as well, so that when he performs the *mitzvah* of *tefillin*, for example, not only has he taken parchment and ink and made them holy but he is also simultaneously hallowing the arm and head to which the *tefillin* is affixed. The flesh is injected with spirituality, so a qualitative change is brought about within it. The same applies to every other *mitzvah*.

This phenomenon explains why the messianic prophecy states, "All 'flesh' shall see together that God has spoken." Rabbi Shneur Zalman, in *Tanya*, clarifies that the Messiah will not ingrain holiness into the world: on the contrary, the world as such will not change at all as a result of his coming, as is stated in the Talmud "the world will still proceed according to its natural order." What will happen is that all the holiness that we ourselves are generating into the world through our performance of God's commandments will become manifest. Thus, "all flesh," even the body, will radiate with holiness since it too has become holy.

Every activity undertaken by a Jew in accordance with God's prescribed command brings holiness into the world. Not only *mitzvos* per se but even eating, drinking, and other physical necessities become holy, provided they are done with the intention of serving God. When a Jew eats so that he will have strength to study Torah and perform the *mitzvos*, he has thereby elevated the food he has consumed.

Furthermore, not only is the food itself elevated, but so are all the stages involved in its preparation, beginning with the planting of the wheat, its harvesting, and including every step to its final preparation in the kitchen. Thus, all the physical effort and energy invested in the preparation and consumption of the food are sublimated by the Jew.

And so the process continues. The Jew's mission will not be complete until every physical object and every human activity bear the stamp of holiness. For there is no area of life for which there is no instruction by the Torah as to how it may be elevated. And slowly but surely, a home for God is built—a place where spirituality and materialism are synthesized together as one and together manifest the presence of the one, unified God.

This task is the calling of the Jews.

OUR ACCOMPLISHMENTS ARE CONCEALED

Unfortunately, in our own times these achievements synthesizing the spiritual and material are hidden. Although undoubtedly the world is becoming spiritualized, the phenomena of transformation are concealed from us. Since we are submerged in the physical dimension and are aware only of what our physical senses perceive, we cannot see the outcome of our observance of Torah and *mitzvos*. In the messianic era, however, God will open our eyes and illuminate the earth with His Light, and then everything will be apparent, "And all flesh shall see."

On the other hand, although our forefathers perceived this reality even in their own lifetime, they did not see the spirituality in the world—not because they were blind to it, as we are today, but because it simply was not there. Their religious duties had no impact whatsoever on creation. But it is precisely within this lack of productivity that we find a superior attribute in the *mitzvos* of our forefathers. The level of their Divine service was spiritually higher than that of our own.

GRANTING HOSPITALITY TO ANGELS: AN EXERCISE IN FUTILITY?

The Torah's narrative of Abraham's incomparable hospitality serves to demonstrate this point. At the beginning of *Parshah Vaeira* the Torah relates how the Almighty revealed Himself to Abraham as he sat at the entrance to his tent awaiting visitors. Suddenly he saw three men, who were really disguised angels, and he excused himself from before God's presence so that he might greet them. Can there be any greater display of love for a *mitzvah* than that? He forfeited an encounter with God to perform the *mitzvah* of hospitality! The Talmud derives from this episode that it is of greater virtue to practice hospitality than to greet the Divine Presence.

Yet, the slightest exertion today on the part of a Jew in fulfillment of the mitzvah of *hakhnosas orhim* (hospitality) is infinitely superior to the accomplishment of Abraham. At the conclusion of Abraham's herculean efforts to provide for his guests, the only thing left was the memory. Nothing had changed. Yet, when a Jew today invites a stranger into his home, feeds him, gives him a bed to sleep in, and provides him water to wash up, he has elevated every minor detail of his efforts. From the wood of the bed to the electricity that provided the guest with light, all have become instruments for a *mitzvah* and are thus consecrated. In contrast, all the fine dishes Abraham prepared, from the "butter and milk" to the "tongues with mustard," were mere food. The Talmud relates that because the visitors were not men but angels, they only feigned eating, but did not actually partake of the food. In reality, then, Abraham fulfilled no *mitzvah* at all since the angels did not even benefit from his hospitality. Indeed it is not possible to be physically hospitable to angels. Why did God, when sending these angels to Abraham, require them to be disguised as men? Abraham was accustomed to seeing angels, so why in this case did the angels come disguised as humans? The simple answer, as explained by the classical biblical commentators, is that God desired to gladden Abraham's heart with human visitors to whom he could be hospitable. So God provided them. One cannot practice *hakhnosas orhim* with angels and hence there was no *mitzvah*. Moreover, Abraham even excused himself from God's presence in order to care for them. What then was the purpose of this episode? Did God want Abraham to leave His presence to accomplish absolutely nothing? To understand the story, we must divorce the episode from any comparison with our own age. For us, good intention accomplishes nothing: it is the act and only the act that is significant. As we can well appreciate, if a poor man with an empty cupboard brings home guests in order to fulfill the *mitzvah* of *hakhnosas orhim* and the guests leave as hungry as they came, not only has he not fulfilled the *mitzvah* but he has also perpetrated a grave injustice. Good intention is insufficient. One must physically cater to and feed one's guests.

Yet, for Abraham the same was not true. Since his were spiritual *mitzvos*, the intention was everything and the act an unimportant outgrowth of the *mitzvah*. For Abraham and his generation, it was the thoughtfulness of the *mitzvah*, the intention one has, that served as its central ingredient. Within this dimension of *mitzvos* he fulfilled the command appropriately. He exerted himself immensely in the pursuit of the *mitzvah*— running, giving orders, providing food. The fact that in the end no one benefited from his efforts was unimportant. The intention was there. Even if there had been a beneficial physical outcome to his hospitality, nothing would have changed. The food and objects used would have remained mundane and unholy.

Today, now that the Torah has been given, it is the positive and beneficial product of one's efforts that counts most of all. Sitting and meditating about the importance of *tefillin* without actually putting them on amounts to nothing.

With this point firmly established, we now return to explain why, notwithstanding the fact that our forefathers fulfilled the *mitzvah* of circumcision exactly as we do, by the command of God, their action was still inferior to our own. This is the topic of discussion in the next chapter.

20

THE SIGNIFICANCE OF PLEASURE, UNDERSTANDING, AND APPRECIATION IN RELIGIOUS WORSHIP

INCREASING THE JEWISH PEOPLE'S MERITS

In establishing the purpose for a multiplicity of *mitzvos*, the *Mishnah* offers this statement: "The Almighty desired to make Israel meritorious. He therefore increased their Torah and *mitzvos*." From this explanation it appears as though the *Mishnah* is set to answer the question, Why did God give the Jewish people so many different *mitzvos*?

But what an odd question this is. Is the *Mishnah* implying with its statement that had God given us only half the amount of *mitzvos* we would have understood the reason for half that number, or 306 commandments? Or had He given us only one commandment, it would have been sufficient? After all, what is the difficulty in understanding the difference between God giving one commandment or 613? If He felt it necessary to give us even one command, surely He can feel it necessary to give us 613 *mitzvos*.

No, the *Mishnah* cannot be referring to a numerical or quantitative dimension. Rather, it is referring to the great variety of qualitative meanings within the *mitzvos. Mitzvos* differ from one another not only in their manner of performance but also in their inner content. Every *mitzvah* has its own inner dimension and spiritual life-force. For example, the *mitzvos* of *tefillin* and *tzitzis* not only look and are performed differently but also possess a totally distinct inner makeup. Thus, there are 613 different contextual frameworks of the *mitzvos.*

DIVERSITY WITHIN THE *MITZVOS*

Commenting on that same *mishnah*, the Talmud explains that, of the 613 commandments, the 248 positive commandments correspond to the 248 limbs in man and the 365 negative commandments correspond to his 365 sinews. This revelation provides even greater insight into the multifarious inner dimensions of the *mitzvos.* The human body is not a composite of identical or even similar parts. Each limb has its own unique design and function. The eye sees, the ear hears, the nose smells, the brain thinks, and the tongue tastes; they look different and they are different. Thus, man does not merely have many limbs, but a great diversity of limbs. And as the limbs differ qualitatively, the same applies to their corresponding *mitzvos.*

This, then, is the *Mishnah's* question: why must every *mitzvah* possess a different inner meaning, different intention, and different meditation? Why could not all *mitzvos* share the same inner content as being God's Will, with the necessity for observance resulting from that fact? What would have been the shortcoming if all *mitzvos* possessed the same inner content and symbolism, so that one performing them could concentrate on one all-inclusive thought and still be accurate for every *mitzvah*?

This question may be asked not only in relation to man but also to God. In *Tikkunei Zohar* it is written that the 248 commandments correspond to the 248 limbs of the King (a term applied to God), and different Divine emanations are anthropomorphically described therein as physical limbs that best personify their function and inner content. This means that each *mitzvah* is connected to a Divine manifestation and embellished with distinct Godly light that identifies it. This insight only strengthens the difficulties about the diversity of *mitzvos*. If indeed *mitzvos* are God's direct Will and are related to His essence, how can there be any discrepancy between them? How can there be a different Godly light associated with each *mitzvah* when the *mitzvos* are related to God's essence and therefore transcend mere light? And how many essences does God have?

Earlier we mentioned the hasidic solution to the profound theological question concerning God's attributes. On the basis of the verse "He is not a man" (and thus He cannot have any anthropomorphic features that would correspond to human limbs), we explained that God's intrinsic essence transcends any description or attribute. It is only once He contracts His essence and descends to a lower level in order to interact with the world that He is called "Merciful," "Wise," "Mighty," and other distinctive attributes.

This explanation shrouds the statement of the *Tikkunei Zohar* in even greater difficulty. We have already emphasized at great length that the special feature of the *mitzvos* given at Sinai was that God had immersed His very essence, the *Anokhi*, into them. Now we are being told that the reason for the great multiplicity in the *mitzvos* is that each corresponds to a Divine limb, which in turn corresponds to the Divine attributes that are present only after God contracts His essence and descends into this world.

The queries above apply to the Torah as well. Why was it necessary for the Torah to be so expansive, not in regard to the multiplicity of ideas, but rather to its multiplicity of content? For example, the *Zohar* maintains that each of the six books of the *Mishnah* corresponds to one of the six Divine emotional attributes (mercy, severity, benevolence, victory, splendor, foundation) and receives its spiritual vitality from the attribute it represents.

A further illustration can be taken from the many disputes between the houses of Hillel and Shammai. Beis Hillel tended to be more lenient than Beis Shammai in their interpretation of the Law. The explanation given for this recurring phenomenon is that the souls of Beis Hillel emanated from the celestial sphere of *hesed*—mercy, and the souls of Beis Shammai from *gevurah*—

severity, and their approach to Torah study was an outgrowth of their spiritual source.

Furthermore, the Torah in its entirety is referred to as *Pardes*, an acrostic for *Peshat*—simple, *Remez*—allusion, *Drush*—homily, and *Sod*—esoteric. This term signifies the four levels at which every Torah passage is understood. And so the Torah resounds with many different opinions, ideals, and principles, with dissenting viewpoints being offered for each. But if the Torah emanates from God's essence, which transcends all division and disunity to the extent that it is referred to as God's wisdom and intellect, how can it contain divisiveness? How can two sages actually disagree in matters of Jewish law?

To answer all these questions, the *Mishnah* declares, "God desired to increase Israel's merits," and in pursuit of this goal "He greatly increased Torah."

BETWEEN A STUDENT AND A SERVANT

Divine worship can be performed in one of two ways. A Jew can serve God as the classic servant, not so much from understanding as from obedience. He does not necessarily appreciate the lofty ideals of Godliness or the sublimity of the *mitzvos*, but he observes them with total faithfulness to his Master.

Alternatively, a Jew can have an intellectual approach to God. His loyalty to God and His commandments is an outgrowth of profound cognitive investigation and a subsequent appreciation of God's greatness. He sees in a *mitzvah* a bridge to the Divine and awakens within himself a burning desire to achieve greater proximity to God by fulfilling the Divine commandments.

Each path has its virtue. The former path involves a total nullification of self to the Almighty. In this scenario, intellectual contemplation and reasoning have no effect on devotion. The individual has in effect transformed himself into the very personification of Divinity. God's Will becomes his own will, and he does not question it nor does he expect emotional fulfillment. On the other hand, devotion that results from intellectual investigation brings about an inner transformation. When one accepts yet struggles to *understand* the inner dimension of God's laws, to foster a natural attraction to them, and to derive pleasure from their observance, one refines one's capacity for intellect, emotion, and pleasure. Instead of losing his existence to God and thereby attaining holiness, such an individual has made his body holy. He is not subjugated to Godliness. He has been transformed into a new being, a Homo spiritus, a Godly human. He has redirected his sense for pleasure so that it no longer enjoys the trivial benefits of this world, but thirsts for an encounter with the Divine.

The former individual, instead of using his gifts to serve God, has ignored them. His intellect does not perceive God's greatness, he has fostered no real affection for spirituality, and his sense of pleasure has remained stifled in earthly pursuits. By virtue of the fact that he first represses and subsequently bends these senses into Godly service, he has become a servant, but he has not undergone any sense of transformation. His intellect, emotion, and pleasure are not an obstacle to Godly devotion, but neither are they vehicles to it. They are just as removed from Godliness as they were before he pledged his loyalty.

The two methods can be summarized thus: The virtue of self-nullification is that one accepts upon oneself the yoke of heaven unconditionally, and the virtue of self-transformation is that one employs the use of all one's faculties in the service of God.

A *MITZVAH* FOR EVERY EMOTION OF THE HEART

The *Mishnah* tells us, "*Ratzah Hakodosh Borukh Hu lezakos es Yisroel lefikhakh hirba la'heim Torah u'mitzvos.*" *Lezakos* can mean "to increase merit," but the word also derives from the root *zakh*, "pure or refined." The statement now reads, "God desired to *refine* the Jewish people: He therefore gave them an abundance of Torah and *mitzvos.*" It was His desire that the individual not only nullify himself to God, but refine and uplift himself, causing an inner transformation. The Divine goal was for man to employ the use of all his faculties in the service of God so that they too become holy.

God therefore formulated abounding diversity within Torah so that the different paths of the mind could explore different avenues and ideas, so that the different emotions of the heart could find expression in different commandments and feelings, and so that man's sense of pleasure could find various types of pleasure within the different *mitzvos*. Had God not instilled within every *mitzvah* its own content and meaning, then man's worship would have been confined to one solitary routine: serving God through negation of self, abrogating any thinking, feeling, or enjoyment. Man would have donned *tefillin*, shaken the *lulav*, and given charity all with the same intention: that this is God's command and ought to be fulfilled. There would be only the most minimal personal involvement, and man would be, in effect, excluded from Divine worship, choosing instead to "go through the motions" mechanically.

But God wanted otherwise. He willed that the earth's inhabitants, in addition to fulfilling the *mitzvos,* become Godly themselves. He thus fashioned every *mitzvah* as a distinct feature, a Divine "limb" or attribute, so that it would have its own content. He then correlated every *mitzvah* to one of man's limbs and sinews so that each *mitzvah* would facilitate the elevation of a different element of man. The result is that man now has in the form of the Torah and its *mitzvos* "motions" that elicit and excite respective "emotions" and personal involvement. In one *mitzvah,* man comes to feel the benevolence of the Creator, and practicing benevolence, he becomes benevolent himself. Similarly, in learning of God's compassion, he comes to love Him. Through still another *mitzvah* he feels God's severity, and by observing the *mitzvah*, he learns to exercise restraint. Moreover, the awe of God's authority brings man to fear of Heaven. And so the same process applies to the *mitzvos* corresponding to all faculties of intellect and emotion.

The result is that Torah encompasses not only man's spiritual faculties—his faith, devotion, and obedience—but also his entire being. The mind learns to comprehend the greatness of God, the heart learns to love and also fear Him, and the sense of pleasure is redirected from earthiness to spiritual fulfillment. Thus, man, in his entirety, becomes holy.

21

ACHIEVING
SIMULTANEOUS DENIAL
AND AFFIRMATION
OF SELF

COMPREHENSIBLE AND
INCOMPREHENSIBLE *MITZVOS*

In his celebrated theological treatise "The Eight Chapters," Maimonides formulates the approach one should imbibe toward good and evil, toward *mitzvah* and sin. Citing King Solomon, "An evil person desireth evil" (Proverbs 21:10), he explains that a person who entertains evil thoughts, even without any intention of acting out the fantasies, is nevertheless called a *rosha*, "evil." If he were not evil, he would not have entertained the thoughts in the first place. Of course, this teaching emphasizes to what degree man must be pure of heart, as well as deed. He should aim to feel a repulsion for evil in the innermost recesses of his heart.

Maimonides does not stop with this statement, but continues with the words of Rabbi Shimon ben Gamliel from the *Mishnah*: "One should not say, 'I have no desire to eat milk and meat simultaneously, or to wear *shaatnez* (mixing of wool and linen), or to have illicit intercourse.' Rather, one's attitude should be, 'Indeed I desire all these. But I cannot because my Father in Heaven has prohibited me from doing so.'"

Rabbi Shimon ben Gamliel's message seemingly contradicts that of King Solomon. In the opinion of Rabbi Shimon ben Gamliel, a truly religious person is not one who abhors sin and evil or who has risen to a level at which temptation no longer taints him. Rather, he may have a strong urge for wrongdoing and may be heavily inclined toward sin, but nevertheless he silences the urge before the command of God. Yet, in the opinion of King Solomon this man is wicked!

Maimonides then reconciles the two verses by explaining that they deal with two different categories of *mitzvos*. King Solomon in Proverbs is discussing *mishpatim*, the *mitzvos* for which there exists a logical explanation, such as the prohibitions against murder and theft, respecting one's parents, and the general preservation of social justice. If a person has an instinct to want to disobey the rational, ethical commandments and bring harm to his fellowman, by all accounts he is evil, "an evil person who desires evil." Yet observance of the *mitzvos* called *hukim*, those that defy comprehension, such as *shaatnez* or the mixing of milk and meat, should be based solely on the command of God. An individual's attitude should be that he desires, for example, to eat nonkosher meat but abstains only "because my Father in heaven has prohibited me from doing so." Maimonides verifies his explanation by pointing out that all the *mitzvos* mentioned by Rabbi Shimon in his statement are *mitzvos* that are intelligible to the human mind.

If we are to accept these words of Maimonides at face value, then he is telling us that the rational commandments should be performed because common sense compels their adherence and the incomprehensible *mitzvos* should be fulfilled solely because God commanded so.

Yet, a proposition of this nature seems grossly inadequate. The first premise for any religious person is that God is the absolute arbiter of good and evil. What He declares righteous is good, and what He prohibits is evil. What an individual or a society thinks is largely irrelevant. God is the supreme arbiter and judge, and it is He who determines what are truth, justice, and goodness. Yet, Maimonides tells us that roughly half the *mitzvos* in the Torah should be observed because common sense declares them to be valuable and virtuous!

Furthermore, why is the individual who has a propensity for social evils considered evil? On the contrary, he should be viewed as the ultimate *tzadik*! Although he has a strong disposition toward those things that even human logic dictates are evil, he nevertheless restrains himself and abides by the prohibitions of his Creator.

Moreover, commenting on the passage "And these are statutes (referring to the logical commandments) that you shall put before them," Rashi writes, "The word *and* is used to compare these *mitzvos* to those enumerated previously (the *hukim*, incomprehensible *mitzvos*). Just as the former are from Sinai, so are the latter." Why was it important for Rashi to corroborate that the *mishpatim* are also Divine commands? The explanation is that this is the Torah's way of telling us that just as the motivation for fulfilling the *hukim* is the command of God, the *mishpatim* should be observed as a result of the same consideration and not because common sense dictates thus.

The same thought is expressed by Rashi. Concerning the biblical passage "And these are the statutes which you are to put before the Gentiles," he writes, "So that even if a Gentile judicial system tried a Jew for his transgression identically to a Jewish court, do not bring him to their courts." Now if the Gentile law is the same as the Jewish court, why not allow a Jew to be tried by the Gentiles? The only explanation can be that the basis for justice in a Gentile court is social order and morality, not Divine law. And the *mishpatim*, far from being mere ethical precepts, are God's commandments and should be treated as such.

With these considerations in mind, should not the attitude toward the logical *mitzvos* be that indeed one should desire them but should refrain from their actualization because of a Divine injunction?

THE BODY AND SOUL OF A *MITZVAH*

Hasidic thought sees a different meaning in the words of Maimonides. Surely, the principal justification for the performance of a *mitzvah* is that it is God's command. This idea cannot be open to debate. After all, the word *mitzvah* itself means command. It was not the intention of Maimonides to postulate a motive for the performance of the two types of *mitzvos*, so that one perform a *hok* because God commanded so and a *mishpat* because doing so is logical. Rather, he was telling us what a *mitzvah* is and what intention man should have when fulfilling it. Thus, he was not saying that one should refrain from eating nonkosher food "because" God commanded him not to do so. Rather, one should concentrate on the fact that God wishes one to feel a desire to eat it, but one should nevertheless abstain in accordance with His command. By the same token, when an individual abstains from robbery, the desirable method of fulfilling the *mitzvah* is to feel as though he has no disposition toward the crime. Stated in other words, these are not *reasons* for *mitzvos* but *kavonos*, "*meditations*," that are to be contemplated during their performance.

Every *mitzvah* is said to possess a body and a soul. The body is the physical act, and the soul is the correct mood or meditation a human is meant to have while performing the act. With regard to physical deeds, all *mitzvos* are equal; their performance is the direct outcome of God's command, which constitutes the sole reason for their performance. However, in terms of the inner feeling of the individual in the course of its execution, there is a difference between a logical and an incomprehensible *mitzvah*.

The proper meditation for a *hok* is that one should feel totally nullified to the Almighty. One should feel that one is accepting the yoke of heaven unconditionally and obeying God's command with the greatest joy, although one cannot fully fathom its inner meaning. Intellectual considerations are insignificant. This is why Rabbi Shimon instructed that one not say "I do not desire them" when fulfilling this type of *mitzvah*, for in this instance it is not God's Will that man find his own reasons for the *mitzvah's* performance. The *mitzvah* should not result from or be accompanied by intellectual examination, but rather by supreme self-nullification.

However, with a logical *mitzvah*, such as honoring one's parents, God desires that man participate intellectually and emotionally in it. The involvement should be so strong that, had

God not commanded the *mitzvah*, an individual's own wisdom would have required him to do so. It is not the intention that he cancel the employment of any personal faculties in the fulfillment of these *mitzvos*. On the contrary, the purpose is to be fully absorbed into the *mitzvah* so that it permeates his very being. Here, the *mitzvah* is meant to cause an inner transformation, to sublimate his body so that it becomes holy. Therefore, he is instructed to feel a repulsion for evil deep within, and if he does not, then he is "an evil person who desires evil." The *mitzvah* has had no effect on him, and he has remained simply a mundane being. In short, in the performance of a rational commandment God welcomes and desires human emotional and intellectual participation.

But why is it that *hok* must be carried out with a feeling of negation and servitude and a *mishpat* with a sense of appreciation, involvement, and attraction?

ACHIEVING SUBJUGATION AND SUBLIMATION SIMULTANEOUSLY

To answer this question we must refer to the preceding chapter. We explained that Godly worship entails two essential ingredients: the subjugation of man, on the one hand, and his sublimation and refinement, on the other. Self-nullification is virtuous in that one gives oneself over to the Almighty totally and unequivocally. He is a faithful servant who has superimposed God's Will on his own. But nullification is incomplete in that all of man's faculties remain unchanged. His devotion to God has not been facilitated by his intellect or emotion, but rather by their negation. Whether he understands or feels is unimportant. What is important is the Will of God.

To satisfy the void left by the lack of participation of man's intellect and emotion in fulfilling God's commandments out of a sense of subjugation and servitude alone, it is necessary to involve intellectual appreciation and emotional stimulation in Godly service so that man can elevate himself and transform the physical into holiness, to construct from the human mind and heart a vehicle to the Divine.

To achieve this dual aim, the Almighty introduced two kinds of commandments. To facilitate self-nullification, He gave supra-rational *mitzvos*, and to enhance the human condition and permeate it with holiness, He gave the logically mandatory *mitzvos,* in whose observance the human being could partici-pate fully. It is therefore vital that in the performance of the *mitzvos* one have the proper intention. When fulfilling a *hok* one must contemplate how one is totally insignificant and as if nonexistent before the Almighty, and when fulfilling a *mishpat* one must be moved by the beauty of the *mitzvah* and appre-hend its essence to the point where the holiness is embedded deep within him.

What this means is that when one is instructed to exercise his fullest ability in understanding a *mitzvah*, the purpose is not that he find rationalizations for its fulfillment. On the con-trary, the only viable basis for the performance of any *mitzvah* is the fulfillment of God's Will. Rather, God desires that the Jew engage all his energy in the performance of a rational command-ment so that the mind is stimulated, the emotion is energized, and the body is generally uplifted and refined.

The last question of this chapter is also the most important. How do we know that it is God's Will that we comprehend these *mitzvos*? His instruction to keep the *mitzvos* did not stipulate that we understand or feel them, just that we observe them!

GOD DESIRES COMPREHENSION AND EXCITEMENT

First, in the case of many *mitzvos*, God Himself follows up the commandment with a reason. For instance, He did not suffice with, "Guard the *Shabbos* and make it holy," but continues with "for God created the world in six days and on the seventh day He rested." The command to observe the festivals is also fol-lowed by a rationalization. For example, in the case of Sukkos: "So that all generations know that the Children of Israel sat in *sukkos*." By specifying these reasons, God is conveying that He wants them to be fulfilled with comprehension and excitement.

Second, in regard to the remaining *mishpatim* that have a rationale that is so blatantly apparent that the Torah does not even bother mentioning it, it was God's intention that we comprehend their necessity. Had this not been so, He would not have created the world in a manner in which they were mandatory. Therefore, because every human being understands that the world cannot function with thievery and murder, we know that we are meant to fulfill those *mitzvos* with profound awareness and sensitivity as to their purpose and necessity.

The Talmud makes an observation that is relevant to this point: "Rabbi Yohanan said, 'Had the Torah not been given, we would have learned modesty from a cat and the objection to thievery from an ant.'" What is the purpose of Rabbi Yohanan's theoretical scenario of "had the Torah not been given"?

In truth, Rabbi Yohanan is not postulating a hypothetical scenario that has no bearing on reality. He is divulging to us that since these *mitzvos* are so apparent that they could have been learned from animals, then it must be God's Will that we fathom their depths and thereby refine our intellect. He wishes the perception of these *mitzvos* to penetrate us to the point where we exclaim, "I have no desire in this! It is repulsive to me." If this does not occur, then the *mitzvah* has not achieved its objective.

In conclusion, then, the general purpose of the superrational *mitzvos* known as *hukim* is the subjugation and nullification of man, and the purpose of the rational *mitzvos* known as *mishpatim* is the total perfection of man. However, this distinction is not necessarily accurate. The truth is that every *mitzvah*—*hok* and *mishpat* alike—possesses both of these aims internally, as we shall explore in the upcoming chapters. First, however, we must provide a critical warning in the next chapter.

22

HANUKKAH AND THE PURITY OF KNOWLEDGE

SO THAT THE TORAH NOT BE TREATED AS A SCIENCE

The individual's devotion to God must comprise two elementary aspects: (1) nullification and the abrogation of self and (2) comprehension, feeling, and participation of self. However, even the desired perception of the *mitzvos* must derive from the subjugation of the individual and his will to fulfill God's command. One must not attempt to fathom the knowledge of the *mitzvos* for one's own sake, but rather because God wants the individual to perform and *grasp* the mitzvah simultaneously.

This principle is of critical importance. If it is not followed closely, the *mitzvah's* entire purpose will be defeated. If an individual's motivation for knowledge into Torah and performing *mitzvos* is to satisfy personal curiosity, even if he wishes to explore the beauty of the *mitzvos*, he is worshiping no one but himself. It is imperative that the thirst for this knowledge be solely for the purpose of fulfilling the Supreme Will.

An understanding of this fundamental principle will shed new light on many talmudic and rabbinic pronouncements. One example is provided below.

DEFILING THE OIL

In its discussion of the miracle of Hanukkah, the Talmud states, "When the Assyrian Greeks entered the Temple, they defiled all the oil that was to be found there. And when the royal Hasmonean House overcame and defeated them, they searched [for oil] but found only one flask that was imprinted with the seal of the High Priest."

This statement presents several difficulties. First, why did the Assyrian Greeks merely "defile" the oil? If their desire was to suspend the lighting of the *menorah*, they should have destroyed the oil altogether. They could simply have poured it on the floor. However, their intention was specifically to blemish the oil, a fact that indicates they were aware of the laws of *tumah* and *teharah*, ritual purity and impurity.

Second, if they were familiar with these laws, then they must have also been aware that their actions would not impede the lighting of the *menorah*. The law stipulates that if the majority of the population is impure, then ritual impurity is ignored, and thus the Jews would have been allowed to use the impure oil for the *menorah*. From this we may deduce that the Assyrian Greeks did not mind that the *menorah* would be lit; their intention was that it be lit with impure oil!

Finally, why does the Talmud emphasize that the flask was found "imprinted with the seal of the High Priest"? Why not state simply that the oil was pure, by which we would automatically understand that the flask was embossed with the seal of the High Priest? The explanation given is that the story of the oil is symbolic of the overall struggle between the Assyrian Greeks and the Jews, a struggle that was essentially a spiritual one.

KEEPING THE WISDOM OF TORAH PURE

Oil is a symbol for intellect and wisdom. The Kabbalah states this fact explicitly. Also the Talmud writes, "Because they were accustomed (to eating) olive oil, wisdom was found amongst them" (*Menahos* 85b). The wisdom of the Jew is, of course, Torah. "For [the Torah] is your wisdom and understanding in the eyes of the Gentiles" teaches that Jewish wisdom is synonymous with Torah.

The oil in the Temple was used for the lighting of the *menorah*, and it was of pivotal importance that the oil be pure, or homiletically speaking, it is critical that the Torah be kept pure. Now the light of the *menorah* illuminated the Temple, which in turn illuminated all the earth, and in actual fact the Temple windows were inverted so that the light was directed outward, signifying the Temple's radiation of spiritual light. This was no small matter either: the essential function of the Temple was to illuminate the earth with pure light, the light of the Torah.

The very conception of ritually "pure" and "impure" is beyond our grasp. Mortal man cannot comprehend what the spiritual quality is that makes one object pure and the other impure. Maimonides goes to great length to emphasize this point: "It is clearly evident that categories of ritual purity and impurity are fixed by Divine decree. They are not of those things that man's wisdom may determine; they are generally *hukim*, laws that defy logic (*Sefer Taharah*; *Hilkhos Mikvaos* 11:12). Thus purity is symbolic of something that transcends man's intellectual grasp.

Therefore, "pure Torah" would signify Torah that is studied with the underlying knowledge that, although it can be apprehended intellectually, its true essence lies at a plane where no intellect can reach it. "Pure Torah" signifies a Torah and *mitzvos* that are fulfilled with intellectual and emotional participation and at the same time with the knowledge that it is God's Torah and it is only His command and His Will that serve as the basis for the fulfillment of the Torah.

The Assyrian Greeks were willing to allow the Jews to light the *menorah* and to study Torah. It must be remembered that Greek civilization basked in intellectual enlightenment. Moreover, the Greeks accepted that the Torah was a book of profound, enriching ideas. What they objected to was "pure oil," pure Torah. They found reprehensible the idea that the Torah is God's Torah whose real essence defies understanding. They could not respect nor tolerate the concept of suprarational commandments.

Rabbi Joseph Isaac of Lubavitch found expression for this idea in the special prayer liturgy recited on Hanukkah: When the wicked Hellenic government rose up against Your people Israel to make them forget Your Torah." It does not state, "to make them forget Torah," but "*Your* Torah."

They had no quarrel with the Jewish Torah if it was only part of the Jews' culture. On the contrary, they wished for the Jews to join their educated, hellenistic society. However, they believed in knowledge for its own sake. Amid the most enlightened culture of all time, the Greeks remained incestuous hedonists who worshiped idols. Their knowledge had no effect on their actions. Indeed it was not meant to have an impact. Wisdom and knowledge were not a means for man's inner transformation, but goals in themselves. The Jewish Torah as God's law and as a code of ethics to elevate man was anathema to them, belittling their concept of wisdom. They wanted a *menorah* that would burn with the light of man.

AM I AS GOOD AS ABBAYE?

They therefore defiled the oil by touching it with human hands, symbolizing the manipulation by man of God's Torah. Their actions reflected their belief that the Torah is mere knowledge and logic, and thus it can be debated, proven, or refuted. It belongs to man, who may do with it what he pleases. The attitude later translates itself into the following appraisal: "Just as Rabbi Akiva and Rabbi Meir, Abbaye and Rava (of the Talmud), Rashi and Tosafos had disputes and offered their opinions with regard to Torah interpretation, so may I. After all, they were mortal men engaging in intellectual debate. Am I any less?"

An individual with this attitude fails to understand that the Rabbis were people whose every thought, speech, and action were dominated by the Will of God. They had achieved complete self-nullification. Their Torah was "pure Torah," and thus they had the merit to grasp the true meaning behind the laws because their intellect became vehicles to the Divine. They penetrated the surface of the commandments in ways that are closed to us, and thus their halakhic opinions had far greater accuracy than our own, going right to the heart of the matter.

To the Jew, the Torah is God's wisdom, not man's. God willed for it to descend to the level of man and clothe itself within the confines of human understanding. The Jew, bearing this knowledge in mind, engages in Torah study with awe, trepidation, and humility, knowing full well that he is dust in the face of the Almighty. He exerts every effort to comprehend Torah. His aim is for the Torah to teach and change him, not for him to teach and manipulate the Torah. He refrains from defiling it with his hands.

The perversion of Torah can exist on many levels. The lowest level is accepting the Torah as nothing more than a collection of human ideas. But there are other, more subtle pollutants, such as the acceptance that, although the Torah was given from Heaven and in its original form it defies human comprehension, nevertheless it is possible and even mandatory for the human to fully apprehend its precepts and fathom its ideas, until he becomes the master of the Torah.

This position is also alluded to in the Hanukkah prayer, "to make them forget Your Torah and violate the decrees of Your Will (*hukei retzonekha*)." Here again the language is very precise. The Hellenists did not object to the performance of *mitzvos* either. They were perfectly willing to allow those in the category of *mishpatim*, such as do not steal or kill, and love your neighbor. What they repudiated were the *hukim*, the laws that defy logic and are kept solely as the command of God.

In truth, they would have allowed even the *hukim*, if it were to comprise part of a national culture of a specific people. The Hellenists did not mind that the Jews wore curious fringes (*tzitzis*) and headdress (*yarmulka*). After all, the Scots wear kilts and the Arabs kaffiyas as part of their cultural heritage. So too the Jews could continue with their unique dietary laws, just as the Japanese and Eskimos have a cuisine that is unique to them. But that these acts be carried out on the supposition that they are God's Will, defying any and all logic, was not allowed. Thus, the prayer reads "*hukei retzonekha*"—"the decrees of *Your* Will." It was the premise that the decrees were God's Will that the Hellenists despised. Thus, as in this case, the Torah can be debased by being secularized and acculturated.

THE ASSUMPTION THAT THE TORAH
MUST HAVE MEANING

There is yet another level of Torah defilement. Let us imagine a teacher who gives a different instruction each day to a certain student, but always accompanies the dictate with a coherent argument. The student slowly becomes accustomed to the fact that each instruction has an important reason for its performance. Then one day the teacher gives an order that is not accompanied by an explanation. The student will nevertheless fulfill the instruction, thinking to himself that just as all the other missions had good reasons, so too must this one but the reason is probably beyond his grasp and so the teacher refrained from divulging it. Thus, the student is fulfilling the command not because he accepts the authority of the teacher, but because he believes there is a good reason.

This a classic example of the performance of a *hok* due to perception and understanding only. Although the reason for the *hok* itself cannot be grasped, in extrapolation of the many *mitzvos* that have coherent explanations the individual puts his "faith" in God that it too has a valid explanation. He realizes that in the light of lofty spiritual concepts, man is but a child and cannot comprehend everything, but he is sure there is a reason and therefore fulfills the command. This man is not serving God, but satisfying his own conscience by doing the right thing.

All the above considerations are the effects of Hellenism and secularism on Torah and *mitzvos*. They will stop at nothing to remove God from the scenario. One may be inspired through the observance of *mitzvos* only so long as it results from personal examination and conclusion. There is no room for accepting the yoke of heaven.

How can this secularization be overcome and this defilement be averted?

BEARING THE SEAL OF THE HIGH PRIEST

The answer is alluded to in the Talmud's emphasis on "the seal of the High Priest." One cannot debate the fallacy of the Hellenist approach on an intellectual level. On the contrary, doing that will submerge the Jew in an intellectual and dialectic debate in order to corroborate the Torah's authenticity, thereby making the observance of Torah dependent on intellectual mastery. The only way to be victorious is with the seal of the High Priest.

In real life, the High Priest is removed from the rest of humanity. He is aloof in holiness and devotion to God. He is the representative of the entire people, but is set apart from them.

There is also a High Priest within each and every Jew. It is the supreme spark of Jewishness that forms the bedrock of one's connection with God. It is aloof from the human elements of the body, because although existing in the body, it has never and can never lose its affinity with God. The High Priest in the Jew is his undetachable umbilical cord to Heaven. This part of the Jew is described as "clamped and clutching You."

One must tap this part of the Jew. In order to fight off the pollutant of Hellenism, one must not wrestle with it, but rise above it. The individual must become conscious of his intrinsic connection and give himself over unconditionally. Then and only then will all interferences dissolve.

But this is only one side of the coin. It is imperative that he have the stamp of the High Priest, but there must also be oil within the flask. Nullification to God is essential, but there must be knowledge and understanding as well. Purity without oil is meaningless. What is necessary is perception and wisdom founded in loyalty and devotion.

Thus, the bedrock into which every *mitzvah* is anchored should be man's unconditional acceptance of God's laws that is coupled with intellectual investigation and feeling, so that he uses all his being in serving the Almighty. These are the two sides of religious worship, and both are essential. Through them, man transforms himself into a vehicle for the Divine.

23

PERSPECTIVE ON THE DIFFERENCES BETWEEN THE SERVANT AND THE STUDENT

Man has a dual role in fulfilling God's commands. On the one hand he must be nullified to the Will of God, and on the other he must exert his full capacity in understanding and appreciating the *mitzvos*. In this chapter we look still deeper into this paradoxical and sometimes contradictory demand.

Obedience can be based on one of two grounds: (1) authority and rule or (2) respect. An individual can act like a servant executing the command of his master out of fear or like a student satisfying the wish of his teacher out of love. Stated in other words, you can fear someone, or you can be in awe of someone. There is a world of difference between the two.

And the difference between them is obvious. The servant shares no desire for the performance of the deed that his master has commanded him to execute. On the contrary, the Talmud says that "a servant is happiest when he is unencumbered and free." He has no pleasure in or understanding of what he is doing and is not moved even to think of it. For him, every task is a burden and is treated as such. Although this attitude may not necessarily affect the quality of his performance, the goal is to put the task behind him. The only reason for performing his master's demands is that, by some weird stroke of luck, he is the slave and his master is the boss.

A student, on the other hand, has developed an affection for his mentor and wants him to be satisfied with his pupil. Not only does he execute his teacher's wishes but he also works on uplifting himself to understand better just what his teacher desires. When he receives a directive from his teacher, he immediately embarks on its fulfillment. Coercion is unnecessary, for he tries to make his will the same as that of this teacher, who is his role model and who he admires and respects.

On the surface, it seems that the student is much closer to his teacher than the servant is to his master, and the former seem to share a superior relationship. But it is not quite that simple.

THE SERVANT IS EXPOSED
TO THE HEART OF HEARTS

There is an inherent shortcoming in the teacher–student relationship. Since their relationship is based on understanding and feeling, the teacher cannot expose all of himself to the student. Since he is older and wiser, there are parts of his character and thought that the student cannot as yet comprehend. The teacher must descend to the level of the student and manifest a miniaturized version of himself. His requests and explanations too must be made to fit the limited capacity of the student. He cannot divulge all of what he really wants, for it will pass right over the student's head. Thus, they share a close, intense, but, at the same time, limited association.

The requests of a master to a slave, on the other hand, are totally uncensored. It is not necessary that the slave understand, only that he perform. The master may thus disclose his intrinsic will so that the slave will perform as required. He need not conceal anything of his essence. He simply gives the command, and it is obeyed.

It would thus appear that the student shares only a superficial, outward relationship with his teacher, whereas the servant has direct access to the master's inner being. The student can fulfill only his teacher's external will, whereas the servant is exposed to his master's heart of hearts. This situation is a direct result of the student's intellectual and emotional approach. Just as it serves to unite him and uplift him to his teacher, it also serves to hamper and limit the relationship. After all, he is still only a student.

THE STUDENT EMBRACES THOUGHT, SPEECH, AND ACTION

But if we examine the relationships from a different angle, the servant's relationship is external because it embraces the master only in deed. His affiliation with his master is only in heeding his words. His intellect, emotion, and sense of pleasure form no part of the relationship whatsoever. The student, however, is linked with his master in thought, speech, and action. Every fiber of his being participates in bridging the gap between him and his mentor. Before long he actually begins to personify his teacher in every aspect and is elevated to his standing.

Who is better? At first we may surmise that, with respect to the quality of what is received from above, the servant has the advantage since the master's intrinsic will is divulged to him, whereas the student receives only a faint glimmer of his teacher's inner self. But when we consider who is more attached, the student has the advantage since his highest faculties form part of his connection, whereas the servant's connection begins and ends with his hands.

Of course, in each case the cause brings about its correlative effect. The aspiration of the student is to rise to the level of his teacher. Accomplishing this goal requires a thorough comprehension of the teacher's thinking and character. To make this possible, the teacher must constrict his intellect to the innate, receptive capacity of his disciple. So whereas the student puts everything he has into the relationship and pushes his own mental capacity to the hilt, the input of the teacher is only marginal and compressed. Yet, the relationship is still intellectual, emotional, and satisfying, and the student's sense for all these things is uplifted.

Conversely, the servant has no desire to reach the heights of his master. His aspirations have been stunted, and he is happy just being left alone, and having one day off a week. But he cannot ignore the fact that he has a master to obey. It is not important that the words of his master are above him, speaking only to his hands. He does not wish to evolve into something better as a result of his obedience. Thus, there is no impediment in the channels of instruction and actualization between the master and servant. Whatever the master says goes, and he holds back nothing.

WE ARE THE SERVANTS, OUR FOREFATHERS, THE STUDENTS

The analogy of these two types of relationship can give us a deeper understanding of the difference between the *mitzvos* of our forefathers and our own. We have mentioned that the *Midrash* refers to the former as "scent." The patriarchs fulfilled *mitzvos*, but brought only an emanation of God into the world, not the substance—God Himself. This is so because they emulated the relationship of a student. They used all their body and all their soul to reach God, but mortal man, being limited, can reach only God's external features, His light and emanation. This is what they generated into the world. They were given no direct Divine commands and thus were oblivious to God's essence, but they were still elevated to a level higher than any other human. They were united with Godly light and permeated with spirituality.

However, they could bring no lasting effect into the physical world. Mere light, however Godly, does not have the power to transform material existence and make it holy.

We, however, who were given the Torah and experienced the revelation of God's substance, His Essence, are privileged to facilitate the enactment of God's Intrinsic Will. Our purpose is to be like servants. Whether or not we understand, we must do. Lacking our forefathers' intellectual insight into the commandments is, unlikely at it may seem, to our advantage. There is no contraction of God in the *mitzvos*. It is not necessary. God enclothed his true Essence into the *mitzvos* for there is nothing limiting His doing so. There is no intermingling of human ideas and apprehension that would be overwhelmed by such action.

On the other hand, we lack the refinement of the forefathers. Because our intellectual and emotional faculties do not embrace the *mitzvah*, they do not soar with it either. In the sense that our forefathers rose to spiritual heights, their service was greater and we remain far lower in comparison.

The *Midrash*'s usage of the word *fragrant* is thus very precise. Not only does it emphasize the fact that the patriarch's *mitzvos* lacked substance but it also points to their virtue of possessing spiritual superiority. Fragrance is something that appeals to the soul. One who faints can be resuscitated with fragrance, for it penetrates directly to the soul. Similarly, the *mitzvos* of the forefathers raised their spiritual faculties to the maximum. Divine light engulfed them and was amalgamated into their souls, not just their deeds.

The *Midrash* states, "The lives of the forefathers are a symbol for their children." Although their *mitzvos* differed from ours, we must learn from them to employ all our talents, intellect, emotion, enjoyment, delight, and soul in the service of God. Because they had this ability, they transmitted it to their offspring.

SYNTHESIZING THE ADVANTAGES OF THE SERVANT AND THE STUDENT

We can now comprehend a contradictory statement of Maimonides concerning the observance of commandments after the giving of the Torah at Sinai. He writes that our own observance of *mitzvos* is based wholly on God's revelation and instruction at Sinai and not on any earlier command, however identical. He then seizes upon the example of *milah*—circumcision—and explains that our performance of the *mitzvah* today is due to God's command to Moses, not to Abraham. Then, amazingly, he says, "for God commanded through Moses that we be circumcised just as Abraham was circumcised." Maimonides is simultaneously making the contradictory statements that there is no affiliation between our *mitzvos* and those of our forefathers, and yet we must still emulate their performance! But if there is no correlation between the two, why should we?

The explanation is that it is the deficiency in the fulfillment of our *mitzvos* that Maimonides is trying to amend. These days we serve God as servants and are thus linked to this essence and not to mere revelation. At the same time, we lack the virtue of the student; our perceptions and feelings are not fully involved and are thus unaffected by our deeds. Our *mitzvos* must therefore be augmented by emulating the wholesomeness of Abraham, Isaac, and Jacob in their religious experience. We must try to apprehend, to the best of our ability, the intellectual dimension and emotional exuberance of the *mitzvos*. We must try our very best to bring as much personal participation into the fulfillment of the *mitzvos* as is humanly possible.

Through the personification of the forefathers' discipline, we synthesize within ourselves the virtues of both the servant and the student. The fundamental aspect of Divine encounter is the deed and will always remain thus for it is the only way of binding oneself with God's Infinite Essence. But it can be enhanced so that the individual participates and is involved to the point where he is both in tune with the infinite as well as holy in his own right.

24

THE JEWISH
AND GENTILE VIEWS
OF RELIGIOUS DEVOTION

There is an an ancient debate between the Jewish people and their Sages and the Gentile nations and their philosophers regarding God's interaction with creation. The Jewish people have a unique approach to the concepts of Divine intervention and providence. King David summed it up well in Psalm 113, speaking of the different levels in the Godhead that we all acknowledge, but examining that part of God with which Jews are most in touch. To the Gentiles belongs verse 5, "The Lord is high above all nations; His glory transcends the heavens." The Jews' reply is in verse 6, "Who is like the Lord our God who dwells on high [yet] looks down so low upon heaven and earth!"

This dialogue is of the highest theological significance. Some nations maintained that it does not seem reasonable that the trivial matters of this earth are important enough to the Almighty that He lower Himself to supervise them. "The Lord is high above all nations," they exclaim. It is beneath His dignity to become involved with unworthy beings such as ourselves. Rather, "His glory transcends the heavens"; he interacts with the heavenly hosts, supervising the existence of the unestimable angels, celestial spheres, and the like. This was principally the view of the great French philosopher René Descartes, who postulated a transcendental God who remains aloof from human affairs and resides primarily in the heavens.

The Jewish position, on the contrary, is that there can be no distinction between heavenly and earthly hosts. God's providence encompasses all equally, from the holiest angel to the lowliest insect.

The basis for the Gentile misconception is that they have failed to disassociate their perception of God from any anthropomorphic considerations. They study God scientifically, mistakenly applying to Him facts obtained from the material world. Instead of perceiving God as totally infinite and defying any description, they view Him as the Supreme Being, a transcendent being, but a being nonetheless. His is the highest existence. Of course, this view implies that the higher and more spiritual the lesser beings, the closer they are to God, because He lurks somewhere "up there" in the celestial heights. Just as a king mixes with the nobility and not with the peasants, likewise God mingles with the angels, but not with men.

GODLY SUPERVISION ENCOMPASSES
LARGE AND SMALL EQUALLY

The truth, of course, is that God cannot even be described as a being, and He certainly cannot be celestially confined to being just "up there." Our conception of a being is that it is something alive, purposeful, and directed, ideas that are not applicable to the spiritual realm. After all, how can any of these aspects be applied to the spirit? The very notion of life and death belongs to the body, not to the spiritual realm. No, we cannot describe Him save to use the word *infinite*, which is a negative description (not finite), automatically divorcing God from any depiction or definition.

In the face of infinity all finite elements are equal. The number one does not lose its value even in the face of a billion. If an individual must insert $1 billion dollars into a vending machine for a pack of cigarettes and has only $999,999,999, he will not receive the pack. He needs that $1 to complete the sum. In the face of infinity, however, all finite quantities are totally nullified, and utterly insignificant.

It would then be ludicrous to say that God focuses more

attention on the higher beings than on the lower because categories of higher and lower are meaningless from God's angle. If we assume that the greatness of a created being will confer greater importance on that being in the eyes of God, then God too must be limited, heaven forbid. If a holy being is more appealing to God than a mundane object, then God is subject to the definitions of "higher" and "lower."

This argument has been the simple, yet crucial basis for the Jewish belief that God regulates everything in His creation, from mighty to minuscule. But this argument alone does not negate the fact that the world is as if nothing before the Almighty, and the creation of the world does not automatically confer upon it enough importance to make it deserving of God's supervision. Man cannot claim that the very fact that God created the world means that He cherishes it and watches over it. This tiny microcosm is as if nonexistent compared to His vastness and is certainly expendable. God is utterly removed from mere material existence.

GODLY INTERACTION BESTOWS SIGNIFICANCE

What does confer significance upon the world is the very fact that God took an interest in it. Why He took an interest we cannot know. We cannot fathom the depths of God's Will. We do know, however, that God took this nothingness and propelled it into infinite significance by caring for it. It is not the world that gives itself value, but the fact that God chose it.

Because the arbiter of the world's significance is God and He chose all of creation, then all of creation is equally important and equally supervised. If God had not conferred importance on the world, we would have been led to believe that the greater value and sublimity of an object, the more special it is to God. Angels and celestial spheres would have by far outweighed plants and animals.

But this is not the case: His Will extends to all things equally. (And amid the creation that God chose, thereby giving it significance, He in turn selected one nation through which to make Himself known to the earth's inhabitants.)

This is the meaning behind the Jewish people's answer, "Who is like the Lord our God who dwells on high [yet] looks down so low upon heaven and earth!" God is so exalted that higher and lower are of equal nonsignificance. Yet, He contracts Himself and condescends to see what is going on below, and because of this interest, He looks at both heaven and earth equally. In fact, for the same reason earth is of far greater significance than heaven.

By extension, God oversees every detail of creation. The same supervision given to occurrences in the heavenly bodies is accorded to a leaf falling from a tree. Every twist and turn in the wind is by providence. Although human beings weigh the worth of everything, to God it is all equal.

Jewish mysticism, in general, and the founder of the hasidic movement, Rabbi Yisroel Baal Shem Tov, in particular, have emphasized more than any other system of religious thought how God is in control of all things in the universe, from the biggest and grandest to the smallest and least significant. Once when the Baal Shem Tov was teaching this doctrine to his students, he walked over to a small leaf that had fallen from a tree. Underneath the leaf was a tiny worm. "You see, my students, if the leaf had fallen with its underside facing the sun, the worm would have died." With this he emphasized how the direction taken by a falling leaf was under God's supervision. The same is true whether or not there is a worm on the leaf or any other way of discerning why this would be of significance to the Almighty.

THE BELIEF THAT GOD CAN ONLY BE UNDERSTOOD THROUGH MAN'S LOFTIER FACULTIES

This dispute extends to other spiritual matters, such as how man should worship the Creator and draw nearer to him. Non-Jewish thinkers maintain that the road to God is through man's higher faculties—his intellect, emotion, and faith or his loftier, more virtuous faculties, if you will. They cannot conceive that mundane deeds could express anything spiritual or bring man closer to God. It is only the metaphysical aspects of man that can bridge the gap to God. Lowly physical activity cannot be

worthy in the eyes of heaven. The attitude of non-Jewish religions toward Godly commands such as the *mitzvos* found in
the Torah—their lack of emphasis on and even criticism of such
acts and the disproportionate emphasis that they put on "faith"
as the sole road to salvation—bears witness to this fact. They
cannot accept that God can be found in something that appears
so un-Godly and ordinary. It is no surprise then that the major
Gentile world religions all advocate transcendence and with-
drawal as opposed to engaging in earthly existence. In light of
our discussions in previous chapters, it may be appreciated that
the Gentile objection to physical acts as a mode of Divine worship applies specifically to the *mitzvos* after *Mattan Torah*, and
not to the *mitzvos* observed by our forefathers. Their *mitzvos*
were essentially duties of the heart and soul and were metaphysi-
cally based. They would in effect bring about the ensuing spiritual emanations, which we bring about today through deed,
merely through the meditations for deeds. Although their
mitzvos also found expression in physical action, the process
was much like the joy felt in the heart that automatically brings
a smile to the face. Because their bodies were so nullified to
their souls, the experiences of the soul found unwitting expression in the body. Therefore, the Gentile nations commend the
religious worship of our patriarchs. They utilized only the highest faculties of mind and soul in the service of the Almighty.

REJECTING PHYSICAL DEED
AS AN AVENUE TO THE DIVINE

What the non-Jewish religions seemingly cannot accept or comprehend are the *mitzvos* given at Sinai, the physical fulfillment
of which is the entire *mitzvah*, with the involvement of mind
and soul only serving to enhance the *mitzvah*. In fact, the physical requirements are so primary that if they are missing in the
minutest detail, such as a *mezuzah* with one broken letter, the
mitzvah is missing in its entirety. All the meditations of the soul
into the sacredness of the *mitzvah* will not help amend that
letter or restore the *mitzvah*. A *mitzvah* kept according to the
letter of the law, however, even if it is devoid of any feeling or

concentration, still warrants the blessing, "Who has commanded us in his *mitzvos*," and the physical object used is hallowed.

"Is this how one worships God? Does God really care whether the letter in the *mezuzah* is whole, or care about the *mezuzah* at all, for that matter? What God desires is man's love, devotion, loyalty, and above all faith. No?" We have all heard these words at some time or other from those who are uninitiated in Jewish thought. The notion of using the material world for religious worship is foreign to them. In *Tehillim* (Psalms) we read, "Why should the nations say, 'Where is their God?'" the homiletics of which imply, "Where is the Godliness in their actions?" All of theological thought is thereby reduced to a superficial outlook whereby "if you can't see or perceive of God being in this particular activity, then He simply is not there."

CAN GOD BE CONCERNED WITH THE MINUTIAE OF LIFE?

The reality is that this grievance is not only heard from non-Jewish thinkers but also from a source within the Jew. The Talmud refers to it as *Hagoy asher bekirbekha*—the "foreign one," which is inside of you, namely, the evil inclination.

Our evil inclination makes use of our superficial understanding of Godliness and attacks our meticulousness in fulfilling the *mitzvos*. "Does God really care if your *tefillin* are this big or that big? When you *daven* the feeling is the same! And so what if you buy a $5 lime-smothered *mezuzah* that took thirty seconds to write. As long as you kiss it and cherish it, you are doing a *mitzvah*. And must you really *daven* with a *minyan* (quorum of ten)? On the contrary, the noise and bustle will disturb your concentration. It is far better to pray at home alone where you can meditate on each and every word." Man can easily be enticed into a superficial outlook whereby the physical element of a *mitzvah* serves the function of awakening the feeling, but is not a goal in itself. So a precise observance of the stipulations of *halakhah* is discarded in favor of the important symbols that the *mitzvos* mistakenly become. If one only spent some time thinking about this conception, it would be seen as totally illogical. The distance between God and man is so infinitely vast that it is impossible for anything human to bridge the gap. Could we really believe for one moment that any of man's physical or spiritual gifts, even maximized to their fullest, has even a faint glimmer of hope of joining man to God?

SELF-PROMPTED HUMAN ACTIVITY IS POWERLESS

Imagine, for instance, a man marooned on a desert island who hears over the radio that a space shuttle will be circling the earth's orbit directly over the coordinates where he is stuck. Could anything the castaway do really serve to alert the astronaut to his presence? Even if he ignited a huge bonfire, would it be noticed by an astronaut who is outside the earth's atmosphere? Of course not. In fact, the only possible means by which the astronaut could communicate with the castaway is if they agreed upon a predetermined frequency for radio communication. In other words, only if the astronaut knows exactly where to look because the castaway has complied with the exact dictates of the astronaut is there any possibility for communication.

The same is true in the God–man relationship. The only possible means for such a link to exist is for the all-powerful God Himself to devise some method for the elevation of man to the infinite. Only He can stipulate that he who does such and such will be united with Me. This is the Torah and *mitzvos*. It is the path that God paved for man to come close and be one with Him. God condescended and told man that he who fulfills His Will and actualizes His command will bring God into his life.

And this is the ultimate irrefutable argument for those who complain that Torah and *mitzvos* are too rigid. The "I want to do my own thing" and "Religion leaves no room for individuality" theories are superficial misconceptions that would have us believe that tiny man by his own limited initiative could find God. How shallow, how vain, how superficial! And how unrealistic! Once the Almighty commands us to take the skin of a cow, write passages from scripture on it, place it into leather boxes, and don them on the hand and head, this is the ladder by which to connect oneself with God, no matter how un-Godly it may seem. It is a *mitzvah* from the root of *tzavta*, meaning "to bind and fasten." Because God enclothed Himself into these physical objects, once man wraps them on his limbs he is binding himself with God.

The implications of this idea are enormous. Had God not instructed us about the process for man's elevation according to His Will, had there not been a revelation at Sinai, there would be absolutely no capacity for man to love God, fear Him, or worship Him. Indeed, man would have remained infinitely removed from God. God would not have even taken notice of man's performance of his own self-motivated actions. Finite devotion in the face of the Infinite is utterly meaningless.

However, the truth is that there is enormous room for the individual within Judaism. Although a *mitzvah* is wholly dependent on its physical apparatus, that alone is insufficient. The same Will of God that desired that man affix a *mezuzah* to his door, thereby giving significance to material substance, also desired that man harbor an appreciation for what he is doing. God desired the inner content of a *mitzvah* not to be concealed and lofty, but rather revealed and appreciated by a human. And the Will of God that makes it obligatory for man to wave a chicken over his head on Yom Kippur eve for "*Kapparot*" is the same Will of God that makes it important for man to know why he is doing it and to foster an appreciation for it. God wants man to be deep and thorough, not shallow and conventional. We do the *mitzvos* because God commanded us to do so, and we try our best to understand them also because God commanded that it be so. And these actions together bring us closer to God.

In pursuit of this lofty goal we beg, "May the Lord our God be with us as He was with our forefathers." Although our connection with God is superior to theirs since our *mitzvos* link us with His Essence, we still pray for their high degree of perception and sensitivity to *mitzvos*. We want the current of the *mitzvos* to electrify our mind and our heart as it did theirs. We want a share in their studentlike, intense, personal relationship with God. We are the heirs to their spiritual fortunes. We therefore have the potential to serve God with the love of the student and the awe of the servant simultaneously.

25

MITZVOS THAT MAKE YOU LIGHT UP

One of the main difficulties in theology is that one can never totally divorce one's approach to God from anthropomorphic thinking. Although man can appreciate that God transcends any human description, even his appreciation of this principle is wholly human and limited. Therefore, man largely ends up seeing God as some exalted being, infinitely higher than man, lurking at the highest celestial peaks like some uniquely special person to which there is no equivalent. In the final analysis, it is still difficult for humans to move beyond the "old man with a long white beard in the sky" conception of the deity that is so familiar to children.

Although it may be difficult to totally divorce our thinking from the material confines of this world, we must exert our utmost to do so. We must push our mental capacity to its limits to orient ourselves toward the spiritual domain. If we do not attempt to do so, we are liable to make gross errors in our conception of God, and our misconception could be in total opposition to halakhah and Scripture.

A classic example of a misconception resulting from a superficial understanding of divinity is the widely acclaimed concept, one central to many major religions, that since God is a supremely spiritual Being, He can have no interest in man's physical actions. The only thing that could interest a spiritual Being of that caliber is man's spiritual faculties. These religions put emphasis on faith, heartfelt devotion, prayer, and the like, but they scorn the Jewish concept of a *mitzvah*. Physical acts, in their opinion, are highly inappropriate and have no real place in the service of God.

THE AGELESS ATTACK ON PHYSICAL DEED AS A MEANS FOR DIVINE WORSHIP

There are various gradations to this misconception, the most radical of which is that there is no room in spiritual worship for a physical deed. One who professes this belief would necessarily have to part with the belief of the giving of the Torah at Sinai or, as has been done, preach a new doctrine advocating abrogation of the Law. The result in either case is the formulation of a religion foreign to Judaism. A far less radical but equally superficial approach is that of one who accepts the Torah mandate for *mitzvos* but understands them as being a medium for awakening greater spiritual feeling than would otherwise have been possible. For example, this individual believes that the sole purpose of eating *matzos* on Pesach is to relive the feelings of servitude and freedom and that the purpose of donning *tefillin* is to arouse the intellect and emotion in the service of God. Other than their spiritual and sentimental arousals, the *mitzvos* serve no purpose.

This approach to *mitzvos* contradicts the very bases of *halakhah*, which maintains that even *mitzvos* that are unaccompanied by an emotional feeling are nevertheless valid. Moreover, even if one is coerced into fulfilling a *mitzvah*, it is still valid. Thus, even if an individual is physically coerced into eating *matzo* that has been forced into his mouth has still fulfilled his obligation, although surely his thoughts at the time were not of the servitude in Egypt. By "fulfilling his obligation," we mean that he has connected himself with the Almighty and generated Godly illumination within the world. Even if he later regrets the distasteful way in which he fulfilled the *mitzvah* and wishes to eat *matzo* again the same night, this time with the proper feeling, he may certainly do so, but he cannot recite the blessing again because he has already observed the *mitzvah*.

The blessing will have been in vain, coming as it does on a *mitzvah* that has been already performed.

Any individual who cannot accept that his actions devoid of intention can bind him with God, and who sees greater virtue in a human emotional attachment to God, has a misguided understanding of the nature of divinity. The fact that he sees a difference between action and feeling in addressing the Infinite is an indication that he has not given thought to what the God–man relationship is all about.

From where did such a gross misconception emerge, and why is it so widespread? Why are these ideas about the most important of acts so foreign to the average reader? Why is it the world consensus that the proper approach of man to God is by intellectual and emotional means, rather than by physical deed? Why is it that we humans innately and intuitively feel respect for faith, prayer, and meditation and a concurrent disdain for action in religious worship?

The answer is that this misleading thought is a reflection of human interaction. The only way in which we humans know how to establish friends, colleagues, and spouses is through emotional channels. Two people who merely exchange favors or other actions are not necessarily attached to each other, but once they begin to feel something for one another, to care for each other, a relationship begins—friendship, love, marriage, and what have you. Emotional attachment is the only thing human beings have between each other, so should it not follow that this is also the proper means by which to attach oneself to God?

SINAITIC REVELATION IS THE ONLY MEANS TO DISCOVER THE DIVINE WILL

Here is where the mistake is made. God is not human and not physical. He is also not limited by any emotion. When a human being is shown love or compassion by another individual, he cannot help but reciprocate.

King Solomon expresses this fact in the Book of Proverbs with his statement, "Like the waters which mirror the face that stares into them, so is the heart of man." Our hearts cannot help but reflect emotions shown to us by other parties. To those who show us kindness we feel attracted, and to those who show us contempt we feel repulsed. But God is not constrained to similar emotional responses. Similarly, God has available to Him avenues far deeper than emotion, such as that of Essence, with which to establish an interpersonal relationship and bond.

Angels may be spiritual, and thus human intellect and emotion, the closest faculties we have to the spiritual, may appeal to them. But the Almighty is totally removed from anything physical or spiritual. Because He is infinite, intellect, emotion, and physical deed are equally meaningless before Him.

Therefore, had God not revealed Himself at Sinai, given us a Torah, and told us the manner in which to serve Him, we would never have known how to connect ourselves with Him. Every avenue we could have possibly taken is still part of the creation and thus intrinsically limited. Every effort would have been for naught. The finite cannot approach the infinite.

It was only once God revealed to man how *He* wanted to be served that intellect, emotion, and physical deed became significant. The only premise for religious feeling derives from God's instruction to man to ponder the greatness of the Creator and thereby come to love and fear Him. The same Will of God established that, even amid all the love and emotion, the only way in which to attach oneself to the Creator is through physical deed. God revealed to us that His primary desire lies in action.

It is true that a natural outgrowth of fulfilling the *mitzvos* is an arousal of feeling and appreciation for God. The celebrated collective work on *mitzvos, Sefer Hahinukh,* emphasizes this point with the words "The deed draws with it the heart" (*mitzvah* 16). But this is only a tributary of the *mitzvah.* The *mitzvah* is the physical act itself. Whether we understand *mitzvos* or not, whether we see any objective in them or not, even if they appear peculiar to us (could God really want this?) is academic. The significance of the *mitzvos* derives from God, not from ourselves, and we try to the best of our ability to find a sense of pleasure in them.

Because God also desired that man become elevated as a result of performing a *mitzvah,* He instilled within every *mitzvah* an inner meditation and meaning corresponding to the different faculties in man. It is incumbent upon us to try to fulfill each *mitzvah* with its corresponding meditation and emotion, and thus *Kavanah* or concentration in the execution of *mitzvos* is of profound importance.

Nevertheless, had the *mitzvos* been utterly devoid of any visible inner content, even, as is written in *Tanya*, quoting from the Talmud, had God instructed us to do something as mundane as chop trees the entire day, we would still be obliged to carry them out with the greatest fervor. God's Will is the only arbiter of the importance of *mitzvos*.

IN DEFENSE OF THE LUBAVITCH *MITZVAH* CAMPAIGN

This, by the way, is the response to *all* those who criticize against the *mitzvah* campaign launched by the Lubavitcher Rebbe just days before the Six-day War in 1967.

Jews were stopped amid their frenzy on the streets and encouraged to put on *tefillin*, shake the *lulav* and *esrog*, eat something in a *sukkah*, and acquire a letter in *Sefer Torah*. Voices cried out: "What kind of *mitzvah* is this? Most of those who acquiesce do not even believe in God. They're only doing it to stop the pestering of the emissary on the street. Do you really, as a result of this one-time *mitzvah*, think they have come any closer to Judaism, Torah, or God? Can you possibly imagine that this single *mitzvah*, fulfilled without any feeling or intention whatsoever, transforms them at all internally?" I even recall on one occasion a learned rabbi in Israel in the heat of a debate telling me, "Putting *tefillin* on a Jew who doesn't believe in God is like putting it on a monkey!"

All these complaints result from a superficial understanding of God and religion. These opponents are under the false impression that the purpose of Torah is to foster a religious awareness among its adherents. They do not appreciate that the physical performance of a *mitzvah* itself is the Will of God, and as such it brings a Jew closer to God and Torah. They view this kind of *mitzvah* as something of an empty shell. Their view reflects a distorted and shallow perception of Judaism.

Additionally, this approach directly contradicts talmudic law. For example, in the case of a rebellious individual who clamorously refuses to observe the *mitzvos*, the Rabbis teach (*Kesubos* 86a), "But if one refuses the performance of a positive command, such as building a *sukka* or shaking the *lulav*, he is coerced until he does so." It is clear from Rashi's commentary on the passage that such physical prodding is not part of a punishment, but a form of coercion to perform the *mitzvah*. Obviously the coercion will serve only to heighten this individual's hostility to Torah, but the Talmud is adamant that a Jewish court should continue the pressure until he has performed the *mitzvah*. Simultaneously, he is obligated to make a blessing sanctifying the act, since doing so will bring him closer to the Almighty whom he rejects.

Thus, the Talmud advocates the use of even somewhat distasteful means to procure a Jew's performance of a *mitzvah*. How much more so is it not only permitted but even obligatory that we encourage the performance of *mitzvos* through appropriate and positive means among our Jewish brethren everywhere. The average Jew walking down the street possesses none of the venom of the Jew being discussed in the Talmud. The passerby usually has had, through no fault of his own, minimal exposure to Judaism and therefore has a lack of interest. If he is antagonistic, his attitude almost always is a result of an ignorance of Judaism and the contempt that may sometimes follow. How dare we abandon him? It is an affront to God and Judaism that he is not treated at all times like a brother.

THE POWER OF A ONE-TIME-ONLY *MITZVAH*

Another consideration is the amazing emotional response these *mitzvos*-on-the-spot elicit from people on the go. How a solitary religious experience in the middle of the street can cause people's eyes to swell, to recount long stories of their Orthodox grandparents, to wail over their child who may have married outside the community, to register in a part-time *yeshivah* program, to buy themselves expensive *tefillin*, or to just walk away feeling Jewish again is beyond our grasp. Usually if one wishes to foster religious identity with a new individual, one must sit through lengthy discussions expounding on the beauty of Judaism and its relevance to contemporary society. But these onetime *mitzvos* that I admit may not be repeated again often achieve the same results! The only plausible explanation is that here we are dealing with something that, far from being an empty shell, is the personification of God's Will that reattaches an individual to His Creator, however momentarily, and simultaneously arouses the congenital convictions all Jews feel for Judaism. None of this would occur if a *mitzvah* lacking feeling were nothing more than a vacuum or shell.

But even ignoring the great success of the campaign and the deep impression it has made on Jews the world over, with many thousands who have reoriented their lives as a result of one encounter, the very fact that a Jew fulfills a *mitzvah* is invaluable. Any further interest in Judaism generated by the encounter is clear profit. Whether a person walks away inspired or indifferent, that moment of connection with God is priceless. The observance of *mitzvos* is not meant as the means by which a Jew returns to Judaism, redirects his material pursuits to spiritual ones, or starts living as an Orthodox Jew. Rather, a *mitzvah* is a goal in itself. It doesn't have to lead to anything else.

So those who scorn the *mitzvah* campaign not only degrade the *mitzvos* performed by the people on the street, but even their own *mitzvos*, for they are demonstrating that, in light of their perception of Torah, even their own *mitzvos* are nothing more than a symbolic gesture aimed at awakening love for God. One who has such a perception must then concede that a *mitzvah* is not God's Will or an end in itself, but rather a means to an end. One who voices such criticism degrades the quality of all *mitzvos* and manifests that he has succumbed to a philosophical outlook that is foreign to Judaism.

One must therefore take the genuine attitude that a religious Jew is not one who feels close to God or meditates on His greatness, but *one who performs mitzvos*. One must, however, simultaneously nurture an appreciation for the deep importance of the understanding, emotion, and pleasure that should accompany a *mitzvah* and give it life.

Our sages equate the physical act of a *mitzvah* to a body and the feeling to the soul or spirit, thus demonstrating that both are essential to its performance. In the words of a noted contemporary theologian, "A *mitzvah* without spirit [feeling] is dead, and a spirit without a body is a ghost!" Thus, as is discussed in the next chapter, meditations are necessary for the elevation of the *mitzvah*, and a *mitzvah* necessary for the elevation of mankind.

26

ILLUMINATING THE EARTH WITH GODLY LIGHT

At the end of the last chapter we paraphrased a saying of our Rabbis, which reads as follows; "A *mitzvah* without intention is like a body without a soul." The *Zohar* adds that "Torah and *mitzvos* without love and fear [of God] do not ascend above and cannot stand before the Almighty."

Now, although one might appreciate that a *mitzvah* done with love and concentration is more desirable by far, how can one say that without these qualities the entire *mitzvah* is worthless and defeated? The importance of this question is greatly magnified in light of our previous discussions that emphasized that the essential portion, indeed the very essence, of every *mitzvah* is the physical deed itself. How then can we now be told that an unfelt *mitzvah* resembles a lifeless body?

HOME: A PLACE FOR ESSENCE TO BE MANIFEST

To answer these questions and better comprehend the nature of Divine worship, we must obtain an understanding, to the best of our limited ability, of the purpose of creation. We have already quoted the words of the *Midrash* proclaiming, "The Almighty desired a dwelling in the lowest world." God desired that this earth be converted into a home for Himself. The way we build that house is by studying Torah and observing its commandments.

What is a house and what does it represent? The Lubavitcher Rebbe (*Likkutei Sihos*, vol. 3, p. 956) explains that a home has two connotations: (1) a place where one resides and (2) a place where man is best able to express his true essence, and just simply be himself. It is in the privacy of their homes that humans feel most comfortable.

Let us elaborate on these two threads. The Talmud declares, "He who has no home is not a man." Why does the possession of a home substantiate a man's being? A person must be real. Someone who is always artificial, always putting on an act, is not an independent, authentic person. There is no time when he can just be himself and not act in accordance with someone else's expectations or conditions. Such a person is not his own man. He belongs to whomever he happens to be with. This is the way most of us are forced to behave around friends, at work, and in public. We must act and dress in accordance with societal expectations.

The only place where a person can be himself is in the privacy of his own home. This is where he finds the security to manifest what he really is without considerations of the judgmentalism or expectations of others. He does not dress up for anybody. He just does what comes naturally to him.

To better illustrate this point, imagine a high public official, such as a king, who under the incessant scrutiny of diplomats, guests, and cheering crowds, must at all times maintain a certain decorum. He cannot laugh when he wants, talk as he pleases, or dress as he would wish, but must do these actions in a manner that befits a king. His body and demeanor are dressed in such thick layers of royal garb that it is almost impossible to see the real man.

Furthermore, he alters his image according to the kind of crowd in front of whom he is appearing. Before his generals, he wears a military uniform. At a state ball, he is in formal attire. And at the coronation ceremony he is in the full robes of majesty.

When the same king sits in his private throne room amid closer acquaintances and confidants, he can relax more and divest himself of some of the garb of royalty, but even then he cannot totally escape demands on his behavior. Only in the privacy of his private living quarters in the company of his intimate family and relatives can he completely remove the mask of sovereignty and be a person in his own right. There he may wear the clothes he pleases, speak in any dialect he wishes, joke the way he likes, and generally express his true and natural self.

Moreover, the *halakhah* states that no one is permitted to see a king unclothed because it would erode his authority. Whenever the king is in the company of other people, he must be clothed. It would be unbecoming for the king to be inappropriately attired. At home of course, there are many occasions when the king will not even be dressed.

Thus, a home or domicile implies a place where man may express his true essence without external impositions that might modify his natural behavior.

GOD DESIRES A PRIVATE DWELLING

This then is the purpose for the creation of this world. God is not satisfied when mere Godly light radiates upon this earth. If He were, He would have had no need to create our world, since the higher, spiritual worlds have a far greater capacity for the radiation and retention of spiritual light.

Furthermore, the light is an external manifestation. It is the king the way he appears in public, the way he manifests himself in accordance with the expectations of his subjects, and so it changes in accordance with the receiving capacity of each individual world, just as the king's demeanor must suit his audience. Our world, being all physical, could receive only a minute, contracted, and finite light. Too much light would overwhelm our infinitesimal existence. No, this world was not needed for the radiation of Godly light, but so that God's Essence might come to reside among us, totally "naked" of any external quality or imposition. Our world was meant to serve as that private residence where the Almighty could remove all garb (contractions) and be totally bare of any eternality until His intrinsic self shined forth.

That wish will not come to fruition until the advent of the
messianic era, when God will reveal His true Essence. As it is
written, "Your Master shall no longer hide," to which the Alter
Rebbe adds, "This means to say, He will not be concealed from
you behind cloaks and garb." In our time, when the reign of
Godly *light* is prevalent, the "garb" that conceals Him is thick
and unpenetrating, for our world in respect to the higher worlds
is like a peasant crowd unaccustomed to the trappings of royalty and we are far removed from the king's close circle of confidants. We are unprepared and as yet undeserving of God revealing His true self to us in all its majesty. But in the World to Come
with the advent of the Messianic Era, the Almighty will remove
all concealments and reside in His home, this world, unmasked
and unveiled.

MITZVOS CONSTITUTE THE BRICKS IN
THE BUILDING OF GOD'S RESIDENCE

However, our observance of Torah and *mitzvos* today is not
ineffective. On the contrary, as was mentioned earlier, when
Moshiah comes, the world will remain the same. What will happen is that all the holiness yielded from the performance of
mitzvos throughout the generations will be revealed to the
naked eye.

Thus, every *mitzvah* we accomplish today adds another brick
to the dwelling. It is specifically *mitzvos* that can be used as
building materials since, as we have already emphasized, God's
intrinsic Essence is found within them. And since what is being
built is meant to house God's Essence, only *mitzvos* will suffice. In other words, every time we fulfill a *mitzvah* it is not
mere Godly light that comes into the world but God Himself
who comes closer. Every *mitzvah* causes Him to descend lower
and lower until we finally succeed in bringing God fully into
our world.

Thus, when a Jew studies Torah or fulfills a *mitzvah*, even if
it is lacking in emotional participation or is coerced (which, of
course, runs contrary to the whole spirit of Judaism), he more
firmly establishes God's presence in this world. He sets this

world up as the residential palace where the King of Kings can manifest his true Essence.

But even this is not the totality of God's Will. God desired not only that He should dwell in the lowest of worlds but that this phenomenon also be revealed. To understand this added dimension, let us return to our analogy of a human king.

Imagine that the king possesses private living chambers where he may be himself, but the chambers are dark. Although the king enjoys complete seclusion and can disregard his public image, there is still a measure of discomfort. The darkness causes a feeling of consternation and unease. It reduces the possibility of complete comfort. Of what good is this reclusive setting if he cannot be totally relaxed? Since the darkness obscures the total manifestation of the inner person and creates an uncomfortable setting, the king's inner essence cannot emerge. Surely, these are not quarters befitting a king.

GOD WISHES TO BE NOTICED

In the same vein, when speaking of a dwelling we mean to emphasize two aspects: It is a place where the king's real self, his essence is found, divorced of any externalities. Second, this fact is realized and apparent, and the dwelling is illuminated.

Thus, when God demands an earthly dwelling, two things are meant: (1) that His intrinsic Essence dwells in the world, and not mere light as exists in the spiritual worlds, where Godly revelation is perceived through a concealing "garment," and (2) that there be nothing to conceal this fact that the world has been transformed to serve as a Godly dwelling.

As has been consistently reiterated throughout this work, this dwelling is being built now through the fulfillment of Torah and *mitzvos* by the Jewish people. Just as there are two aspects of the dwelling so must there be a corresponding duality within Torah and *mitzvos*.

The foundation of the dwelling is laid by the physical fulfillment of the *mitzvah* alone. Since the Almighty has enclothed His Essence in Torah, every *mitzvah* performed brings His Essence into this world. But if the physical performance is lacking in meditation, feeling, and emotion, a fundamental aspect of the dwelling is missing. The house is existent, but it lacks illumination. It is shrouded in darkness.

Still worse, when one performs a *mitzvah* with improper intention, say, as a cultural or ethnic gesture, or as a habit, or for a reward, he clothes the *mitzvah* in a garb foreign to Godliness. He causes God to descend into thick robes. God's presence in the world is concealed in *klippah*, a dark covering. Thus, not only is the dwelling dark but there are even obstacles that prevent God's manifestation.

THE DIFFERENCE THAT LOVE AND FEAR CAN MAKE

Conversely, when a *mitzvah* is permeated with love and fear of the Almighty—that is, when the *mitzvah* radiates within the individual—it causes the Godliness within it to radiate as well. Thus, although it is not an absolute prerequisite that a *mitzvah* be the natural outcome of deep contemplation and a realization of the greatness of the Holy One, blessed be He, a *mitzvah* that includes these prerequisites is far greater.

To be sure, even a small iota of the physical performance of the *mitzvah* is more significant than all the love and emotion accompanying it. If even one letter of the parchment in the *tefillin* is erased, the entire *mitzvah* is invalid. In other words, the king is not present at all. All the floodlights in the entire world can illuminate the dwelling, but the king is simply nowhere to be found. A radiant *mitzvah* that is missing God's presence is doubtlessly worthless. When a *mitzvah* is performed with improper intention, its quality is blemished. A king deserves a perfect home. It can be appreciated then why the Talmud encourages man to "always study Torah even with improper intention, for improper intention later leads to its fulfillment with the proper intention." Of fundamental importance is the performance of the *mitzvah* for whatever reason. For, even if the *mitzvah* at present is a little dark, the light can be added later. We are taught that when a person later returns to the same *mitzvah* and this time fulfills it with the proper intention, he simultaneously illuminates *all* his previous fulfillments of the same *mitzvah* so that its darkness is dispelled.

TESHUVAH BRINGS BACK LIFE

This is the concept of *teshuvah*, repentance. Repentance implies not only that one returns from sin but also that one returns to illuminate his previous *mitzvos* that had been left in the dark. Thus, through repentance one raises the overall quality of his service unto God. One need not fulfill all the same *mitzvos* again, but merely radiate light within them.

This too is why our sages equate a *mitzvah* without intention to a dead body. The Rabbis did not state that the *mitzvah* is totally worthless. It is a complete body, but it is missing life. As long as the body is existent, there is a place for the soul to reside, whether it inhabits the body immediately or later. If the physical act of the *mitzvah* is lacking, however, then both the body and the soul are missing. In this case, a body will have to be created from anew and a soul found to animate it.

Therefore it is the act that is essential, and the individual is always encouraged to perform a *mitzvah* for whatever reason. Sooner or later he will return and provide the *mitzvah* with new life.

And once we have illuminated the entire dwelling, once we have brought God's light to all corners of the earth, we will have ushered in the Messianic Era, a time when "the earth shall be filled with the knowledge of the Lord as the waters of the sea cover the ocean floor" (Isaiah 11:2).

May it happen in all of our lifetimes, *NOW*!!

Index

About the Author

Rabbi Shmuel Boteach serves as a rabbi to the students of Oxford University and as the director of the Oxford University L'Chaim Society. Under his directorship the L'Chaim Society has become the second-largest student organization in Oxford University's history, with over 2,000 Jewish and non-Jewish members, and has recently opened a branch in London. He has brought Mikhail Gorbachev, Elie Wiesel, Bob Hawke, Javier Perez de Cuellar, Yitzhak Rabin, Yitzhak Shamir, Christiaan Barnard, Leonard Nimoy, Simon Wiesenthal, Boy George, and Admiral William Crowe, to name a few, to speak at Oxford, as well as sending his weekly essays on Jewish life and moral issues to thousands of people in twenty-eight different countries via fax and internet. He is also the author of several books, including *Dreams* (1991), *The Wolf Shall Lie with the Lamb* (1993), *Moses of Oxford* (1994), *Wrestling with the Divine* (1995), and *The Jewish Guide to Adultery* (1995). He is a sought-after lecturer on a wide variety of Jewish, personal, and social issues and has addressed audiences around the world. Rabbi Boteach, an American, divides his time between Oxford and London, England, with his Australian wife, Debbie, and their five young children.